Sloan Edward Lennox

The Salt Lake City directory and business guide, for 1869

Sloan Edward Lennox

The Salt Lake City directory and business guide, for 1869

ISBN/EAN: 9783337712167

Printed in Europe, USA, Canada, Australia, Japan

Cover: Foto ©Suzi / pixelio.de

More available books at **www.hansebooks.com**

THE

SALT LAKE CITY

DIRECTORY

AND

BUSINESS GUIDE,

FOR 1869.

COMPILED AND ARRANGED BY E. L. SLOAN.

COPY RIGHT SECURED.

SALT LAKE CITY, UTAH:
PUBLISHED BY E. L. SLOAN & CO.
1869.

GENERAL INDEX.

INDEX TO ADVERTISERS.

INTRODUCTION.

IN presenting the Salt Lake City Directory and Business Guide for 1869 to the public, it is necessary to briefly state the causes which have delayed its publication for several weeks beyond the time originally fixed upon for issuing it. In procuring the information contained in it much more labor was required, and longer time had to be devoted to it, than was at first believed would be necessary. The greater portion of the matter contained in it was also delayed on its transit to the printers by the heavy snow storms which impeded travel through the Rocky Mountains in February and March.

No pains have been spared to make the work a reliable one for future reference; and every change of business which has occurred from the completion of the canvass for the Business Directory, up to the work being put to press, has been carefully noted as far as information could be obtained.

The compiler begs to express his obligations for favors received in obtaining information to the Hon. George A. Smith, historian; A. W. Street, Esq., P. M., Salt Lake City; Robert Campbell, Esq., Recorder of Salt Lake City; Jesse W. Fox, Territorial Surveyor General; Hon. L. E. Harrington, American Fork; and Walter Thompson, Esq., Ogden, County Clerk of Weber County.

Respectfully,

THE PUBLISHERS.

SKETCH OF MORMONISM.

Joseph Smith, the founder of the organization, was born in Sharon, Windsor county, Vermont, December 23d, 1805. His father's name was Joseph and his mother's Lucy; and their family consisted of six sons and three daughters of whom the future prophet was the third son. When he was in his fourteenth year his father moved to Manchester, Ontario county, New York, having previously resided four years in Palmyra in the same county. While in Manchester, and during a religious revival, he was, as he states in his autobiography, the subject of religious impressions; during which, while praying in the woods one day, he had the first vision, two glorious personages appearing to him, who communed with him. Some three and a half years afterwards, on the 21st of September, 1823, he had a second vision and received a communication relative to the plates upon which the Book of Mormon was inscribed. These plates, his history states, he obtained possession of on the 22d of September, 1827, from the place of their deposit, on the west side of a hill convenient to Manchester, the village where he resided. The plates were enclosed in a box, covered with a stone, and had been there for some 1400 years, having been buried by an ancient inhabitant of this continent named Moroni. The characters on them had been principally inscribed by Mormon, hence the title of the work.

Being poor and with the work of translating the records before him, in his exigencies he obtained assistance from a gentleman named Martin Harris; and in April, 1829, he made the acquaintance of Oliver Cowdery, a school teacher, who became his amenuensis, and the work of translating commenced immediately. The Book of Mormons, was put in the hands of the printers; but before it was published a church was organized on the 6th day of April, 1830, in the house of Mr. Peter Whitmer, Fayette, Seneca county, New York. Thus the Empire State not only produced the plates, from which the book was translated, but can claim the honor of the organization of that society which is the greatest problem of the century. Six members composed this church on its organization, a small beginning for the thousands into which it has grown and the power and influence acquired in the short space of thirty-eight years. The Book of Morman was published, preaching and proselytizing were prosecuted with vigor, though the missionaries of the new faith were mostly uneducated, and churches were raised up in a number of places in a few months.

Early in 1831 a settlement was made at Kirtland, Ohio, and this may be called the first "gathering-place" of the church—a central point to wards which all who received the faith should converge. In July of the same year a lot was selected and dedicated, for a Temple, at Independence, Jackson county, Missouri. Here a printing press was set in operation and a periodical, the *Evening and Morning Star*, was published by Judge W. W. Phelps. Trouble broke out at Independence, between the settlers of the new faith and others inhabiting that region, and a mob tore down the printing office, tarred and feathered some of the prominent Mormons, abused others, and inflicted losses on the fraternity, in the destruction of property, to a very large amount. The Mormons were obliged to leave, and most of them fled into and settled in Clay county, in the same state. The Jackson county mob influenced the citizens of Clay county, and after a time the refugees had again to leave, this time settling in unoccupied territory, which received the name of Caldwell county, as well as in Davis and other adjacent counties, in Missouri. In three years they made wonderful improvements in their new location, for industry has ever been a prominent characteristic of the organization. At this time they were viewed with suspicion by many pro-slavery citizens there, who classed them as abolitionists, many of them having com from states where the abolition theory was gaining ground. For this cause, and because their industrious habits conflicted with the dissipated customs of a class always too well known in frontier settlements, as well as for religious reasons, troubles again broke out and the entire Mormon community was compelled to leave the state. Their next settlement was at Commerce, Hancock county, Illinois, where in a short time they built the city of Nauvoo, which was duly chartered by the state Legislature. They had built a temple at Kirtland, which was an immense effort in its size and costliness for so small and poor a body of people as they then were. But in Nauvoo one was commenced on a scale proportionately greater to correspond with their increased numbers, wealth and importance. This they finished, but before it was completed, their Prophet, Joseph Smith, and his brother Hyrum Smith, the Patriarch of the Church, were murdered in Carthage, where they were imprisoned on a charge of treason. The Missouri enemies of the prophet and his followers, had never ceased their efforts against him and his people, preferring charge after charge which were disposed of by the courts, he always obtained an acquittal; until this last charge, when the mob would not wait for the result of a trial, but shot him and his brother dead while in prison under guard, wounding at the same time Elder John Taylor, one of the Twelve Apostles. They held Governor Ford's pledge for their safety at the time. This was on the 27th of June, 1844.

Soon after the Mormons were compelled to leave Illinois, and took up their line of march in February, 1846, for the then almost unknown west. That Fall and Winter the main body of the refugee Saints located in the neighborhood of the Missouri River, near what is now Council

Bluffs and Omaha, where temporary settlements were formed. Next Spring, President Brigham Young started westward with 143 pioneers, broke a road, forded streams and built bridges from the Missouri over the great plains and through the Rocky Mountains, arriving in Salt Lake Valley on the 21st of July, 1847. As soon after as possible the main body followed, a provisional State government was formed, gentlemen were sent to Washington to represent the new colony; and in 1849 a Territorial government was granted to them for the Territory of Utah. Since that time they have prospered exceedingly; their cities, towns and settlements number about two hundred with a population of nearly 150,000 souls. Besides these there are branches of the Church in many parts of the United States; and in Europe the communicants of the faith number nearly 20,000. Their missionary efforts have been directed to every country where religious toleration would permit them to carry and disseminate their views. Most European and some Asiatic nations, as well as Australia and several of the Pacific Islands, have given proselytes to the faith; and almost all the old members of the Church are native born citizens of the Union, which still adds largely to the believers in the latter-day dispensation.

The Church is organized with a First Presidency of three; a Council of Twelve Apostles; a Patriarch; a quorum of High Priests of indefinite number; sixty-four quorums of Seventies; an Elders' Quorum; a Presidency of three and a High Council of twelve for each Stake of Zion; a Presiding Bishop for the Church with two Counselors; a Bishop for each Ward; a Priests' quorum; a Teachers' quorum; and a Deacons' quorum.

The present authorities of the Church are:

Brigham Young, President; George A. Smith his first and Daniel H. Wells his second counselor.

Orson Hyde, President of the Quorum of the Twelve Apostles, and Orson Pratt, Sr., John Taylor, Wilford Woodruff, Ezra T. Benson, Charles C. Rich, Lorenzo Snow, Erastus Snow, Franklin D. Richards, George Q. Cannon, Joseph F. Smith and Brigham Young, Jr., members.

John Smith, Patriarch.

John Young, President of the High Priests' Quorum; Edwin D. Wooley and Samuel W. Richards counselors.

Joseph Young, President of the first seven Presidents of the Seventies, and Levi W. Hancock, Henry Harriman, Albert P. Rockwood, Horace S. Eldredge, Jacob Gates, and John Van Cott, members of the first seven Presidents of the Seventies.

Edward Hunter, Presiding Bishop, Leonard W. Hardy and Jesse C. Little, his counselors.

George A. Smith, Historian and general Church Recorder, and Wilford Woodruff, assistant.

CHRONOLOGICAL EVENTS OF UTAH.

1847. *July 24th*—Pioneers, numbering 143 men, enter Salt Lake Valley, having left the Missouri river April 14th. The day of their arrival they commenced plowing and planting potatoes. A thunder shower wet the ground slightly in the afternoon.

July 29th.—A portion of the Mormon Battalion, numbering about 150, under command of Captain Brown, arrive, having come from Pueblo to Fort Laramie and thence west. They were accompanied by a party of immigrants from the State of Mississippi.

July 31st.—Great Salt Lake City laid out, in square blocks of ten acres each, eight lots to the block, and streets eight rods wide, running at right angles. Latitude of northern boundary of Temple block, ascertained by meridian observations of the sun by Prof. Orson Pratt, Sr., 40 deg., 45 min., 44 sec. Longitude, obtained by lunar distances, taken by the sextant and circle, 111 deg., 26 min., 34 sec., west of Greenwich. Altitude above sea level 4,300 feet.

August 25th.—President Brigham Young and about seventy of the Pioneers start east for "Winter Quarters," on the Missouri river, to assist their immigration forward.

August 26th.—The colonists had laid off a fort, built twenty-seven log houses, plowed and planted eighty-four acres with corn, potatoes, beans, buckwheat, turnips, etc., and had manufactured 125 bushels of salt.

1848. *May 31st.*—President Brigham Young organizes the immigrants of the faith coming west, at Winter Quarters, into companies for the journey. They numbered 1,891 souls, with 623 wagons.

August 9th.—Great Salt Lake City fort contains 450 buildings, with three saw mills and a flouring mill in the city, and others in course of construction.

August 10th.—Feast given in Great Salt Lake City to celebrate the First Harvest gathered in the Great Basin.

September 20th.—President Young arrives with his company.

Davis and Weber counties settled.

1849. *February 5th.*—Mercury 33 deg. below zero in Great Salt Lake City.

March 8th.—Memorial sent to Congress for a State Government.

March 9th.—Election held under the Provisional Government of the State of Deseret. Brigham Young elected governor; Willard Richards, secretary of state; N. K. Whitney, treasurer; H. C. Kimball, chief justice; John Taylor and N. K. Whitney, associate justices; Daniel H. Wells, attorney general; Horace S. Eldredge, marshal; Albert Carrington, assessor and collector of taxes; and Joseyh L. Heywood, surveyor of highways, etc. Magistrates were also elected.

May 27th.—Parties from the east *en route* for the California gold mines first arrive.

August 28th.—Captain H. Stansbury arrive to commence his survey.

October 6th.—Perpetual emigration Company organized.

Utah, Tooele and Sanpete Counties settled. First Indian war.

Deseret Dramatic Association organized. Robert Campbell, president ; re-organized again in 1850.

1850. *February 22d.*—Earthquake shock felt in Great Salt Lake Valley.

June 15th.—" Deseret News" published.

July 4th.— Parley's canon opened for travel under the name of " The Golden Pass."

August 28th.—Captain Stansbury completes his survey.

September 9th.—Act of Congress, organizing Utah Territory, approved.

Ogden City located.

October.—Brigham Young appointed Governor of Utah Territory.

December 8th.—" Thirty families left Salt Lake City, including 118 men, with 600 head of stock and 101 wagons, led by Elder George A. Smith, and in January following arrived at and settled the county of Iron, by building a fort at Parowan."

Council House ready for occupation this fall.

1851. *January 3d.*—First criminal trial by jury held in the provisional State of Deseret.

January 11th.—Great Salt Lake City incorporated, Jedediah Morgan Grant, first mayor.

Charters granted to Ogden, Provo, Manti and Parowan cities.

October 29th.—Fillmore City located as the seat of government for and the capital of Utah territory.

Millard, Box Elder and Carson counties settled.

1852. *January 16th.*—Tabernacle, capable of seating nearly 3000 persons, finished.

February 14th.—Territorial Legislature memorialize Congress for a Pacific railroad and telegraph line.

July 27th.—Thermometer 127 deg. in the sun in Great Salt Lake City.

September 3d.—First company of P. E. Fund immigrants arrive from Europe with thirty-one wagons, A. O. Smoot, captain ; met by the First Presidency, Captain Wm. Pitt's band, and many leading citizens.

September 4th.—Treaty made with the chiefs of the Utes and Shoshones in Great Salt Lake City.

Juab and Washington counties settled, the latter in the spring and the former in the fall.

Post offices established at American Fork, Springville and Payson, Utah county; Salt Creek (Nephi), Juab county; and Fillmore City, Millard county.

1853. *February 14th.*—The ground for the Temple, in Temple Block, consecrated.

April 6th.—Corner stones of Temple laid.

August 29th.—Resolution adopted by city council, in compliance with expressed request of the inhabitants, to build a Spanish wall around Great Salt Lake City. The wall was twelve feet high; six feet thick at base, tapering to two feet and six inches six feet from the ground; and preserving that thickness to the top. It was about nine miles in length. Portions of it still stand in a dilapidated condition.

September 26th.—Captain J. W. Gunnison, U. S. Topographical Engineers, and seven men killed by Indians, near the swamps of the Sevier, twenty miles from the Sevier river, in revenge for killing an Indian and the wounding of two others by a company of immigrants for California.

Second Indian war.

Social Hall erected.

Summit and Green River counties settled.

1854. *January 7th.*—John C. Fremont with nine whites and twelve Delaware Indians, arrived at Parowan in a state of starvation. One man had fallen dead from his horse near the settlement, and others were nearly dead. Animals and provisions were supplied, and after resting to the 20th they departed.

March 11th.—Dr. Williard Richards, second counselor to President Young and editor of the "Deseret News," died.

May 23d.—Patriarch John Smith died.

April 7th.—Jedidiah M. Grant chosen counselor in place of Willard Richards.

July.—Grasshoppers make their appearance and do much damage.

Deseret alphabet produced.

Seventies' Hall built.

1855. *January 1st.*—Iron made by the Deseret Iron Company.

January 20th.—Walker, the celebrated Utah Chief, died at Meadow Creek.

July 1st.—Molasses made from beet at the sugar factory.

September.—Deseret Horticultural Society organized.

Various societies organized during the early part of the year

Gents' Furnishing Goods, cheap, at HELLMAN & CO.'S, Salt Lake City.

62   CHRONOLOGICAL EVENTS.

among which and most prominent, were the "Universal Scientific Society;" the "Polysophical Society;" "Deseret Philharmonic Society;" and "Deseret Typographical Association."

Grasshoppers do serious damage to crops, destroying nearly everything green in many parts of the territory.

Morgan county settled.

1856. *January 26th.*—Express carrying company organized to carry express from Missouri River to California, and shares taken to stock a thousand miles of the road at a mass meeting held in Great Salt Lake City.

March 17th.—Convention met in Great Salt Lake City to prepare constitution and memorial to Congress for admission as a State.

March 27th.—Constitution and memorial adopted, George A. Smith and John Taylor elected Delegates to present them to Congress.

September 26th.—First hand-cart companies arrive under charge of Captains Edmund Ellsworth and D. D. McArthur. They were met by the First Presidency of the church, a brass band, a company of lancers, and a large concourse of influential citizens.

December 1st.—Jedediah M. Grant died.

December 8th.—Legislature meet in Fillmore, organized and adjourned to Great Salt Lake City.

December 18th.—Legislature meets in the Social Hall, Great Salt Lake City.

Beaver and Cache counties settled.

1857. *January 4th.*—Daniel H. Wells chosen second counselor to Pres. B. Young, in the place of J. M. Grant.

April 23d.—A company of about seventy missionaries start and cross the plains east with hand-carts, making the trip in forty-eight days.

July 11th.—Alfred Cumming of Georgia appointed Governor of Utah.

July 24th.—Judge Stoddard arrives without the mails, the post master at Independence having received orders not to forward them. General Harney with two thousand infantry and a proportionate number of artillery and cavalry ordered to Utah.

August 7th.—First part of the "Army of Utah," consisting of the tenth infantry and Phelphs' Battery, arrive at Fort Kearney.

1858. *March 21st.*—The citizens of Great Salt Lake City, and the settlements north of it agree to abandon their homes and go south, all the information derived from eastern papers being that the approaching formidable army was sent to destroy them. Destination when starting, supposed to be Sonora.

April 10th.—Governor A. Cumming and Col. T. L. Kane, with

Boys' Clothing, in any quantity, low, sold by HELLMAN & CO., Salt Lake City.

CHRONOLOGICAL EVENTS. 63

a servant each, having left the "army of Utah" to proceed to Salt Lake City, arrive with an escort of Mormons with whom they had accidentally met on the way.

April 15th.—Governor Cumming reports having arrived and been treated everywhere "with respectful attention."

April 19th.—Governor Cumming and Col. Kane visit the Utah library, where J. W. Cummings showed them the records and seal of the U. S. District Court, said to have been burnt up, which was one of the reasons why the army was ordered to Utah.

June 7th.—Powell and McCullough, Peace Commissioners, arrive in Great Salt Lake City.

Kane county settled.

1860. *April 7th.*—George Q. Cannon chosen one of the Twelve Apostles.

1861. *April 23d.*—Two hundred wagons, with four yoke of cattle each, carrying about 15,000 lbs. of flour, started for the Missouri river to bring on the poor of the immigration.

October 18th.—First telegram crosses the overland wire, from Utah, sent to President Abraham Lincoln by President Brigham Young.

October 24th.—First telegram sent to San Francisco by President B. Young.

1862. *January 22d.*—Constitution again adopted, with memorial for admission of Utah as a State, with the name of "Deseret." George Q. Cannon and W. H. Hooper elected to present them to Congress.

March 6th.—Salt Lake Theatre dedicated.

May 21st.—Two hundred and sixty-two wagons, 293 teamsters, 2,880 oxen, carrying 143,315 lbs. of flour, sent from Utah to assist the poor of the immigration across the plains and mountains.

December 10th.—Governor Harding delivers his annual message, extra copies of which the Legislature will not publish, viewing it insulting.

1863. *January 29th.*—Col. P. E. Connor attacks a band of Shoshone Indians in a ravine near Bear river, and defeats them. Known as Bear river battle.

March 22d.—Overland mail, with four passengers, attacked by Indians near Eight Mile Station, Tooele county. Driver killed and one passenger wounded. Judge Mott, who was in the coach, took the reins, drove for life, and escaped.

April 5th.—Battle of Spanish Fork cannon, between 140 cavalry, (C. V.) under Col. G. S. Evans, and 200 Indians. Lieut. F. A. Teale was killed. The Indians were defeated.

May 18th.—384 wagons, 488 teamsters, 3,604 oxen, taking

225,969 lbs. flour, start to assist the poor of the immigration. 4,300 lbs. of Utah grown cotton sent East for sale with the teams dispatched to assist the immigration.

Rich and Wasatch counties settled.

1864.   *July 4th.*—*Daily Telegraph* issued, T. B. H. Stenhouse, proprietor and editor; semi-weekly issued October 8th, same year.

1865.   *January.*—Sevier and Piute counties organized.

 April 10th.—Proposition make to build a telegraph line in Utah.

 June 5th.—Treaty made by Col. O. H. Irish with the principal chiefs in the Territory, at Spanish Fork, Reservation Farm.

 June 8th.—Hon Schuyler Colfax and party arrive.

 June 11th.—Colfax and party address the citizens in front of the Salt Lake House.

 June 13th.—Governor Doty died.

 July 14th.—Hon. J. M. Ashley addresses an audience, in the Bowery, at the celebration on the national anniversary.

 October.—First issue of the *Deseret News*, semi-weekly.

 November.—First Hebrew marriage celebrated in Salt Lake City.

1866.   *May 31st.*—First circumcision of Hebrew child in G. S. L. City.

 June 11th.—Indian war. Gen. Wells and militia start for Sanpete to protect the settlements there.

1867.   *March 21st.*—Deseret Telegraph Company organized.

 July 19th.—Grasshoppers arrive in vast quantities.

 October 6th.—First conference held in new Tabernacle.

 November 21st.—*Deseret Evening News issued.*

1868.   *January 29th.*—Act approved changing the names of Great Salt Lake city and county to Salt Lake City and Salt Lake County.

 June.—Union Iron Company commence operations at Pinto county.

 June 19th.—Ground broken on the U. P. R. R. in Weber canon.

 June 22d.—Heber C. Kimball, first counselor to Pres. Young, died.

 Grasshoppers destroy a large portion of the crops in the Territory.

 October 6th.—George A. Smith chosen first counselor in place of Heber C. Kimball.

MAYORS OF SALT LAKE CITY.

Name.	Term Com'd.	Term Expired.
Jedediah M. Grant	Jan. 11, 1851	Dec. 1, 1856
Abraham O. Smoot	Jan. 2, 1857	Feb. 12, 1866
Daniel H. Wells	Feb. 12, 1866	Present Mayor.

No Washing Machine equals the "HYDRAULIC," F. A. MITCHELL, Sole Ag't.

TERRITORY OF UTAH.   65

TERRITORY OF UTAH.

UTAH occupies an area of about 65,000 square miles, which includes large tracts of wild and mountainous country. It extends from the 37th to the 42d parallels of north latitude; and from the 109th to the 114th degrees of longitude. About 130,000 acres are under cultivation; of which, in 1867, over 80,000 were planted in cereals; nearly 2,000 in sugar cane, from which molasses was made; some 6,800 in root crops; nearly 200 in cotton; 900 in apple orchards; 1,000 in peaches; 75 in grapes; and 195 in currants; while 30,000 were in meadow; of this about 94,000 acres had to be irrigated, at a cost during the year, in making canals, dams for irrigation purposes, cleaning out ditches, etc., of nearly $247,000. The result of the grasshopper visitation in 1868 presents details far below the average of other years. Even in 1867, the loss to the cereals, and part of the fruit and root crops, averaged over one-sixth of the whole, as compared with former years and with the promise for harvest before the insects appeared.

Correct returns of mineral operations in the Territory have not been made. Gold has been found in small quantities in various parts of the Territory, as the result of extensive prospecting, but not to an extent that pays for outlay, although during the summer of 1868 a number of men were at work in Bingham's Canon, in the Oquirrh range, on the west side of Salt Lake Valley. Silver has also been found in the Wasatch Mountains, east side of the Valley, in Cottonwood Canon, but it has not paid remuneratively for working.

Iron ore exists in vast quantities in several parts of the Territory. In Iron county, works were erected in 1852, and a small quantity of iron was made, but the lack of the proper fuel compelled a cessation of the works, which were ultimately abandoned. In Summit county, iron ore exists to a considerable extent.

On the Pinto, Iron county, the Union Iron Company commenced operations in June, 1868, with Ebenezer Hanks, president; S. M. Blair, Peter Shirts and Robert Ritchey, directors, and Chapman Duncan, agent. On the first of January, 1869, they had two furnaces in operation, with another in course of erection; and had a fair prospect of being successful.

Coal is found extensively, but principally in the neighborhood of Coalville, in Summit county. Fresh veins were discovered up Echo Canon during the construction of the grade for the U. P. R. R., in August of 1868. An excellent quality of coal is also obtained in Sanpete, which is used extensively for blacksmithing purposes.

MEN'S, BOYS' and CHILDREN'S BOOTS Exceedingly Cheap, at DUNFORD & SONS.

2

Copper, lead, bismuth, limestone, etc., exist in considerable quantities in the Territory.

The following, with some slight and necessary corrections, is taken from *the Great West and Union Pacific Railroad Guide*, published by The American News Company, New York:

" Settlements were made in Utah as early as July, 1847. It originally formed part of Mexico, but by the treaty of Guadaloupe Hidalgo, in 1848, it was ceded to the United States. The comparatively small beginning in 1847 has grown and lengthened, until now the settlements extend to a distance of three hundred miles north and south ; and wherever a valley can be found that can be watered, there you will find the industrious, uncomplaining settlers, making an honest living in a way most congenial to nature and most conducive to health, by the cultivation of the soil. Not only are the ordinary vegetables and cereals produced, but in the southern part of the Territory they are raising cotton, the product of free white labor, thereby removing the objection of some of our eastern friends to the use of this necessary article. In a word the desert has been converted into the fruitful field, and the frowns of nature exchanged for smiles of gladness.

" The country for the most part is mountainous, interspersed with valleys, which can only be cultivated by irrigation.

" The melting of the snow in the mountains affords in ordinary seasons sufficient water to cultivate the valleys successfully.

" The summers are very warm and dry; the winters generally mild and open. The fall of snow is light in the valleys and heavy in the mountains. The climate may be said to be invigorating and healthful, fevers and pulmonary complaints being almost unknown.

" The soil, which, to a very great extent, is formed of the mountain washings, consists principally of gravelly loam, and is well adapted to the growth of wheat and other cereals.

" Wheat is indeed the great staple product of the Territory. In good seasons the average yield per acre is about twenty-five bushels. Sixty to seventy bushels are not unfrequently obtained; and in some instances as high as eighty bushels have been raised from a single acre.

" Oats, barley, rye, and flax are cultivated with great success.

" All kinds of vegetables grow astonishingly large, and of a superior quality.

" In Washington county, in the southern part of the Territory, large fields of cotton are cultivated, the growth of which will be sufficient in a few years to supply all the wants of the people. In 1863 quite a considerable quantity of cotton was exported to the States at remunerative prices.

" Madder, indigo, figs, grapes, and other tropical fruits are also raised in this part of the country.

"Timber is scarce, and being found only in the mountains and 'kanyons,' is very difficult of access. As a consequence of this, houses are costly to build, and rents are proportionately high.

"The climate and soil of Utah are particularly adapted to the production of fruit; and her citizens, no doubt, feeling the promptings of an internal as well as external nature, have improved their opportunities for cultivation. Apples, pears, peaches, apricots, plums, grapes, currants and other fruits are produced, not only in great abundance, but of a superior quality.

In addition to flouring and other mills necessary for the support of the Territory, woolen and cotton factories are being established in different parts of the country for home supplies."

The property value of Utah, according to the Territorial Auditor's Report for 1868, was $10,533,872; and the amount of tax assessed on it, for the same year, $52,669. Of these amounts, Salt Lake county owned property assessed at $4,379,652.80; and was taxed, for Territorial purposes, $21,898.26. The Territory has no debt; but in the Treasurer's hands, at the close of the last fiscal year, was a balance of $17,000, not drawn for the purposes for which it had been appropriated.

There are in the Territory 186 school districts, having 226 schools, on the rolls of which are the names of about 13,000 pupils. The teachers number 306, who received for the the year $61,839.

The population of the Territory is estimated at 130,000.

The government is vested in Executive, Judicial and Legislative departments.

The Executive consists of a Governor and Secretary; the Judicial of a Chief Justice and two Associate Justices; and the Legislative, of an Assembly composed of thirteen Councilors and twenty-six Representatives.

FEDERAL OFFICERS.

Governor—Charles Durkee, of Wisconsin.
Secretary—Edwin Higgins, of Michigan.
Chief Justice—Charles C. Wilson, of Illinois.
Associate Justices—Thomas J. Drake, of Michigan, and Enos D. Hoge, of Illinois.
Clerk of Supreme Court—W. I. Appleby, of Utah.
Superintendent of Indian Affairs—F. H. Head, of Wisconsin.
Assessor of Internal Revenue—A. L. Chetlain, of Illinois.
Collector of Internal Revenue—R. T. Burton, of Utah.
Surveyor General—J. A. Clark, of Illinois.
U. S. Attorney—C. H. Hempstead, of California.
Marshal—Josiah A. Hosmer, of Utah.

TERRITORIAL OFFICERS.

Treasurer—David O. Calder.
Auditor—William Clayton.
Attorney General—Zerubbabel Snow.
Surveyor General—Jesse W. Fox.
Marshal—John D. T. McAllister.
Road Commissioner—Theodore McKean.
Librarian—Wm. C. Staines.
Recorder of Marks and Brands—William Clayton.
Sealer of Weights and Measures—Nathan Davis.
Superintendent of Common Schools—Robert L. Campbell.

MEMBERS OF THE EIGHTEENTH LEGISLATIVE ASSEMBLY.

OFFICERS OF COUNCIL.

President—George A. Smith.
Secretary—Patrick Lynch.
Assistant Secretary—Charles W. Stayner.
Sergeant-at-Arms—J. D. T. McAllister.
Messenger—Charles W. Carrington.
Foreman—Charles W. Smith.
Chaplain—Joseph Young, Sr.

MEMBERS OF COUNCIL.

Salt Lake, Tooele, Summit and Green River counties—Wilford Woodruff, Albert Carrington, A. O. Smoot and Joseph A. Young.
Davis and Morgan counties—Hector C. Haight.
Weber and Box Elder Counties—Lorenzo Snow.
Cache and Rich Counties—Ezra T. Benson.
Utah and Wasatch Counties—L. E. Harrington and Aaron Johnson.
Sanpete and Sevier Counties—Orson Hyde.
Millard and Juab Counties—Thomas Callister.
Beaver, Iron and Piute Counties—George A. Smith.
Washington and Kane Counties—Erastus Snow.

OFFICERS OF THE HOUSE OF REPRESENTATIVES.

Speaker—Orson Pratt, Sr.
Chief Clerk—Robert L. Campbell.
Assistant Clerk—Joseph C. Rich.
Sergeant-at-Arms—S. H. B. Smith.
Messenger—Abinadi Pratt.
Foreman—George W. Slade.
Chaplain—W. W. Phelps.

REPRESENTATIVES.

Washington and Kane Counties—William Snow.
Iron County—Silas S. Smith.
Beaver and Piute Counties—John R. Murdock.
Millard County—F. M. Lyman.
Juab County—Jonathan Midgley.
Sanpete and Sevier Counties—W. S. Seely and George Taylor.
Utah County—Wm. B. Pace, David Evans and Albert K. Thurber.
Wasatch County—Abraham Hatch.
Summit County—William W. Cluff.
Salt Lake County—John Taylor, Albert P. Rockwood, Enoch Reese,
Orson Pratt, Sr., Brigham Young, Jr. and Joseph F. Smith.
Tooele County—John Rowberry.
Davis and Morgan Counties—Wm. R. Smith and Willard G. Smith.
Weber County—Chauncey W. West and Lorin Farr.
Box Elder County—Jonathan C. Wright.
Cache and Rich Counties—Peter Maughan and Charles C. Rich.

SALT LAKE CITY.

SALT LAKE CITY is situated at the foot of a spur of the Wasatch
mountains, its northern limits running up unto the "bench," or elevated
portion of the valley, which reaches to the base of the mountains. It
can be approached from the east by two canons—Emigration canon,
through which nearly all travel formerly passed, and which debouches
in the valley between three and four miles from the city; and Parley's
canon, through which the stage road runs. The mouth of the latter
canon is some six miles from the city, in a southeasterly direction, and
the road between them runs past a tannery, two woolen mills, and a
paper mill, all worked by the water of the creek that dashes down the
canon hollow. The scenery in each is bold and impressive, the mountain sides of these passes in the Wasatch range rising with wild abrupt-
ness from extremely narrow gorges, and covered on their summits with
pine, maple, oak, and other kinds of timber, extensively used for lum-
bering purposes and fire wood. Nearly thirty miles to the south the
mountain range juts across the valley, partially separating it from Utah
valley, which contains the lake of the same name. To the west of the
valley rises the Oquirrh range of mountains; and north of them, about
twenty miles from the city, in a westerly direction, lies Salt Lake, with

several mountainous islands jutting out of its bed, which have been utilized for herd grounds, sheep ranges, and salt boiling. The streets in the main portions of the city are laid out at right angles, and run north and south, east and west. They are 132 feet wide, with rivulets of water gurgling down each street, used for irrigation, and for culinary purposes where wells are not sunk. The culture of shade trees, which have a rapid and healthy growth from these streams, is much encouraged ; and as almost every lot has an orchard, when the summer foliage clothes fruit and shade tree with a full covering of green, the picture which the city presents is then exceedingly pleasant and beautiful. The blocks contain ten acres each, and were originally laid out to contain eight lots to the block; but the growth of business, and other causes, have changed this design in the centre of the city, where the buildings are erected closer together. In the 20th ward, the northeast portion of the city, which is a survey of more recent date than the first settled part, the blocks contain only two and a half acres each, and the streets are proportionately narrow ; and a portion of the 17th and 19th wards, in the northwest part, contains crooked and irregular streets, caused by the peculiar character and irregularities of the ground.

The city contains about 25,000 inhabitants. It has several tanneries, grist mills, the woolen factories mentioned before, the paper mill, a pail factory, steam wood working factories, furniture factories, large adobe yards, brick yards, etc., etc. Its City Hall, not long built, cost $70,000, yet the corporation is entirely free from debt.

The government is vested in a Mayor, five Aldermen, and nine Councilors.

MUNICIPAL ORGANIZATION.

Mayor—Daniel H. Wells.
Marshal—John D. T. McAllister.
Recorder—Robert Campbell.
Treasurer—Paul A. Schettler.
Aldermen—Henry W. Lawrence, Samuel W. Richards, Alonzo H. Raleigh, Jeter Clinton, Alexander C. Pyper.
Councilors—R. T. Burton, Isaac Groo, Theodore McKean, John Sharp, William S. Godbe, Peter Nebeker, Thomas Jenkins, George J. Taylor, Heber P. Kimball.

STANDING COMMITTEES.

On Public Laws—Raleigh, McKean and Taylor.
On Ways and Means—Richards, McKean, Godbe, Sharp and Nebeker.
On Claims—Pyper, Burton and Sharp.
On Improvements—Lawrence, Burton, Groo, Jenkins and Taylor.
On Unfinished Business—Raleigh, Godbe and Kimball.

On Elections—Richards, Sharp and Kimball.
On Police—Clinton, Lawrence, Groo, Burton and Sharp.
On Public Grounds—Lawrence, Richards, Godbe, Nebeker and Pyper.
On Revision—Clinton, Burton and McKean.
On License—Richards, Groo and Lawrence.
On Public Works—Raleigh, Jenkins and Nebeker.
On Finances—Pyper, Godbe and Taylor.
On Cemetery—Groo, McKean and Taylor.
On Market House—Clinton, Groo and Lawrence.

CITY OFFICERS.

City Attorney—Hosea Stout.
Chief of Police—Andrew Burt.
Chief Engineer of Fire Department—John D. T. McAllister.
City Business Agent—Isaac Groo.
Inspector of Buildings—A. H. Raleigh.
Inspector of Liquors—Robert Campbell.
Inspector of Stock—H. J. Faust.
Market Master—Andrew Burt.
Sealer of Weights and Measures—Nathan Davis.
Surveyor—Jesse W. Fox.
Quarantine Physician—Jeter Clinton.
City Sexton—Joseph E. Taylor.

PUBLIC BUILDINGS.

THE TEMPLE.
Temple Block.

COUNCIL HOUSE.
Corner of S. T. and E. T.

CITY HALL.
1st S. bet. 1st and 2d E.

COURT HOUSE.
Corner of 2d W. and 2d S.

CITY PRISON.
Rear of City Hall.

SEVENTIES' HALL.
1st E. bet. 1st and 2d S.

BATH HOUSE.
Northwest of city on State road.

PENITENTIARY.
Four miles southeast of city.

PLACES OF AMUSEMENT.

THEATRE.
Corner of 1st E. and 1st S.

SOCIAL HALL.
1st E. bet. S. T. and 1st S.

MUSIC HALL.
1st S. bet. 1st and 2d W.

BILLIARD HALLS.
E. T. bet. 1st and 2d S., and 2d S. bet. E. T. and 1st E.

CHURCHES.

TABERNACLES
Temple Block.

ASSEMBLY ROOMS.
Of 13th, 14th and 8th wards, and Independence Hall, 3 S. bet. E, and W. T.

WARD MEETING HOUSE.
In each ward.

LITERARY, SCIENTIFIC AND BENEVOLENT.

Lectures are delivered on miscellaneous subjects, in various parts of the city, during the winter months. Debating clubs, organized annually, also hold regular meetings. Female relief societies are organized, one in each ward, which minister to the wants of the necessitous.

EDUCATIONAL.

UNIVERSITY OF DESERET.

Mercantile department of the University of Deseret, classes meet in Council House. Prof. J. A. Park, principal.

MORGAN'S COMMERCIAL COLLEGE.

East side of E. T. bet. 2d and 3d S. John Morgan, M. A., principal.

UNION ACADEMY.

Near Washington Square, 16th ward. Dr. H. I. Doremus, principal.

RAGERS' SEMINARY.

13th ward assembly rooms.
A ward school in each ward, and private schools in several.

CEMETERIES.

CITY CEMETERY.

Northeast of city.

CAMP DOUGLAS CEMETERY.

Contiguous to Camp.

HOT AND MINERAL SPRINGS.

Warm springs one mile north of city, and hot springs three miles north, on state road.

GUIDE TO THE PUBLIC BUILDINGS, ETC., IN SALT LAKE CITY.

THE TEMPLE.

Not yet completed, situated near the east centre of Temple Block. The ground was consecrated February 14th, 1853; corner stones laid April 6th following, sixteen feet below the surface of the ground. Its total length is 186½ feet; width 99 feet; and covers an area of 21,850 feet.

THE TABERNACLE.

Inside Temple Block. First opened to public worship October 6th, 1867, though then unfinished. It is an oblong, 250 feet from east to west, by 150 feet from north to south. The roof is a single oval span, 80 feet high with the ceiling 65 feet above the flooring, and rests on 46 square pillars of red cut sandstone. It is capable of seating about 8,000 persons; and has an organ in course of construction, inside the building, said to be the largest in the United States. Entrances to building from S. and W. Temple streets.

OLD TABERNACLE.

Erected in 1851 of adobies, now used for public worship during winter; stands south of the New Tabernacle on the same block; is 126 feet by 64 feet, and can seat over 2,500 persons.

COUNCIL HOUSE.

Northeast corner of block between S. and E. Temple streets; erected 1849, of red sandstone, two stories, 45 feet square, now occupied by University of Deseret and Commercial Bazaar.

COURT HOUSE.

Southwest corner of block between 2d W. and 2d S. streets; cost about $20,000. The U. S. Supreme Court, the U. S. and Territorial Courts, for the 3d judicial district, and the Probate Court for Salt Lake county, are held here. Underneath are the cells of the county prison.

CITY HALL.

1st S. between 1st and 2d E. streets, 60 feet square, two stories; cost $70,000. Contains the Mayor's, Recorder's and City Treasurer's offices; an Alderman's and Justice's Court room; Council Chamber; Territorial Library; City Attorney's office, and that of the Adjutant General of the Nauvoo Legion—the territorial militia. The sessions of the Legislative Assembly are held in this hall.

CITY PRISON.

Rear of City Hall. Strongly built of cut sandstone; the blocks have an inch and a half ball laid between each two to prevent criminals cutting through the cement. Cost, over $30,000.

SEVENTIES' HALL.

1st E. between 1st and 2d S.; 50 feet by 30 feet; principally used for free public lectures.

THEATRE.

Corner of 1 E. and 1 S.; 144 feet by 80 feet, in the main building, but an addition of 28 feet to the north end makes it 172 feet in length. The auditorium is divided into parquette, first or dress circle, second and third circles, and is capable of seating nearly 1,700 persons. The circle, balconies and proscenium are tastefully finished in white and gold. The stage is 80 feet deep, and at the back are the green room, large scene room, the copyist's room, manager's office, with a number of dressing rooms up stairs. Other dressing rooms, atelier, machinist's work room, etc., are also in the rear of the main building.

The Box office is on the west side of the portico in front, which is furnished with fluted columns.

SOCIAL HALL.

1 E. bet. S. T. and 1st S. streets; 73 feet by 33 feet; built 1853; formerly used for theatrical purposes and social parties; now devoted to balls and parties.

MUSIC HALL.

1st S. bet. 1st and 2d W. streets; used for concerts, balls, parties, etc.

INDEPENDENCE HALL.

7th ward, 3 S. bet. E. and W. T.; used for lectures, meetings, parties, and school purposes. Episcopal service and other religious meetings held in it.

THIRTEENTH WARD ASSEMBLY ROOMS.

2d S. bet. 1st and 2d E.; used for ward and general meetings, concerts, etc.

Each ward in the city has a hall, or meeting-house, used for ward and general meetings.

BATHS AND SPRINGS.

CITY BATHS.

Northwest of city, on State road north, are plunge and private baths. The water of these baths is of a highly medicinal quality.

Dr. Charles T. Jackson, of Boston, made an analysis of the water in 1849. The following is his report:

"Three fluid ounces of the water on evaporation to entire dryness in a platina capsule gave 8.25 grains of solid, dry, saline matter.

Carbonate of Lime and Magnesia	0.240	1.280
Per Oxide of Iron	0.040	0.208
Lime	0.545	2.907
Chlorine	3.454	18.421
Soda	2.877	15.344
Magnesia	0.370	2.073
Sulphuric Acid	0.703	3.748
	8.229	43.981

It is slightly charged with Hydro Sulphuric Acid Gas, and with Carbonic Acid Gas, and is a pleasant, saline, mineral water, having valuable properties belonging to saline sulphur springs."

The usual temperature is laid down at 102 degrees F.

HOT SPRINGS.

Two miles further north are the Hot Springs, very similar in quality and component parts to the Warm Springs, but issuing from the foot of a rock at the base of the mountain in a stream as thick as an ordinary sized man's leg, and of boiling heat. Close by, to the west, is a beautiful little lake, some three miles long by a little over a mile in breadth, which is formed from the waters of these springs and is known as the "Hot Spring Lake." It is fringed with a growth of trees, looks very pretty in the summer, and in winter, when frozen over, is a favorite resort for skating parties.

COURTS.

THE SUPREME COURT.

Holds its sittings in the Court House, southwest corner of block on 2d South and 2d West.

UNITED STATES AND TERRITORIAL DISTRICT COURT FOR THIRD JUDICIAL DISTRICT.

In Court House.

COUNTY COURT.

In Court House.

ALDERMAN'S AND JUSTICE'S COURTS.

In City Hall.

SECRET SOCIETIES.

Masonic.

MOUNT MORIAH LODGE, NO. 70, A. F. & A. M.

Regular communication of Mount Moriah Lodge, No, 70, A., F. & A. M. held at Masonic Hall the second and fourth Monday of each month.

Members of Sister Lodges and sojourning Brethren in good standing, are cordially invited to attend.

W. M.—Joseph F. Nounnan.

Sec.—Sol. Siegel.

WASATCH LODGM, NO. 8, A. F. & A. M.

Regular communications of Wasatch Lodge, No. 8, A. F. & A. M., held at Masonic Hall, on second and fourth Fridays of each month.

Sojourning and visiting Brethren, in good standing are invited to attend.

W. M.—R. H. Robertson.

Sec.—John Cunnington.

Independent Order of Odd Fellows.

UTAH LODGE, NO. 1.

Hold their regular meetings in Odd Fellows' Hall, Main street, on Thursday evening of each week at 7 o'clock.

Brethren in good standing are invited to attend.

N. G.—Nathan Ellis.

Sec.—R. Wolfer.

Independent Order of Good Templars.

CAMP DOUGLAS LODGE, NO. 1.

Holds its regular meetings at the Good Templars' Hall at Camp Douglas on Wednesday evening of each week at 6 o'clock.

Sojourning Brethren in good standing are respectfully invited to attend.

W. C. T.—S. Elwell.

W. S.—E. W. Stiles.

BANKS.

The Banking Companies doing business in Salt Lake City are those of Wells, Fargo & Co., whose general agent for all purposes in this region is Theodore F. Tracey, Esq.; and Hussey, Dahler & Co., managed by Warren Hussey, Esq.; the latter having purchased the "Miners' National Bank." Both are undoubted in credit and reliability.

HOTELS.

The principal hotels are the Salt Lake House, F. Little, proprietor, situated on the east side of East Temple street. The Townsend House, J. Townsend, proprietor, situated on the corner of First South and West Temple streets. The Revere House, conducted by Mr. Shurtliff, Second South street, near First East. The Mansion House, E. Tufts, proprietor, on the corner of First East and Third South streets. The Delmonico, run by Mr. Greenwald, situated on the west side of East Temple street, and the Pacific House, F. Reich, proprietor, East Temple, between Second and Third South streets.

POST OFFICE.

Salt Lake City Distributing Post Office; West side East Temple street, between South Temple and 1 South.

Postmaster—A. W. Street.

OFFICE HOURS.

General Delivery Open.................................8 a. m.
     "   "   Closes ....6 p. m.
     "   "   Sundays...........................12 to 1 p. m.
Outside door open......................................6 a. m. to 9 p. m.
For money orders and registering letters...........10 a. m. to 4 p. m.

TIME OF ARRIVAL AND CLOSING OF MAILS.

		CLOSE.		ARRIVE.	
		A. M.	P. M.	A. M.	P. M.
EAST—Daily		5.30			
" Local—					
" Coalville, Wanship and Heber, Thursdays		5.30			
WEST—Daily		6.00			
" Local—					
" Tooele, Stockton, Deep Creek		6.00			
" Grantsville, Thursdays		6.00			
NORTH—Idaho, Washington and Oregon, carrying territorial mail to Bear River, daily		5.30			
" Due, daily				8.00	
" Virginia, Montana, daily		5.30			
" Due, daily				8.00	
" Helena, Montana, alternate days		5.30			
" Due, alternate days				8.00	
" Morgan county, Thursdays		5.30			
" Due, Saturdays				8.00	
" Cache Valley, Mondays and Thursdays		5.30			
" Due Wednesdays and Saturdays				8.00	
" Bear Lake, Thursdays		5.30			
" Due, Saturdays				8.00	
SOUTH—Provo, daily, except Sunday		7.30			
" Due, daily					11.00
" Fillmore, Mondays, Wednesdays and Fridays		7.30			
" Due, Tuesdays, Thursdays and Saturdays					11.00
" St. George and Arizona, Mondays and Fridays		7.30			
" Due Tuesdays and Saturdays					11.00
" Sanpete county, Mondays and Fridays		7.30			
" Due, Tuesdays and Saturdays					11.00
" Fairfield and Cedar Valley, Thursdays,		7.30			
" Due, Fridays					11.00
WEST Jordan and Herriman, Thursdays		5.30			7.00

The time of arrival and closing of mails is subject to frequent changes.

RATES OF DOMESTIC POSTAGE.

LETTERS.

The standard single rate weight is ½ ounce avoirdupois.

Single rate letter, throughout the United States...... 3 cents
For each additional ½ oz. or fraction................. 3 "
Drop-letters, for local delivery, single rate.......... 2 "
" where there is no local delivery, single rate 1 "
Advertised letters are charged extra............... 1 "

These postages must be prepaid by stamps.

NEWSPAPERS.

The standard single rate is 4 ounces avoirdupois.

Daily (seven times a week)............ 35 cents per quarter.
  "   (six   "   )............ 30   "
Tri-weekly......................... 15   "
Semi-weekly........................ 10   "
Weekly............................. 5   "

These rates must be prepaid quarterly or yearly ; for full security they should be paid at the office where the paper is received. One copy of a weekly newspaper may be sent free by the publisher to each subscriber who resides in the county where the paper is published.

PERIODICALS.

The standard single rate is 4 ounces avoirdupois.

Semi-weekly.................... .... 6 cents per quarter.
Monthly............................ 3   "
Quarterly.......................... 1   "

TRANSIENT PRINTED MATTER.

Books, for each single rate of 4 oz. avoirdupois............. 4 cents.
Circulars, not exceeding three in one envelope constituting a
    single rate... 2 cents.
Miscellaneous mailable matter (embracing all pamphlets, occa-
    sional publications, transient newspapers, book manuscripts
    and proof-sheets, whether corrected or not, maps, prints,
    engravings, sheet music, blanks, flexible patterns, samples
    and sample cards, photographic paper, letter envelopes,
    postal envelopes or wrappers, cards, paper, plain or orna-
    mental, photographic representations of different types,
    seeds, cuttings, bulbs, roots, and scions), in one package to
    one address, for each single rate of 4 ounces avoirdupois.. 2 cents.

[By a decision of the Post Office Department, manuscripts and proofs passing between authors and editors of magazines and newspapers are not regarded as passing "between authors and publishers," and must pay letter postage.]

Prepayment by stamps is required for all postage on transient printed matter.

The maximum weight of any package of printed or miscellaneous matter is 4 pounds avoirdupois.

REGISTRATION.

Letters may be registered on payment of a fee of fifteen cents, but the government takes no responsibility for safe carriage or compensation in case of loss.

MONEY ORDERS.

All principal post offices now receive small sums of money and issue drafts for the same upon other post offices, subject to the following charges and regulations.

On orders not exceeding $20.................... 10 cents.
Over $20 and not exceeding $30................. 15 cents.
Over $30 and not exceeding $40................. 20 cents.
Over $40 and not exceeding $50................. 25 cents.

No fractions of cents to be introduced in an order. United States Treasury Notes or National Bank Notes only received or paid.

The order is only payable at the office upon which it is drawn.   The order should be collected within one year from its date. After once paying an order, by whomsoever presented, the Department will be liable to no further claim.

RATES OF POSTAGE BETWEEN THE UNITED STATES AND THE BRITISH NORTH AMERICAN PROVINCES.

LETTERS.

The standard single rate is ½ ounce avoirdupois.

To or from the Dominion of Canada, irrespective of distance, if prepaid, 6 cents; otherwise...................... 10 cents.

To and from other British North American Provinces, for a distance of not over 3,000......................... 10 "

For any distance over 3,000............................ 15 "

Prepayment optional except to Newfoundland, to which prepayment is compulsory.

PRINTED MATTER.

The regular United States rates must be prepaid, but these only pay for transportation to the boundary line; a second fee is charged on delivery by the Provincial post office.

LIST OF POST OFFICES IN UTAH TERRITORY, FEB. 1869.

Name of Office.	County.	Name of Office.	County.
Alpine City	Utah.	Millville	Cache.
American Fork	Utah.	Minersville	Beaver.
Adamsville	Beaver.	Mona	Juab.
Bear River	Box Elder.	Morgan	Morgan.
Beaver	Beaver.	Moroni	Sanpete.
Brigham City	Box Elder.	Mountain	Morgan.
Bloomington	Rich.	Mount Pleasant	Sanpete.
Bennington	Rich.	New Harmony	Washington.
Big Cottonwood	Salt Lake.	North Ogden	Weber.
Cedar City	Iron.	Ogden City	Weber.
Cedar Valley	Utah.	Panaca	Washington.
Centreville	Davis.	Paradise	Cache.
Coalville	Summit.	Portage	Box Elder.
Croyden	Morgan.	Paragoonah	Iron.
Deep Creek	Tooe e.	Parowan	Iron.
Deseret	Millard.	Paris	Rich.
Draper	Salt Lake.	Payson	Utah.
Duncans' Retreat	Kane.	Peoa	Summit.
Easton	Weber.	Pine Valley	Washington.
Enterprise	Morgan.	Pinto	Iron.
Evanston	Summit.	Plain City	Weber
Ephraim	Sanpete.	Pleasant Grove	Utah.
Echo City	Summit.	Providence	Cache.
Fairfield	Utah.	Provo City	Utah.
Fairview	Sanpete.	Richmond	Cache.
Farmington	Davis.	Rockville	Washington.
Fillmore City	Millard.	Riverdale	Weber.
Fish Haven	Rich.	St. Charles	Rich.
Fountain Green	Sanpete.	Slatersville	Weber.
Franklin	Cache.	Salt Creek	Juab.
Gunnison	Sanpete.	Salt Lake City	Salt Lake.
Grantsville	Tooele.	Santaquin	Utah.
Gilmer	Summit.	Summit	Iron.
Harrisburg	Washington.	Scipio	Millard
Heber City	Wasatch.	Smithfield	Cache.
Holden	Millard.	Spanish Fork	Utah.
Herriman	Salt Lake.	Springdale	Kane.
Huntsville	Weber.	Springtown	Sanpete.
Hyde Park	Cache.	Springville	Utah.
Hyrum	Cache.	Spring Lake Villa	Utah.
Kananaville	Iron.	Stoker	Davis.
Kanosh	Millard.	Saint George	Washington.
Kaysville	Davis.	Toquerville	Washington.
Lavan	Juab.	Tooele	Tooele.
Lehi City	Utah.	Union	Salt Lake.
Liberty	Rich.	Virgen City	Washington.
Logan	Cache.	Wanship	Summit.
Lynne	Weber.	Washington	Washington.
Manti	Sanpete.	Weber	Morgan.
Meadow	Millard.	Wellsville	Cache.
Mendon	Cache.	West Jordan	Salt Lake.
Midway	Wasatch.	Willard	Box Elder.

SALT LAKE COUNTY.

Salt Lake County covers an extent of over 400 square miles, a considerable portion of which is under cultivation. To the west of Jordan river, which runs northward through the valley, is a large tract of land lying within the county, which is principally used as a range for cattle. Large amounts have been expended to bring the water of the Jordan out, and carry it through canals to irrigate portions of this land, and the result is numerous productive farms where but a short time ago were rabbit brush and scant herbage for cattle. The population of the county is between 30,000 and 35,000.

COUNTY OFFICERS.

Probate Judge—Elias Smith.
County Clerk—E. W. East.
District Attorney—Zerubbabel Snow.
Sheriff—Robert T. Burton.
Recorder—Edwin D. Woolley.
Treasurer—Theodore McKean.
Assessor—Robert T. Burton.
Coroner—H. S. Beatie.
Notaries Public—John T. Caine, William Clayton, Patrick Lynch and W. W. Phelps.
Superintendent of Common Schools—Robert L. Campbell.
Selectmen—Reuben Miller, Robert J. Golding and Isaac Stewart.

DISTANCES FROM SALT LAKE CITY.

By Union Pacific Railroad.
EAST.

Salt Lake City to—	Distances from point to point.	Total Distance.	Altitude.
			4,300
Ogden	39	39	4,320
Weber Canon	10½	49½	4,654
Echo	32	81½	5,764
Wasatch	23½	105	6,880
Bryan	108	213	6,310
Cheyenne	345	558	7,040
Sidney	102	660	
North Platte	123	783	2,790
Omaha	291	1,074	965
Chicago	493	1,567	625
Philadelphia	824	2,391	
Chicago to New York	898	2,465	Tide.
Chicago to Boston	1,017	2,584	

By Central Pacific Railroad.
WEST.

Salt Lake to City—	Distances from point to point.	Total Distance.	Altitude.
			4,300
Ogden	39	39	4,320
Brigham City	21	60	4,330
Bear River	3	63	4,266
Promontory	29	92	4,943
Monument Point	27	119	4,290
Humboldt Wells	142	261	5,650
Elcho	60	321	5,030
Argenta	64	385	4,575
Winnemucca	72	457	4,365
Reno	170	627	4,525
Summit	49	676	7,042
Colfax	51	727	2,448
Sacramento	54	781	56
San Francisco (via Sacramento river)	120	901	Tide.
Portland, Oregon (by Ocean)	642	1,543	
Victoria, V. I. (by Ocean)	753	1,654	
Panama, C. A. (by Ocean)	3,280	4,181	

DISTANCES FROM SALT LAKE CITY.

NORTH.

By Wells, Fargo & Co.'s Stages,

TO HELENA AND FORT BENTON, M. T.

Salt Lake City to—	Distance from point to point.	Total distance.
Centreville	12	12
Farmington	5	17
Ogden	22	39
Brigham City	22	61
Bear River	23	84
Malad City	32	116
Carpenters'	33	149
Ross Fork	47	196
Taylor's Bridge	42	238
Desert Wells	37	275
Pleasant Valley	46	321
Black-tailed Deer	51	372
Virginia	50	422
White-tailed Deer	65	487
Helena	59	546
Fort Benton	140	686

TO BOISE CITY.

Salt Lake City to—		
Bear River	84	84
Curlew	50	134
City of Rocks	47	181
Mountain Meadows	38	219
Overland Ferry	41	260
King Hill	50	310
Canon Creek	40	350
Boise City	43	393

SOUTH.

Salt Lake City to—	Distance from point to point.	Total distance.
Provo	48	48
Fillmore	112	160
St. George	180	340
San Bernardino	385	725
Los Angeles	55	780

SALT LAKE CITY

DIRECTORY

ABBREVIATIONS:

bet..between
cor..corner
E..east
es...east side
E. T..East Temple
lab...laborer
N..north
ns...north side

N. T...North Temple
res...residence
S...south
ss...south side
S. T...South Temple
wd..ward
ws..west side
W. T...West Temple

Abel Elijah, carpenter, 10th wd. 3d S. bet. 8 and 9 E.

Adair I. S. auctioneer, with J. K. Trumbo

Adams Ellis E. teamster, 20th wd. Maple, cor. Fruit

Adams B. L. farmer. 1st wd. 7 E. cor. 8 S.

Adams Hannah, wid. 7th wd. 3 S. bet. E. and W. T.

Addoms John, bookkeeper, with L. Reggel, res. 15th wd. 3 W. bet. S. T. and 1 S.

Adkins George, mason, 11th wd. S. T. cor. 7 E.

Adkins William R. gardener, 20th wd. Spruce, bet. Fir and Wall

Admire Charles, cooper, 17th wd. bet. 1 and 2 N.

Afelts John, tanner, 1st wd. bench bet. 7 and 8 S.

Airmet John, carpenter, 20th wd. Elm, cor. Prospect

Ajax William, commission merchant, 11th wd. 8 E. bet. 2 and 3 S.

Albach A. manager, " Reporter " office

Albern William, lab. 19th wd. 5 W. bet. 3 and 4 N.

Albion James, architect, 15th wd. 1 S. bet. 4 and 5 W.

Albion James, lab. 6th wd. 2 W. bet. 5 and 6 S.

Alder George A. (Dunford & Sons), hats, boots and shoes, es. E. T. bet. 1 and 2 S. res. 14th wd. S. T. bet. 1 and 2 W.

Alexander Charles, lab. 12th wd. 4 E. bet. 2 and 3 S.

Alford John, salesman, with G. Goddard, res. 19th wd. cor. Central and Currant

Allen William L. N. cabinetmaker, 20th wd. S. T. cor. Locust
Allen Samuel, lab. 1st wd. 7 S. bet. 8 and 9 E.
Allen Joseph M. (Allen & Co.), stoves and tinware, ws. E. T. bet. 1 and
    2 S. res. 7th wd. 4 S. cor. 1 W.
Allen Thomas, lab. 15th wd. 4 W. bet. 2 and 3 S.
Almond James, gardener, 19th wd. 3 W. bet. 3 and 4 N.
Almond John B. salesman, with Allen & Co. res. 14th wd. 2 S. bet. 1
    and 2 W.
Alpine John, freighter, 13th wd. 1 E. bet. 2 and 3 S.
Ames John, baker, 13th wd. S. T. bet. 1 and 2 E.
Anderson James, moulder, 6th wd. 3 W. bet. 3 and 4 S.
Anderson A. glovemaker, 2 S. bet. E. T. and 1 E.
Anderson William, carpenter, 6th wd. 5 S. bet. 2 and 3 W.
Anderson Neils, carpenter, 3d wd. 6 S. bet. 1 and 2 E.
Anderson Andrew, bricklayer, 2d wd. 8 S. bet. 3 and 4 E.
Anderson Mrs. wid. 10th wd. 6 S. bet. 8 and 9 E.
Anderson Henry, 11th wd. 8 E. bet. 2 and 3 S.
Anderson Ole C. shoemaker, 20th, Birch, cor. Garden
Anderson A. tailor, 8th wd. 2 E. bet. 4 and 5 S.
Anderson Robert, clerk, 13th wd. 1 S. bet. 1 and 2 E.
Anderson W. F., M. D. physician and surgeon, 13th wd. 2 E. bet. 2 and
    3 S.
Anderson George, herdsman, 20th wd. Elm, cor. Bluff
Andres Frantzen, glovemaker, 1 S. bet. E. T. and 1 E.
Andrew F. H. blacksmith, 7th wd. 4 S. bet. E. and W. T.
Andrews Chester, lab. 15th wd. 4 W. bet. S. T. and 1 S.
Andrews Joseph, with David Day, res. 13th wd. 3 S. bet. E. T. and 1 E.
Angell Trueman O. architect, 1st wd.
Angell Albert, shinglemaker, 20th wd. Wall, cor. Fir
Ansel Eric, shoemaker, 8th wd. E. T. bet. 5 and 6 S.
Angell John O. shinglemaker, 20th wd. Wall, cor. Oak
Appleby William I. attorney at law and clerk Supreme Court, office, at
    res. 14th wd. 1 S. bet. W. T. and 1 W.
Appleby William P. clerk, 7th wd. 3 S. bet. W. T. and 1 W.
Applegate Joseph, teamster, 17th wd. N. T. cor. 1 W.
Armstrong Frank, contractor, 11th wd. 1 S. bet. 6 and 7 E.
Armstrong Thomas E. bookkeeper, with Kimball & Lawrence, res. 14th
    wd. 1 S. bet. W. T. and 1 W.
Arnold George, lab. 17th wd. 2 W. cor. 2 N.
Arnold Henry, keeper of baths, res. 19th wd. at Warm Spring Baths
Arnold Orsen, teamster, 13th wd. 3 E. bet. 1 and 2 S.
Arnold Joseph H. lab. 19th wd. 2 N. bet. 5 and 6 W.
Ashman James, lab. 10th wd. 9 E. bet. 3 and 4 S.
Ashman William, shoemaker, 10th wd. 5 S. bet. 7 and 8 E.

Ashton Edward, shoemaker, 15th wd. 6 W. bet. 1 and 2 S.
Asmussen Carl, watchmaker and jeweler, E. T. bet. S. T. and 1 S.
Asper William, carpenter, 19th wd. cor. Quince and Quaking Asp
Assay William, carpenter, 5th wd. 6 S. bet. 3 and 4 W.
Atkins Reuben, shoemaker, 2d wd. 7 S. bet. 3 and 4 E.
Atkinson Jane, wid. 7th wd. 3 S. bet. W. T. and 1 W.
Attey Stephen, farmer, 8th wd. 1 E. cor. 4 S.
Attley Henry, pressman, Deseret News office, res. 15th wd. 6 W. cor. 1 S.
Atwell Wm. carpenter, 20th wd. cor. Fruit and Quaking Asp
Atwick Wm. farmer, 15th wd. 8 W. bet. S. and N. T.
Atwood Minor G. farmer, 12th wd. 1 S. bet. 5 and 6 E.
Atwood Orville, teamster, 12th wd. 2 S. bet. 4 and 5 E.
Atwood Millen, farmer, 13th wd. 1 E. bet. 2 and 3 S.
Atwood William, carpenter, 19th wd. 4 N. bet. 1 and 2 W.
Atwood Charles B. clerk, with W. B. Wilkinson, res. 19th wd. 5 N. bet.
    1 and 2 W.
Auerbach & Levy, fancygoods, E. T. bet. 1 and 2 S.
Auerbach & Bros. general merchandize, ws. E. T. bet. 1 and 2 S.
Aubrey Thomas, painter, 14th wd. 3 S. cor. W. T.
Auger Sarah, wid. 6th wd. 4 S. bet. 3 and 4 W.
Austerman J. shoemaker, 19th wd. Beet
Aveson R. compositor, Telegraph office, res. 20th wd.
Axton John, lab. 12th wd. 6 E. bet. 1 and 2 S.
Ayland William T. warehouseman, 7th wd. 3 S. bet. E. and W. T.
Ayrton William, gardener, 15th wd. 1 S. bet. 3 and 4 W.

B

Badley George, farmer, 10th wd. 3 S. bet. 9 and 10 E.
Baggs John, shoemaker, 9th wd. 3 S. bet. 4 and 5 E.
Baguley Joseph, lab. 11th wd. 10 E. bet. 2 and 3 S.
Bailey Anna, wid. 16th wd. 2 N. bet. 3 and 4 W.
Bailey John, trader, 4th wd. 1 W. bet. 7 and 8 S.
Bain John, painter, 20th wd. Spruce cor. Prospect
Baker Mr. physician, 13th wd. 2 E. bet. 2 and 3 S.
Baker Harry, assistant property man at theatre, res. 14th wd. E. T. bet.
    2 and 3 S.
Baldwin James, lab. 17th wd. 2 W. bet. 1 and 2 N.
Baldwin Nancy, wid. 15th wd. 2 S. cor. 5 W.
Ball John P. shoemaker, 3d wd. 1 E. cor. 7 S.
Ballan William, watchmaker, ws. E. T. bet. S. T. and 1 S. res. 17th wd.
    2 N. bet. W. T. and 1 W.
Bamford Charles, lab. 8th wd. 3 E. bet. 3 and 4 S.

Barfoot Joseph L. warterproofer, 3d wd. 3 E. cor. 7 S.

Barker Joseph (B. & Wells), gunsmith and cutler, ns. 2 S. bet. E. T. and 1 E. res. 20th wd. S. T. cor. Ash

Barker Andrew, lab. 13th wd. 3 E. bet. 2 and 3 S.

Barlow J. M. watch and clockmaker, 15th wd. 1 S. cor. 3 W.

Barnard John, teamster, 20th wd. Maple, cor. Fruit

Barnes James, mason, 19th wd. 2 N. bet. 1 and 2 W.

Barnes Mark, gardener, 11th wd. 6 E. bet. S. T. and 1 S.

Barnes John S. trader, 8th wd. E. T. bet. 3 and 4 S.

Barney Royal, carpenter, 8th wd. E. T. bet. 4 and 5 S.

Barnum Charles D. carpenter, 15th wd. 1 S. bet. 3 and 4 W.

Barrows E. variety store, 2 S. bet. E. T. and 1 E.

Barth Wm. & Bro. boots and shoes, ns. 2 S. bet. E T. and 1 E.

Barton William, carpenter, 20th wd. Chesnut, cor. Bluff

Barton George, clerk, with Kahn Bros. res. 15th wd 3 S. bet. 4 and 5 W.

Baskin R. N. attorney at law, E. T. bet. 1 and 2 S.

Bassett C. H. (B. & Roberts), general merchandise, whol. and ret. ws. E. T. bet. 1 and 2 S. res. 14th wd. S. T. cor. 2 W.

Bassett A. C. asst. supt. Western Union Telegraph office, es. E. T. bet. S. T. and 1 S.

Bates William, shoemaker, 9th wd. 4 E. bet. 5 and 6 S.

Bath William, lab. 19th wd. 4 W. bet. 3 and 4 N.

Bauman & Co. druggists, ws. E. T. bet. 1 and 2 S.

Bayliss William, cabinetmaker, 20th wd. S. T. cor. Beach

Bayliss Ephraim, teamster, 19th wd. 5 N. cor. 1 W.

Beach Aaron, lab. 7th wd. 1 W. bet. 4 and 5 S.

Beadle J. H. editor of Reporter, E. T. cor. 2 S.

Bean Joseph, carpenter, 11th wd. 8 E. bet. S. T. and 1 S.

Beatie H. S. salesman, wholesale Co-operative Association, res. 7th wd. E. T. cor. 3 S.

Beck Robert, carpenter, 8th wd. 6 S. bet. E. T. and 1 E.

Beck Jonas N. painter, 19th wd. 5 N. bet. 1 and 2 W.

Beck Elizabeth, wid. 19th wd. 5 N. bet. 1 and 2 W.

Beck Mary, wid. 2d wd. 5 E. bet. 7 and 8 S.

Bedell Edmund, engineer, 13th wd. 1 S. bet. 2 and 3 E.

Beers John, tinner, at late R. C. Sharkey's, res. 13th wd. 3 E. bet. S. T. and 1 S.

Beeston James, commission merchant, 14th wd. 1 S. cor. 1 W.

Beezley Eleazer, shoemaker, 19th wd. bet. Quince and Central

Bell William, cabinetmaker, 20th wd. S. T. cor. Walnut

Bell Joseph, lab. 11th wd. S. T. bet. 7 and 8 E.

Bell Edward, carpenter, 11th wd. 8 E. cor. 2 S.

Bell Henry C. chief clerk stage dept. Wells, Fargo & Co.'s office

Bennett Richard, engineer, 20th wd. bet. Fir and Oak

Benson Andrew B. clerk, with Kimball & Lawrence, res. 19th wd. cor. Central and Peach

Bently Joseph, weaver, 10th wd. 3 S. cor. 9 E.

Bertrand L. A. gardener, 12th wd. 6 E. bet. 2 and 3 S.

Best Alfred, dealer in stoves and tinware, ws. E. T. bet. 1 and 2 S. res. 7th wd. W. T. bet. 3 and 4 S.

Best James, lab. 15th wd. 3 W. bet. S. T. and 1 S.

Bevans Andrew, teamster, 9th wd. 5 S. cor. 5 E.

Beynon Edward, lab. 12th wd. 3 S. bet. 5 and 6 E.

Bimal Charles B. wheelwright, 7th wd. 1 W. bet. 4 and 5 S.

Binder William L. carpenter, 15th wd. 2 S. bet. 3 and 4 W.

Biorkman P. E. tailor and glover, 14th wd. S. T. bet. W. T. and 1 W.

Birchall Thomas, lab. 8th wd. 1 E. bet. 5 and 6 S.

Bircumshaw Joseph, weaver, 11th wd. 9 E. cor. S. T.

Bircumshaw Wm. builder, 9th wd. 5 S. bet. 3 and 4 E.

Bircumshaw Thomas, at J. R. Clawson's

Bird James, cabinet maker, ss. 2 S. bet. E. T. and 1 E. res. 14th wd. W. T. bet. 1 and 2 S.

Bird Edmund F. carver in wood, 15th wd. 3 S. bet. 2 and 3 W.

Bird Henry, lab. 6th wd, 4 W. bet. 3 and 4 S.

Blackhurst David, lab, 7th wd. 4 S. bet. W. T. and 1 W.

Blackhurst Jane, wid. 7th wd. cor. W. T. and 4 S.

Blair Edward, farmer, 1st wd. 8 E. cor. 8 S.

Blair S. M. attorney-at-law, 1st wd.

Blazard John H. wheelwright, 14th wd. 1 S. bet. E. and W. T.

Blonquist L. A. G. shoemaker, 17th wd. 1 W. bet. N. and S. T.

Blunt Joseph, shoemaker, 20th wd. cor. Oak and Garden

Blythe John L. farmer, 13th wd. 1 E. bet. 2 and 3 S.

Boaz Wm. tinner, 13th wd. 2 S. bet. E. T. and 1 E.

Bockholdt Dirk, clerk to collector R. T. Burton, res. 15th wd. 3 W. bet. 2 and 3 S.

Bodell Joseph, butcher, 13th wd. 2 S. bet. 1 and 2 E.

Bodinger T. Van, miner, 16th wd. 1 N. bet. 3 and 4 W.

Bollin Wm. tailor, 17th wd, Crooked

Bollwinkle Frederick, farmer, 19th wd, 2 N. bet. 1 and 2 W.

Bolser John, carpenter, 15th wd. 4 W. cor. S. T.

Bolter John, bartender at Eddins' beer saloon, res. 13th wd. 3 S. bet. E. T. and 1 E.

Bolto Frank, carpenter, 3d wd. 3 E. bet. 6 and 7 S.

Bond George, dyer and scourer, ws. E. T. bet. 1 and 2 S. res. 13th wd. 3 S. bet. 1 and 2 E.

Booth John, clockmaker, 10th wd. 8 E. bet. 3 and 4 S.

Booth Joseph, farmer, 1st wd. 8 E. bet. 6 and 7 S.

Booth Thomas, freighter, 7th wd. 2 W. bet. 5 and 6 S.

Booth Mary, wid. 20th wd. Maple, cor. Fruit
Boswick George, tinner, 7th wd. 3 S. bet. W. T. and 1 W.
Bourne George E. clerk with Jennings & Co. res. 14th wd. 3 S. bet. W. T. and 1 W.
Bovier Edward, farmer, 19th wd. 2 N. bet. 3 and 4 W.
Bowan David, farmer, 1st wd. 7th E. bet. 6 and 7 S.
Bowk John, carpenter, 16th wd. N. T. bet. 4 and 5 W.
Bowlding Richard, lab. 15th wd. 3 W. bet. 2 and 3 S.
Bowman Thomas, blacksmith, 11th wd. 9 E. bet. S. T. and 1 S.
Bowman Wm. sr. lab. 11th wd. 1 S. bet. 7 and 8 E.
Bowman Wm. jr. lab. 11th wd. 1 S. bet. 7 and 8 E.
Bowring Henry E. (B. & Crow), ws. E. T. bet. S. T. and 1 S. res. 12th wd. 1 S. bet. 3 and 4 E.
Box Thomas, freighter, 17th wd. 1 N. cor. 1 W.
Boyce John, farmer, 16th wd. 5 W. bet. N. and S. T.
Boyd George, lab. 5th wd. 2 S. bet. 4 and 5 W.
Boyle George, shoemaker, 20th wd. cor. Hickory and Fruit
Bradfield Charles, blacksmith, 8th wd. 5 S. bet. 2 and 3 E.
Bradford Larkin, tinner, 9th wd. 5 E. bet. 4 and 5 S.
Brain Edward, builder, 20th wd. Pine, cor. Garden
Braiser Richard, farmer, 2d wd. 8 S. bet. 2 and 3 E.
Brasher John L. bartender, S. L. House, 14th wd. W. T. bet. 2 and 3 S.
Bratton Howard, engineer, 13th wd. 1 E. bet. 2 and 3 S.
Brazer George, groceries and provisions, 1 S. bet. E. T. and 1 E.
Brazier Wm. sr. carpenter, 4th wd. 7 S. bet. W. T. and 1 W.
Brazier Wm. jr. carpenter, 4th wd. 7 S. bet. W. T. and 1 W.
Brett John, shoemaker, 15th wd. 1 S. bet. 4 and 5 W.
Brewer James, harnessmaker, 11th wd. 2 S. cor. 7 E.
Brewer Wm. freighter, 20th wd. Birch, cor. S. T.
Brewster Frederick, locksmith, 19th wd. cor. Quince and Currant
Bridge Joseph, lab. 16th wd. N. T. bet. 5 and 6 W.
Brighton Wm. S. lab. 11th wd. 1 S. bet. 8 and 9 E.
Brim Alexander, tanner, 1st wd. 9 E. cor. 7 S.
Bringhurst Samuel, wagonmaker, 8th wd. 3 S. bet. E. and 1 E.
Britner Charles, auctioneer, es. E. T. bet. 2 and 3 S.
Britner & Friedman, auctioneers and commission dealers, E. T. bet. 2 and 3 S.
Britton Richard, jeweler, 6th wd. 4 S. bet. 4 and 5 W.
Broadbent Jesse, lab. 20th wd. Oak, cor. High
Broadbent Levi, farmer, 19th wd. 5 N. bet. 2 and 3 W.
Broadhurst Samuel, wheelwright, 14th wd. 1 S. bet. 1 and 2 W.
Brockbank Isaac, saddler, 8th wd. 1 E. cor. 4 S.
Brocklehurst John, lab. 20th wd. High, bet. Fir and Oak
Brookbank Samuel, lab. 1st wd. 9 E. bet. 7 and 8 S.

Brooks James, plasterer, 7th wd. 5 S. bet. W. T. and 1 W.

Brooks J. G. boarding house, 8th wd. 2 E. cor. 4 S.

Brooks Philip, carpenter, 12th wd. 6 E. bet. S. T. and 1 S.

Brooks Edmund, salesman, with D. Grenig, res. 12th wd. 6 E. bet. S. T. and 1 S.

Broomhead Wm. carpenter, 17th wd. 1 W. bet. N. T. and 1 N.

Brough John, tailor, 4th wd. 1 W. bet. 7 and 8 S.

Brown Wm. clerk at A. Best's, res. 20th wd. Pine, cor. Wall

Brown T. D. (T. D. B. & Son), books and stationery, es. E. T. bet. 1 and 2 S. res. 14th wd. W. T. bet. 1 and 2 S.

Brown James (T. D. B. & Son), books and stationery, res. 14th wd. W. T. bet. 1 and 2 S.

Brown W. O. telegraph operator, Western Union Telegraph office

Brown Samuel W. shoemaker, 2d wd. 4 E. bet. 8 and 9 S.

Brown John, clerk, 1st wd. 8 E. bet. 6 and 7 S.

Brown Alfred, carpenter, 4th wd. 3 W. bet. 6 and 7 S.

Brown James S. miner, 17th wd. 1 W. bet. N. and S. T.

Brown William, farmer, 15th wd. 2 W. bet. S. T. and 1 S.

Brown Joseph, fisherman, 15th wd. 3 W. cor. S. T.

Brown Albert, carpenter, 5th wd. 3 W. bet. 6 and 7 S.

Brown Samuel, carpenter, 5th wd. 7 S. bet. 3 and 4 W.

Brown John, carpenter, 7th wd. 1 W. bet. 3 and 4 S.

Brown C. compositor, Telegraph office, res. 12th wd.

Brown Benjamin P. farmer, 15th wd. 4 W. bet. 1 and 2 S.

Brown Benjamin, farmer, 8th wd. 6 S. cor. W. T.

Brown Mary, wid. 15th wd. 2 S. bet. 4 and 5 W.

Brown John, lab. 3d wd. 3 E. cor. 7 S.

Brown Homer, lab. 7th wd. 6 S. bet. W. T. and 1 W.

Brown John, confectioner, E. T. bet. S. T. and 1 S.

Brown Thomas, shinglemaker, 15 wd. 1 S. bet. 4 and 5 W.

Brown George H. (A. C. Pyper & Co.), general merchant, E. T. bet. S. T. and 1 S. res. 12th wd. cor. 1 S. and 4 E.

Brown Samuel J. carpenter, 4th wd. 7 S. bet. 3 and 4 S.

Brown James, confectioner, next door west of theatre

Brown R. H. clerk, with Pyper & Co.

Brown M. engineer, 12th wd. 5 E. bet. 2 and 3 S.

Browning O. T. (B. & Houtz), dry goods and groceries, ns. 2 S. bet. E. T. and 1 E. res. 12 wd. 3 E. bet. 3 and 4 S.

Browning James, bookkeeper, 7th wd. 3 S. bet. W. T. and 1 W.

Browning Wesley, clerk, 7th wd. W. T. bet. 5 and 6 S.

Brumell Henry, miller, 1st wd. 7 E. cor. 7 S.

Brunker Thomas, mason, 11th wd. 9 E. bet. 2 and 3 S.

Bruntin Eric F. blacksmith, 2d wd. 4 E. cor. 7 S.

Bryan Daniel G. sawyer, 1st wd. 7 E. cor. 7 S.

Buckley Joseph, lab. 3 E. cor. 8 S.

Bull Joseph, compositor, 17th wd. 1. N. bet. 1 and 2 W.

Bullock Charles, lab. 16th wd. 5. W. bet. N. and S. T.

Bullock Thomas, clerk, 14th wd. 1 S. cor. W. T.

Bullock Alexander, lab. 8th wd. 1 E. bet. 5 and 6 S.

Bunch George M. letter clerk, Wells, Fargo & Co.'s office

Bundy George, farmer, 4th wd. 6 S. bet. E. and W. T.

Bune George, wheelwright, 11th wd. 9 E. bet. 2 and 3 S.

Bunot Joseph, watchmaker, 20th wd. cor. Peach and Fruit

Bunting Mary A. wid. 1st wd. W. T. bet. 4 and 5 S.

Bunting James L. boots and shoes, ws. E. T. bet. S. T. and 1 S.
res. 11th wd. S. T. bet. 6 and 7 E.

Burchnell James, clerk, 1st wd. bet. 1 and 2 N. res. 17th wd.

Burgess William, lumberman, 15th wd. 5 W. bet. S. T. and 1 S.

Burnett Gerrit B. lab. 10th wd. 5 S. bet. 9 and 10 E.

Burns James, lab. 10th wd. 9 E. bet. 5 and 6 S.

Burns Robert, farmer, 12th wd. 3 S. cor. 4 E.

Burnswood Joseph, blacksmith, 5th wd. 6 S. bet. 4 and 5 W.

Burrell George, lab. 7 S. cor. 7 E.

Burt Andrew, chief of police, 20th wd. Maple, cor. Fruit

Burt John, lab. 5th wd. 8 S. bet. 3 and 4 W.

Burt Alexander, lab. 6th wd. 4 W. bet. 5 and 6 S.

Burton William, lab. 6th wd. 3 W. bet. 4 and 5 S.

Burton R. T. sheriff, Salt Lake county, res. 15th wd. 2 W. cor. 2 E.

Burton John, carpenter, 6th wd. 6 S. bet. 2 and 3 W.

Burton Joseph, lab. 6th wd. 3 W. bet. 4 and 5 S.

Bury James, harnessmaker, 3d wd. 6 S. bet. 1 and 2 E.

Busby William, farmer, 16th wd. 5 W. bet. 1 and 2 N.

Busby John, lab. 10th wd. 5 S. cor. 8 E.

Busby Joseph, lab. 13th wd. 2 S. bet. 1 and 2 E.

Bustle James, lab. 15th wd. 5 W. bet. 1 and 2 S.

Butcher S. M. lab. 6th wd. 4 W. bet. 5 and 6 S.

Butler Ann, wid. 10th wd. 6 E. cor. 4 S.

Butler John, butcher, 19th wd. 3 W. bet. 3 and 4 N.

Butterwood Thomas, lab. 14th wd. 1 W. bet. 2 and 3 S.

Butterworth Edmund, adobiemaker, 15th wd. 3 S. cor. 4 W.

Buttle William, lab. 6th wd. 5 S. bet. 3 and 4 W.

Buttler John O. lab. 16th wd. S. T. bet. 3 and 4 W.

Byers Thomas, carpenter, 14th wd. 1 W. cor. 2 S.

Byland Ebulon, carpenter, 16th wd. S. T. cor. 4 W.

C

Cahoon William F. carpenter, 12th wd. 4 E. bet. S. T. and 1 S.

Caine John T. (Clawson & C.), manager and lessee Salt Lake theatre, res. 20th wd. Chesnut, cor. Garden

Camomile Daniel, basketmaker, 7th wd. 2 W. cor. 4 S.

Calder David O. commission and forwarding merchant, res. 20th wd. cor. Pine and Garden

Calder William, salesman, res. 17th wd. bet. N. T. and 1 N.

California Corral, 2 S. cor. W. T.

California House, 1 S. nr. E. T.

Callaghan M. B. hardware, E. T. bet. 1 and 2 S.

Callister Thomas, farmer, 17th wd. N. T. bet. W. T. and 1 W.

Callister Edward, tailor, 7th wd. 4 S. bet. W. T. and 1 W.

Calton William F. wellsinker, 11th wd. 7 E. bet. 2 and 3 S.

Cameron Daniel, enginedriver, 15th wd. 3 W. bet. 2 and 3 S.

Camp James, trader, 15th wd. 3 S. bet. 3 and 4 W.

Campbell Robert, city recorder, 12th wd. S. T. bet. 3 and 4. E.

Campbell David, lab. 1st wd. 6 E. bet. 6 and 7 S.

Campbell R. L. supt. common schools, 14th wd. W. T. bet. 1 and 2 S.

Campbell James, teamster, 20th wd. Elm, cor. Prospect

Campbell Alexander, teamster, 12th wd. 5 E. bet. S. T. and 1 S.

Campe John H. photographer, 9th wd. 5 S. bet. 3 and 4 E.

Campkin George, bootmaker, 17th wd. 1 W. bet. 1 and 2 N.

Cannon Geo. Q. one of the 12 Apostles, editor Deseret News and Juvenile Instructor, res. 17th wd. 1 W. bet. N. and S. T.

Cannon Angus M. business agt. Deseret News, res. 15th wd. 2 W. bet. S. T. and 1 S.

Cannon Marsena, photographer, 17th wd. 1 W. bet. N. and S. T.

Capener William, carpenter, 13th wd. 1 S. bet. 2 and 3 E.

Care William, stagedriver, 13th wd. 2 E. bet. S. T. and 1 S.

Careless George, leader of orchestra in theatre, res. 7th wd. 4 S. bet. W. T. and 1 W.

Carlisle George, wagonmaker, 17th wd. 2 W. bet. 1 and 2 N.

Carlson Carl, carpenter, 2d wd. 4 E. bet. 6 and 7 S.

Carr George, clerk, 13th wd. S. T. cor. 2 E.

Carrington Albert, 17th wd. cor. N. and E. T.

Carson John, teamster, 7th wd. 4 S. cor. W. T.

Carter J. M. attorney at law, (C. & Marshall), room at O. Hydes, N. T. bet. E. and W. T.

Carter Robert, newsdealer, 2 S. bet. E. T. and 1 E. res. 5 S. bet. 3 and 4 E.

Carter Charles, photographer, es. E. T. bet. 1 and 2 S. res. 13th wd. 1 E. bet. 1 and 2 S.

Carter Thomas, farmer, 12th wd. 2 S. bet. 4 and 5 E.

Cartwright John (Co operative Pottery), 8th wd. 1 E. bet. 5 and 6 S.

Case Andrew, brickmaker, 8th wd. 1 E. cor. 5 S.

Cassidy Samuel H. trader, 8th wd. 4 S. bet. E. and 1 E.

Caste E. M. furniture maker, 1 E. bet. 2 and 3 S. res. 20th wd. cor. Chesnut and Bluff

Castleton James, gardener, 20th wd. cor. Cherry and Garden

Cater William, lab. 9th wd. 5 S. bet 5 and 6 E.

Cates Michael, carpenter, 19th wd. 3 N. bet. 1 and 2 W.

Chadd Michael, greengrocer, ws. E. T. bet. S. T. and 1 S. res. 15th. wd. 1 S. bet. 5 and 6 W.

Chambers Francis, carpenter, 20th wd. Elm, cor. High

Chamblain Richard, carpenter, 8th wd. 5 S. bet. 1 and 2 E.

Chamblain Thomas, carpenter, 8th wd. 5 S. cor. 2 E.

Chamberlain Joseph, lab. 15th wd. 4 W. bet. S. T. and 1 S.

Chandler George, butcher, Meat Market, res. 20th wd. Fruit, bet. Poplar and Willow

Chapman Welcome, stonecutter, 12th wd. 4 E. bet. S. T. and 1 S.

Charles Robert, gunsmith, 10th wd. 6 S. bet. 8 and 9 E.

Charles Thomas W. trader, 12th wd. 2 S. cor. 5 E.

Chase Sisson A. farmer, 1st wd. 8 E. bet. 8 and 9 S.

Chase Benoni, lab. 10th wd. 7 E. bet. 4 and 5 S.

Chatfield George, lab. 15th wd. 5 W. bet. S. T. and 1 S.

Cheshire George, shoemaker, 10th wd. 7 E. cor. 6 S.

Cheshire Thomas, lab. 9th wd. 3 S. cor. 6 E.

Chestney James, lab. 7th wd. 1 W. bet. 4 and 5 S.

Childs T. W. groceries and provisions, cor. 2 S. and 1 E.

Chislett John (Chislett & Co.), dry goods and groceries, es. E. T. bet. 1 and 2 S. res. 7th wd. E. T. bet. 4 and 5 S.

Chong Ping, Chinese tea dealer, 2 S. nr. E. T.

Christianson Ludvig, sawyer, 2d wd. 4 E. bet. 7 and 8 S.

City Hall, 1 S. bet. 1 and 2 E.

Clampitt John, special mail agent, room at O. Hydes, 17th wd.

Clark John, bookkeeper, res. 15th wd. 1 S. bet. 3 and 4 W.

Clark John A. surveyor general, Little's row, 2 S. near E. T.

Clark John, shoemaker, 16th wd. 5 W. bet. N. T. and 1 N.

Clark George, barber, ss. 2 S. bet. E. T. and 1 E. res. 3d wd. E. T. bet. 6 and 7 S.

Clark A. L. harnessmaker, Railroad Shops, 13th wd.

Clark Amos, blacksmith, 19th wd. Central, bet. Apricot and Currant

Clawson John R. ice cream saloon, 1 S. bet. E. T. and 1 E.

Clawson George, wheelwright, 14th wd. 1. W. bet. 1 and 2 S.

Clawson H. B. (Eldredge & C.), general merchandise, ws. E. T. bet. S. T. and 1 S. res. 12th wd. S. T. cor. 3 E.

Clayton Joseph, teamster, 14th wd. W. T. cor. 1 S.

Clayton John, cutler, ws. E. T. bet. 2 and 3 S. res. 20th wd. Oak, cor. Bluff

Clayton William, accountant and notary public, office in Eldredge & Clawson's, res. 17th wd. N. T. bet. 1 and 2 W.

Cleary James F. shoemaker, 17th wd. 2 W. bet. N. and S. T.

Cleghorn Robert, clerk, with Godbe & Co. res. with Michael Earl, 20th wd.

Clemmons ——, land office, Little's row, 2 S. near E. T.

Cliff Albert, lab. Bench, bet. 8 and 9 S.

Clifton Charles, stonemason, 7th wd. 5 S. bet. 1 and 2 W.

Clinton Jeter, police magistrate and justice of the peace, res. 13th wd. 2 E. bet. 1 and 2 S.

Clive Claude (C. & Reid), bakery and provisions, ss. 2 S. bet. E. T. and 1 E.

Clowes John C. operator in W. U. Telegraph office, res. 18th wd.

Cobb James T. school teacher, 13th wd. 1 E. bet. S. T. and 1 S.

Coberstrom O. bootmaker, 1 S. bet. E. T. and 1 E.

Cochran James, lab. 16th wd. 7 W. cor. 2 N.

Cohn L. (Cohn & Co.), dry goods, ws. E. T. bet. 1 and 2 S.

Colebrook Charles, millinery, ws. E. T. bet. S. T. and 1 S. res. 14th wd. 1 S. cor. 1 W.

Coles G. S. currier, 19th wd. 2 W. cor. 5 N.

Colestensen N. S. lab. 8th wd. 2 E. bet. 3 and 4 S.

Collet Richard, shoemaker, 19th wd. cor. Central and Quince

Collins Maria, wid. 14th wd. 1 W. bet. 2 and 3 S.

Collins Robert, lab. 20th wd. cor. Beach and Fruit

Colorado Corral, 2 S. near S. T.

Colwell Robert, boarding house keeper, 1 S. near E. T.

Combs William W. painter and glazier, 7th wd. W. T. bet. 3 and 4 S.

Condie Gibson, Sr. farmer, 6th wd. 5 S. bet. 4 and 5 W.

Condie Gibson, Jr. lab. 6th wd. 3 W. bet. 5 and 6 S.

Condie Thomas, farmer, 4th wd. 1 W. cor. 7 S.

Conley Charles, shoemaker, 14th wd. 3 S. bet. E and W. T.

Counegieter Jacob W. baker, 17th wd. 1 N. bet. 1 and 2 W.

Cook Frederick, Sr. lab. 5th wd. 7 S. bet. 2 and 3 W.

Cook Frederick, Jr. lab. 5th wd. 7 S. bet. 2 and 3 W.

Cook John R. teamster, 14th wd. 1 S. bet. 1 and 2 W.

Cook Joseph, lab. 4 E. bet. 5 and 6 S.

Coon John, lab. 16th wd. 1 N. bet. 3 and 4 W.

Cooper William (Cooper Bros.), dry goods and groceries, ws. E. T. bet. 1 and 2 S. res. 7th wd. 3 S. cor. 1 W.

Cooper Charles, news and toy dealer and plasterer, ws. E. T. bet. S. T. and 1 S. res. S. T. cor. 1 W.

Cooper Samuel (C. Bros.), dry goods and groceries, ws. E. T. bet. 1 and 2 S. res. 7th wd. 3 S. bet. 1 and 2 W.

Cooper Thomas, shoemaker, 20th wd. Wall, cor. Beech

Cope Jane, wid. 1st wd. 7 E. bet. 8 and 9 S.

Corbett Daniel, farmer, 2d wd. 5 E. cor. 7 S.

Corbett John, teamster, 2d wd. 7 S. bet. 4 and 5 E.

Corless John, teamster, 4th wd. 7 S. cor. E. T.

Corless Henry, lab. 4th wd. E. T. bet. 7 and 8 S.

Corless Wm. teamster, 4th wd. 7 S. bet. E. and W. T.

Corless Thomas, farmer, 4th wd. 7 S. bet. E. and W. T.

Corless Edward, farmer, 4th wd. 7 S. bet. E. and W. T.

Coneroy Richard, teamster, 11th wd. 8 E. bet. S. T. and 1 S.

Cottam John, sr. chair mender, 16th wd. 5 W. bet. N. T. and 1 N.

Cottam John, jr. carpenter, 16th wd. N. T. cor. 5 W.

Cotterell Charles, plasterer, 14th wd. S. T. bet. W. T. and 1 W.

Cotterell Wm. lab. 12th wd. 3 S. bet. 5 and 6 E.

Cottle Henry, blacksmith, 20th wd. Hickory, cor. Bluff

Coulam Henry, carpenter, 11th wd. 8 E. cor. 2 S.

Coulam John, sr. carpenter and joiner, 11th wd. S. T. bet. 7 and 8 E.

Coulam John, jr. joiner, 11th wd. 7 E. cor. S. T.

Coult James, plasterer, 11th wd. 7 E. bet. 1 and 2 S.

Coult Wm. teamster, 9th wd. 5 S. bet. 5 and 6 E.

Court House, 14th wd. 2 S. cor. 2 W.

Covey Enoch, teamster, 12th wd. 3 S. bet. 5 and 6 E.

Covey Hyram, teamster, 12th wd. 2 S. bet. 5 and 6 E.

Covey Joseph, teamster, 12th wd. 2 S. bet. 5 and 6 E.

Cowan Andrew, plasterer, 4th wd. 3 W. bet. 6 and 7 S.

Cowan Hannah, wid. 5th wd. 6 S. bet. 2 and 3 W.

Cowan Wm. clerk, res. 8th wd. E. T. bet. 5 and 6 S.

Cowley John M. cooper, 7th wd. 2 W. bet. 4 and 5 S.

Cowley Wm. tailor, ws. E. T. bet. 1 and 2 S. res. 19th wd. 6 W. bet. 2 and 3 N.

Cox Samuel, lab. 20th wd. S. T. cor. Cherry

Cox Henry, blacksmith, 20th wd. S. T. cor. Cherry

Cox Edward, carpenter, 16th wd. N. T. bet. 3 and 4 W.

Crabtree Charles, lab. 10th wd. 8 E. cor. 5 S.

Crabtree Wm. carpenter, 11th wd. 2 S. bet. 8 and 9 E.

Craddock John, lab. 20th wd. High, bet. Oak and Elm

Cram Charles S. architect, 7th wd. 5 S. cor. 1 W.

Crandall Jacob, sawyer, 17th wd. N. T. bet. W. and 1 W.

Crane Abner, blacksmith, 8th wd. 4 S. bet. E. and 1 E.

Crane John, laborer, 10th wd. 9 E. bet. 3 and 4 S.

Crawford Samuel, carder, 14th wd. 3 S. bet. 1 and 2 W.

Cripes Charles, ropemaker, 16th wd. 6 W. bet. 1 and 2 N.

Crismon Charles, freighter, 14th wd. 1 W. cor. 2 S.

Crismon George, freighter, 14th wd. 1 W. bet. 1 and 2 S.

Crocherou George W. clerk with Kimball & Lawrence, res. 8th wd. 3 E. bet. 5 and 6 S.

Crockwell John, M. D. physician, ss. 1 S. bet. E. T. and 1 E. res. 9th wd. 4 E. bet. 5 and 6 S.

Croff Wm. C. blacksmith, 14th wd. 2 S. bet. 1 and 2 W.

Crompton Stephen, shoemaker, 11th wd. 2 S. bet. 6 and 7 E.

Crompton Mrs. C. tailoress, 13th wd. 3 S. cor. 1 E.

Cronyn George (C. & Perris), ws. E. T. bet. 1 and 2 S. bds. with F. Perris

Cross Daniel, lab. 11th wd. S. T. cor. 7 E.

Crow Charles H. (Bowring & C.) saddlery, ws. E. T. bet. S. T. and 1 S. res. 11th wd. 9 E. cor. 1 S.

Crowther Sarah, wid. 8th wd. 3 E. bet. 3 and 4 S.

Crowther Wm. lab. 4th wd. 7 S. bet. 1 and 2 W.

Crowther Edward D. carpenter, 12th wd. 3 S. bet. 4 and 5 E.

Crowther James, adobemaker, 7th wd. W. T. bet. 5 and 6 S.

Crowther William B. lab. 16th wd. N. T. bet. 7 and 8 W.

Croxall Jonah, Co-operative Pottery, cor. E. T. and 5 S. res. 7th wd. 1 W. bet. 3 and 4 S.

Croxall Mark, business manager, W. U. Telegraph office, res. 14th wd. W. T. bet. S. T. and 1 S.

Cullen John, stonemason, 1st wd. 6 S. bet. 6 and 7 E.

Culmer Alfred, carpenter, 20th wd. cor. Ash and Fruit.

Cumberland Charles, blacksmith, 16th wd. 5 W. bet. N. T. and 1 N.

Cummings Samuel A. farmer, 9th wd. 5 S. bet. 5 and 6 E.

Cummings Benjamin F. millwright, 14th wd. 2 S. bet. W. T. and 1 W.

Cummings James W. foreman, Brigham Young's woolen factory, res. 14th wd. 2 S. bet. W. T. and 1 W.

Cundick Francis, lab. 3 S. bet. 5 and 6 E.

Cunningham J. N., M. D. ns. 1 S. bet. E. T. and 1 E.

Cunningham Lucinda, wid. 15th wd. 3 W. cor. 1 S.

Cunningham R. blacksmith, railroad shops

Cunnington John, merchant, (Stayner & C.), cor. E. T. and 2 S. res. 7th wd. 5 S. bet. W. and 1 W.

Currie James, blacksmith, 14th wd. 3 S. bet. E. and W. T.

Curtis Edwin, tinner, 13th wd. S. T. cor. 2 E.

Curtis Theodore, sackmaker, ws. E. T. bet. 2 and 3 S. res. 7th wd. W. T. cor. 4 S.

Curtis ——, wid. 6 E. bet. 5 and 6 S.

Curtis Foster, saddler, 7th wd. E. T. bet. 3 and 4 S.

Cushing Henry, shoemaker, 20th wd. S. T. bet. Maple and Elm
Cushing James, farmer, 11th wd. S. T. cor. 8 E.
Cushing Robert, shoemaker, 8 E. bet. 1 and 2 S.
Cuthbert Edward, blacksmith, 6 E. cor. 7 S.

D

Daft Alexander J. dry goods and groceries, 2 S. bet. E. T. and 1 E. res.
    7th wd. 3 S. bet. E. and W. T.
Daft Sarah A. wid. 8th wd. E. T. bet. 4 and 5 S.
Dale James, lab. 13th wd. 2 E. bet. 1 and 2 S.
Dallas Samuel B. cabinetmaker, 17th wd. 1 W. bet. N. T. and 1 N.
Dangerfield Jabez, lab. 11th wd. 2 S. cor. 10 E.
Daniels Abigail, wid. 2 E. cor. 7 S.
Davey Charles, propr. Emigration Corral, res. 4th wd. 2 W. bet.
    7 and 8 S.
Davidson Samuel, shoemaker, 10th wd. 7 E. cor. 5 S.
Davies Joseph, lab. 4th wd. E. T. bet. 7 and 8 S.
Davies William, lab. 20th wd. Fruit cor. Cherry
Davies Brigham, lab. 4th wd. E. T. bet. 7 and 8 S.
Davies Theodore, lab. 19th wd. bet. Apricot and Plum
Davies William, plasterer, 10th wd. 7 E. bet. S. T. and 1 S.
Davies Morgan, plasterer, 10th wd. 7 E. bet. S. T. and 1 S.
Davies John C. provision dealer, 17th wd. 1 N. bet. 1 and 2 W.
Davies Edward W. carpenter, 17th wd. 2 W. bet. N. T. and 1 N.
Davies Edwin W. carpenter, 17th wd. W. T. bet. N. T. and 1 N.
Davies S. David, clerk, with Jennings & Co. res. 17th wd. S. T. bet. 1
    and 2 W.
Davis Nathan, bishop, 17th wd. res. N. T. bet. W. T. and 1 W.
Davis Mary, wid. 4 E. bet. 6 and 7 S.
Davis Martha, wid. 16th wd. 5 W. cor. N. T.
Davis Samuel (D. & Cohn), clothing store, es. E. T. bet. 1 and 2 S.
Davis David E. lab. 6 E. bet. 6 and 7 S.
Davis M. L. physician, office at Godbe's Exchange Bldgs. res. 7th wd.
    3 S. bet. E. T. and W. S.
Davis William, teamster, 20th wd. S. T. cor. Hickory
Davis John S. trader, 8th wd. 2 E. cor. 4 S.
Dawson Joseph W. (Field & D.), ss. 2 S. bet. E. T. and 1 E.
Day David, provisions and general merchandise, ws. E. T. bet. 1 and 2
    S. res. 14th wd. 3 S. bet. E. and W. T.
Day Hugh, wheelwright, 16th wd. S. T. cor. 5 W.
Day Naomi, wid. 16th wd. 5 W. cor. N. T.
Day Mrs. milliner, 2 S. bet. E. T. and 1 E.

Daynes John, watchmaker, 1 S. bet. E. T. and 1 E. res. 20th wd. Oak, bet. S. T. and Fruit

Deage William, lab. 16th wd. 4 W. bet. N. T. and 1 N.

Debenham Henry, shoemaker, 2 S. bet. E. T. and 1 E. res. 17th wd. 1 N. bet. 1 and 2 W.

Decker Charles, lumber merchant, 9th wd. 6 S. cor. 5 E.

Decker Rubie, bookkeeper, 12th wd. 2 S. bet. 4 and 5 E.

Delmonico Hotel, E. T. near 2 S.

DeLong Palmer, blacksmith, 13th wd. 2 S. bet. 1 and 2 E.

Demmins Moses, farmer, 1st wd. 8 E. bet. 8 and 9 S.

Dent George, lab. 20th wd. Poplar, cor. Fruit

Derr William, nurseryman, res. 16th wd. 1 N. bet. 2 and 3 W.

Derrick Zachariah, engineer, 12th wd. 6 E. cor. 2 S.

Deseret News, office, cor. S. and E. T.

Deseret Telegraph, office, S. T. east of E. T.

Deuel O. M. farmer, 15th wd. 4 W. cor. S. T.

Deuel Amos C. gardener, 15th wd. 1 S. cor. 4 W.

Devey John, blacksmith, 8th wd. W. T. bet. 5 and 6 S.

Dewey Albert, policeman, 8th wd. 2 E. cor. 4 S.

Dewey Frank, ns. 2 S. bet. E. T. and 1 E. res. 8th wd. 4 S. bet. 2 and 3 E.

Dick John, lab. 11th wd. S. T. bet. 8 and 9 E.

Dick David, lab. 11th wd. S. T. bet. 8 and 9 E.

Dick James, lab. 11th wd. S. T. bet. 8 and 9 E.

Dickson Robert, teacher, 14th wd. 2 S. bet. 1 and 2 W.

Diehl Chris. hairdresser, es. E. T. bet. 1 and 2 S. res. 13th wd. 1 E. cor. 3 S.

Digo Frederick, lab. 2d wd. 5 E. cor. 8 S.

Dilworth Eliza, wid. 8th wd. 3 E. bet. 4 and 5 S.

Dinwoodey Henry, cabinetmaker, furniture dealer and undertaker, ws. E. T. bet. S. T. and 1 S. and bet. E. and W. T. res. 7th wd. 1 W. bet. 3 and 4 S.

Dixon Henry, clerk, 11th wd. 7 E. bet. S. T. and 1 S.

Domen Edward, lab. 5th wd. 3 W. bet. 7 and 8 S.

Domvill James, saddler, 4th wd. 6 S. bet. 2 and 3 W.

Domvill Thomas, joiner, 7th wd. 6 S. bet. W. T. and 1 W.

Donelson Charles M. cooper, ws. E. T. bet. S. T. and 1 S. res. 13th wd. 2 S. bet. 1 and 2 E.

Donkin T. pressman, Telegraph office, res. 7th wd.

Doolittle John, furnituremaker, 7th wd. W. T. bet. 3 and 4 S.

Doremus H. I. Dr. Union Academy, res. 17th wd. 2W. bet. 1 and 2 N.

Dougall William B. operator, Deseret Telegraph Line, res. 2 S. bet. 2 and 3 E.

Douglass Graham, lab. 16th wd. 1 N. bet. 4 and 5 W.

Douglas, William, blacksmith, 8th wd. 2 E. cor. 3 S.

Douglas J. boarding house keeper, 1 S. nr. E. T.

Dowden Edwin, clerk, with Naisbitt & Hindley, 14th wd. 1 W. bet. S. T. and 1 S.

Drackett Anna, wid. 8th wd. 2 E. bet. 4 and 5 S.

Drake Thomas J. associate justice, bds. with J. W. Stevens, 13th wd.

Drake Horace, farmer, 12th wd. 5 E. bet. 1 and 2 S.

Driver George, lab. 3d wd. E. T. cor. 7 S.

Druce Henry, engraver, ns. 2 S. bet. E. T. and 1 E. res. 19th wd. 3 N. cor. 3 W.

Druce John, carpenter, 12th wd. 1 S. cor. 5 E.

Dudman James, lab. 5 S. bet. 4 and 5 E.

Duffin Abraham, lab. 6 S. bet. 3 and 4 E.

Duke John J. clerk, res. 12th wd. 5 E. bet. 2 and 3 S.

Duke Albert R. clerk, res. 12th wd. 5 E. bet. 2 and 3 S.

Dumbill James, harnessmaker, 5th wd. 6 S. bet. 2 and 3 W.

Dunbar Wm. C. provision dealer, ws. E. T. bet. 1 and 2 S. res. 20th wd. cor. Fir and Garden

Duncan Homer, farmer, 16th wd. 2 W. bet. N. and S. T.

Duncan James, farmer, 15th wd. 3 W. bet 2 and 3 S.

Duncan Wm. farmer, 1st wd. 8 E. bet. 6 and 7 S.

Duncanson David, blacksmith, 15th wd. 1 S. cor. 6 W.

Dunford George, (D. & Sons), hats, boots and shoes, es. E. T. bet. 1 and 2 S. res. 17th wd. S. T. bet. W. T. and 1 W.

Dunford Wm. bookkeeper, 16th wd. 2 W. bet. N. and S. T.

Dunlap Sarah, wid. 2d wd. 8 S. bet. 3 and 4 E.

Dunn T. C. tobacco and cigars, E. T. bet. 1 and 2 S.

Durnford James, stonemason, 19th wd. 5 n. cor. 1 W.

Dutton James, lab. 1st wd. 6 S. cor. 9 E.

Dwiggins James, saddler, 20th wd. Pine, cor, High

Dwyer James, newsdealer, Post-office building, res. 17th wd. 1 N. bet. W. and 1 W.

Dye Robert, stonemason, 20th wd. cor. Fruit and Oak

Dyer Wm. C. engine driver, 17th wd. 1 W. bet. N. T. and 1 N.

Dykeman John, carpenter, 16th wd. 4 W. cor. 1 N.

Dykeman John H. carpenter, 16th wd. 4 W. cor. 1 N.

E

Eagan Nancy, wid. 14th wd. 2 S. cor. 2 W.

Eardly Bedson, (Co-operative pottery store), res. 7th wd. 1 W. bet. 4 and 5 S.

Eardly James, (Co-operative pottery store), res. 3d wd. E. T. bet. 6 and 7 S.

LEAST, SEWS THE EASIEST AND THE BEST, F. A. MITCHELL, SOLE AGT.

SALT LAKE CITY DIRECTORY. 103

Earl Michael, (Thirkell & E.) tailors, 1 S. bet. E. T. and 1 E. res. 20th wd. Locust, cor. Fruit

Earl Jonathan, farmer, 10th wd. 9 E. bet. 4 and 5 S.

East Edward W. clerk, county court office, in Court House, res. 14th wd. 1 S bet. 1 and 2 W.

Eastman O. F. saddler, 17th wd. 2 W. bet. 1 and 2 N.

Eccles David, salesman, 10th wd. 6 S. cor. 9 E.

Eccles Henry, stonecutter, 15th wd. 2 S. cor. 3 W.

Eddington Wm. general trader, 14th wd. 1 W. bet. 2 and 3 S.

Edginton Walter W. machinist, 11th wd. 8 E. bet. 1 and 2 S.

Edward Alexander, carpenter, 19th wd. cor. Central and Plum

Edwards Wm. farmer, 4th wd. W. bet. 6 and 7 S.

Edwards Joseph, stonemason, 2d wd. 4 S. bet. 5 and 6 E.

Edwards John, carpenter, 6th wd. 3 W. bet. 3 and 4 S.

Egan Howard, 17th wd.

Eighth Ward Assembly Rooms, 4 S. bet. 1 and 2 E.

Elder Joseph B. cooper, 14th wd. 2 S. bet. 1 and 2 W.

Eldredge Elnathan, farmer, 16th wd. 4 W. bet. N. T. and 1 N.

Eldredge Horace S. (E. & Clawson), gen. merchandize, whol. and ret. ws. E. T. bet. S. T. and 1 S. res. 13th wd. 1 S. cor. 2 E.

Elephant Corral, Charles C. Hart, ns. 2. S. near E. T.

Elgutter Solomon, clerk, with Davis & Cohn

Eliason Olef L. watchmaker, ws. E. T. bet. 1 and 2 S. res. 20th wd. Bluff, cor. Ash

Ellerbeck Thomas, chief clerk at Brigham Young's office, res. 17th wd. 1 N. bet. 1 and 2 W.

Ellis Edmund, cooper, 17th wd. 1 N. bet. 1 and 2 W.

Ellis Nathan, merchant, res. at O. Hyde's 17th wd.

Elstrom Charles, lab. 11th wd. 1 S. bet. 9 and 10 E.

Elsworth Edward, lab. 8th wd. 3 S. bet. E. and 1 E.

Elvers Carl, warehouseman, at F. A. Mitchel's, res. 17th wd. N. T. bet. W. T. and 1 W.

Ely John, lab. 13th wd. 2 E. cor. 1 S.

Emigration Corral, Washington square, Charles Davey, propr.

Emory Henry, warehouseman, 16th wd. 7 W. bet. S. and N. T.

Empy Nelson, contractor, 12th wd. 1 S. bet. 3 and 4 E.

Ence Godlieb, miller, 19th wd. 2 W. cor. 5 N.

Engler J. (Cohn & Co.), ws. E. T. bet. 1 and 2 S.

Engstrom John, ss. 1 S. bet. E. T. and 1 E.

Ensign Samuel, millwright, 8th wd. 3 S. bet. 2 and 3 E.

Ensign Samuel N. farmer, 8th wd. 3 S. bet. 2 and 3 E.

Ensign Calvin, carpenter, 13th wd. 2 E. bet. 2 and 3 S.

Ensign L. A. lab. 13th wd. 3 S. bet. 2 and 3 E.

Entwistle Edwin, lab. 16th wd. 6 W. bet. 1 and 2 N.

Eoff Alfred, chief clerk, Wells, Fargo & Co.'s local Express dept.

Erickson Eric G. tailor, 1st wd. 7 E. cor. 6 S.
Erickson Peter, carpenter, 8th wd. 2 E. bet. 3 and 4 S.
Eruger John, cabinetmaker, 10th wd. 6 E. cor. 4 S.
Erskine Archibald, tailor, res. 20th wd. Locust, cor. Garden
Evans David W. phonographer, 20th wd. Chestnut, bet. Bluff and
    Wall
Evans James, carpenter, 20th wd. Spruce, cor. Wall
Evans William (Midgely & E.), painter, 2 S. bet. E.' and W. T. res. 12th
    wd.
Evans John, tailor, 3d wd. 7 S. bet. E. T. and 1 E.
Evans John T. lab. 16th wd. S. T. bet. 6 and 7 W.
Evans Peter, plumber, 9th wd. 3 E. bet. 3 and 4 S.
Evans Joseph, blacksmith, 16th wd. N. T. bet. 7 and 8 W.
Evans John E. compositor, Telegraph office, res. 9th wd. 3 E. bet. 3 and
    4 S.
Evans Hugh, saddler, 16th wd. 7 W. bet. N. T. and 1 N.
Evans David, lab. 2d wd. 4 S. bet. 5 and 6 E.
Evans William, lab. 16th wd. 7 W. bet. 1 and 2 N.
Evans Samuel S. architect, 6th wd. 4 W. bet. 4 and 5 S.
Evans John, teamster, 7th wd. 5 S. bet. W. T. and 1 W.
Evans Benjamin P. lab. 16th wd. 2 N. cor. 5 W.
Evans M. Charles, (Wallace & E.), es. confectionery and fancy groceries,
    E. T. bet. 1 and 2 S. res. 7th wd. 4 S. bet. 1 and 2 W.
Evans David, carpenter, 7th wd. 3 S. bet. 1 and 2 W.
Evans Moses, blacksmith, 17th wd. 1 W. bet. N. and S. T.
Evans Evan, lab. 15th wd. 1 S. bet. 6 and 7 W.
Evans Martha, wid. 15th wd. 1 S. bet. 5 and 6 W.

F

Fagan M. painter and glazier, Railroad Shops, 13th wd.
Fairclough Mary, wid. 4th wd. 2 W. cor. 8 S.
Fairclough James, enginedriver, 4th wd. 2 W. bet. 6 and 7 S.
Fairclough James, lab. 5th wd. 2 W. bet. 6 and 7 S.
Fairclough Mary A. wid. 5th wd. 8 S. bet. 2 and 3 W.
Fairclough Peter, stonemason, 7th wd. 5 S. cor. 2 W.
Fallon Henry, cabinetmaker, 13th wd. S. T. cor. 2 E.
Faraday John, enginedriver, 4th wd. E. T. bet. 7 and 8 S.
Farnsworth M. F. clerk, 14th wd. 3 S. bet. 1 and 2 W.
Farrer Benjamin, carpenter, 4th wd. 4 W. bet. 6 and 7 S.
Faust H. I. (F. & Houtz), livery stables, ss. 2 S. bet. E. T. and 1 E. res.
    14th wd. W. T. bet. 1 and 2 S.

given quantity of water than any other water-wheel. F. A. Mitchell, sole agt.

SALT LAKE CITY DIRECTORY. 105·

Fawdon Thomas, shoemaker, 12th wd. 3 E. bet. S. T. and 1 S.

Fawkes John, stonecutter, 2d wd. 5 E. bet. 3 and 4 S.

Felt Nathaniel H. cashier at Jennings & Co.'s, res. 17th wd. E. T. bet. and 1 N.

Fenton Thomas, nurseryman, 6th wd. 4 W. bet. 4 and 5 S.

Ferguson Jane, wid. 14th wd. 1 S. bet. 1 and 2 W.

Field H. (Kelson & F.), bakers and confectioners, ws. E. T. bet. 1 and 2 S.

Field Jesse (F. & Dawson), bakers, 2 S. bet. E. T. and 1 E.

Fielding Amos, match manufacturer, 4th wd. 3 W. bet. 7 and 8 S.

Fielding James sr. miner, 6th wd. 3 W. bet. 3 and 4 S.

Fielding James jr. lab. 6th wd. 3 S. bet. 5 and 6 E.

Fielding Mary A. wid. 16th wd. 1 N. cor. 4 W.

Fielding Amos, farmer, 5th wd. 8 S. bet. 2 and 3 W.

Fife Adam, lab. 10th wd. 3 S. bet. 9 and 10 E.

Fifteenth Ward School House, 1 S. bet. 3 and 4 W.

Findlay Hugh, match and ink manufacturer, ws. E. T. bet. S. T. and 1 S. res. 17th wd. Central

Firman Daniel R. lab. 14th wd. 2 S. cor. W. T.

Fisher Edward, lab. 19th wd. Beet, bet. Peach and Pear

Fisher Joseph, lab. 10th wd. 9 E. bet. 3 and 4 S.

Fisher Thomas, lab. 6th wd. 4 W. bet. 5 and 6 S.

Fisher ——, wid. 10th wd. 6 E. bet. 4 and 5 S.

Fisher William, teamster, 16th wd. 1 N. bet. 5 and 6 W.

Fletcher Edwin F. carpenter, 8th wd. 3 E. bet. 3 and 4 S.

Fletcher K. plasterer, 8th wd. 3 E. bet. 3 and 4 S.

Fleualen Emily, wid. 7th wd. E. T. cor. 3 S.

Flint William, lab. 19th wd. 3 W. bet. 2 and 3 N.

Flower John, shoemaker, 19th wd. cor. Quince and Plum

Folsom William H. achitect and builder, 14th wd. S. T. cor. 1 W.

Foot George Rev. Episcopal clergyman, 12th wd. 1 S. bet. 4 and 5 E.

Foot Henry Rev. Episcopal clergyman, 12th wd. 1 S. bet. 4 and 5 E.

Force Charles E. prompter at Theatre, bds. at Stephen Lee's

Ford John, lab. 13th wd. 2. E. cor. 2 S.

Ford ——, wid. 9th wd. 5 S. bet. 5 and 6 E.

Fordham Elijah, carpenter, 16th wd. 2 W. bet. N. T. and 1 N.

Fordham Herbert, woodcutter, 17th wd. N. T. bet. W. T. and 1 W.

Foreman Joseph, cooper, 14th wd. S. T. bet. W. T. and 1 W.

Forester Robert, gardener, 11th wd. 7 E. bet. 2 and 3 S.

Forsall Alfred, lab. 20th wd. Pine, cor. Summit

Foss Ezra C. farmer, 14th wd. W. T. bet. S. T. and 1 S.

Foster William C. copyist at theatre, res. 20th wd. cor. Prospect and Pine

Foster William, weaver, 4th wd. bet. 7 and 8 S.

Foster Joseph, stonecutter, 16th wd. N. T. bet. 7 and 8 W.

Foster William, farmer, 8th wd. 1 E. bet. 5 and 6 S.

Foster William L. lab. 15th wd. 3 S. bet. 2 and 3 W.

Foster William H. woodturner, es. E. T. bet. 2 and 3 S. res. 7th wd. W. T. bet. 3 and 4 S.

Foster William, soapmaker, 5th wd. 8 S. bet. 3 and 4 W.

Fotheringham Ann, wid. 16th wd. S. T. bet. 6 and 7 W.

Foulger John, tailor, 20th wd. cor. Beech and Fruit

Fourteenth Ward Assembly Rooms, 1 S. bet. W. T. and 1 W.

Fourth Ward Meeting House, 7 S. cor. W. T.

Fowkes Reuben, lab. 7th wd. 1 W. bet. 3 and 4 S.

Fowler H. C. blacksmith, 20th wd. Fir, cor. Wall

Fowler Allan, M. D. es. E. T. bet. 1 and 2 S.

Fowler Samuel, gardener, 11th wd. 1 S. bet. 6 and 7 E.

Fowles William, shoemaker, 16th wd. 1 N. bet. 6 and 7 W.

Fox Jesse W. territorial surveyor, 14th wd. 1 S. bet. 1 and 2 W.

Frame Archibald, mason, 11th wd. S. T. bet. 8 and 9 E.

Francis John, engineer, 16th wd. N. T. bet. 5 and 6 W.

Frantz A. glovemaker, 2 S. bet. E. T. and 1 E.

Frazer Andrew, farmer, 6th wd. 4 W. bet. 3 and 4 S.

Fredericksen Johannes, teamster, 20th wd. cor. Fruit and Walnut

Free Preston, farmer, 12th wd. 4 E. bet. 1 and 2 S.

Free Absalom, farmer, 12th wd. 1 S. bet. 3 and 4 E.

Freebairn Archibald, pressman, 5th wd. 3 W. bet. 6 and 7 S.

Freeze James, clerk, 11th wd. 7 E. cor. 2 S.

Freholt Jensen, lab. 2d wd. 3 E. bet. 6 and 7 S.

Frost Burr, blacksmith, 8th wd. 3 S. cor. 2 E.

Freund F. W. & Bro. armorers and gunsmiths, es. E. T. bet. 1 and 2 S.

Fry John J. salesman, with Eldredge & Clawson, res. 15th wd. S. T. bet. 5 and 6 W.

Fryer Robert, lab. 12th wd. 2 S. cor. 3 E.

Fuins William, lab. 20th wd. High, bet. Spruce and Pine

Fullmer Junius, farmer, 6th wd. 4 S. bet. 2 and 3 W.

Fullmer Eugene, stonecutter, 6th wd. 4 S. bet. 2 and 3 W.

Fullmer David, farmer, 6th wd. 3 W. bet. 4 and 5 S.

Fullmer Alma L. farmer, 9th wd. 4 E. bet. 3 and 4 S.

Furster John B. weaver, 9th wd. 6 E. bet. 4 and 5 S.

Fustctar Endrick, stonemason, 7th wd. 4 S. cor. 1 W.

G

Gage John, lab. 14th wd. 2 W. bet. W. T. and 1 W.

Gaisford George M. clerk, res. 10th wd. 7 E. cor. 4 S.

Galbraith John H. lab. 12th wd. 3 S. cor. 4 E.

Gale Albert, carpenter, 19th wd. cor. Central and Pear

Gallacher John, baker in Grenig's bakery

Gallacher M. baker in Grenig's bakery

Gamble Thomas, peddler, 8th wd. 5 S. bet. E. T and 1 E.

Ganz Abraham, tobacconist, es. E. T. bet. 1 and 2 S. res. 14th wd. 2 S. bet. E. and W. T.

Garrett Levi, butcher, meat market, res. 20th wd. S. T. cor. Poplar

Gates Jacob, farmer, 13th wd. 2 E. cor. 2 S.

Gentry Saul, blacksmith, 20th wd. S. T. cor. Poplar

George John, lab. 19th wd. 3 W. bet. 2 and 3 N.

George Owen, shoemaker, 17th wd. S. T. bet. W. T. and 1 W.

George Henry, tailor, 3d wd. 2 E. bet. 6 and 7 S.

Gerber John, homeopathist physician, 15th wd. 2 W. bet. S. T. and 1 S.

German William, clerk, 11th wd. 6 E. cor. 1 S.

Gibbs Gideon, carpenter, 16th wd. N. T. cor. 4 W.

Gibbs Horace, lab. 17th wd. 1 W. bet. 1 and 2 S.

Gibby William, carpenter, 7th wd. 1 W. bet. 4 and 5 S.

Gibby Thomas, carpenter, 7th wd. 1 W. bet. 2 and 1 N.

Gibson Alexander, teamster, 20th wd. Elm, cor. Prospect

Gibson William, teamster, 20th wd. Elm, cor. Bluff

Gibson Jacob, farmer, 9th wd. 3 S. bet. 3 and 4 E.

Gibson John, teamster, 20th wd. Elm, bet. Fruit and Garden

Gilbert William, general merchandise, Bank Buildings, ws. E. T. bet. 1 and 2 S. res. 14th wd. W. T. bet. 1 and 2 S.

Giles Thomas D. harper, 15th wd. 6 W. bet. 1 and 2 S.

Gill Richard, barber, ns. 2 S. bet. E. T. and 1 E. res. 20th wd. S. T. cor. Maple

Gillespie Peter, stonecutter, 16th wd. N. T. bet. 7 and 8 W.

Gillespie Mary, wid. 15th wd. S. T. bet. 6 and 7 W.

Gillet John A. carpenter, 9th wd. S. cor. 5 E.

Gillet Horace E. blacksmith, 9th wd. 4 E. bet. 4 and 5 S.

Gillet Granville, teamster, 9th wd. 4 E. cor. 4 S.

Gillet Carlos, teamster, 9th wd. 5 S. bet. 4 and 5 E.

Glade James, baker, Salt Lake House, res. 8th wd. 5 S. bet. E. T. and 1 E.

Gleason Eliza A. wid. 3d wd. 6 S. cor. 2 E.

Glen Alexander, lab. 4th wd. 6 S. bet. 1 and 2 W.

Glen John, lab. 11th wd. 10 E. bet. 2 and 3 S.

Goble George, lab. 17th wd. cor. W. and N. T.

Godbe Anthony, teller in Hussey, Dahler & Co.'s bank

Godbe W. S. (G. & Co.), drugs, medicines and liquors, Exchange Bldgs. cor. E. T. and 1 S. res. 13th wd. 1 E. bet. 2 and 3 S.

Goddard Joseph, clerk, 12th wd. 2 S. bet. 3 and 4 E.

Goddard Stephen, trader, 13th wd. 2 E. bet. 2 and 3 S.

Goddard George, provision dealer, es. E. T. bet. 1 and 2 S. res. 13th wd. 2 S. bet. 2 and 3 E.

Godfrey George, lab. 10th wd. 4 S. cor. 9 E.

Golding Robert J. tanner, 17th wd. 1 N. bet. 1 and 2 W.

Golightly Richard, Globe bakery, E. bet. S. T. and 1 S. res. 8th wd. 3 S. bet. 1 and 2 E.

Golightly Thomas, carpenter, 17 wd. 1 W. bet. 1 and 2 N.

Goodman William N. carpenter, 11th wd. 9 E. bet. 1 and 2 S.

Goodman Thomas, gardener, 12th wd. 5 E. cor. 2 S.

Gorringe William, saddler, 19th wd. cor. 1 W. and Pear

Goss F. tailor, 6th wd. 6 S. bet. 4 and 5 W.

Gover Morris, lab. 19th wd. cor. Apricot and Central

Graham John C. actor, 12th wd. 2 S. bet. 4 and 5 E.

Graham William C. watchcase maker, 1st wd. 8 S. cor. 9 E.

Grandhand John L. hatter, 4th wd. 7 S. cor. 1 W.

Grant Robert, cabinetmaker, 8th wd. 6 S. bet. E. T. and 1 E.

Grant Rachel, wid. 13th wd. E. T. bet. S. T. and 1 S.

Grant George D. farmer, 13th wd. 2 S. bet. 1 and 2 E.

Graves Henry, stock dealer, 8th wd. E. T. bet. 4 and 5 S.

Gray Andrew S. farmer, 15th wd. 4 W. cor. S. T.

Gray John, shoemaker, 9th wd. 4 E. bet. 5 and 6 S.

Gray Alfred, moulder, 11th wd. 7 E. bet. S. T. and 1 S.

Gray John, carpenter, 13th wd. 1 E. bet. 2 and 3 S.

Greames Thomas, shoemaker, 19th wd. bet. Central and Beet

Greaves Robert, lab. 19th wd. 4 N. bet. 1 and 2 W.

Green Mary A. dressmaker, 14th wd. 1 S. bet. E. and W. T.

Green William, shoemaker, 2d wd. 3 E. cor. 6 S.

Greene John Y. freighter, 12th wd. 2 S. bet. 4 and 5 E.

Gregg W. C. picture frame maker and gilder, 13th wd.

Gregory Ann, wid. 3d wd. 1 E. bet. 6 and 7 S.

Gregory Lucy, wid. 8th wd. 2 E. cor. 6 S.

Grenig Daniel, bakery and groceries, es. E. T. bet. 1 and 2 S. res. 15th wd. 4 W. cor. 3 S.

Griffen W. W. carpenter, 13th wd. 1 S. bet. 2 and 3 E.

Griffen William, lab. 10th wd. 9 E. bet. 3 and 4 S.

Griffin ——, blacksmith, railroad shops

Griggs Charlotte, wid. 15th wd. 2 W. bet. 2 and 3 S.

Griggs Thomas, salesman, with Eldredge & Clawson, res. 15th wd, 2 W. bet. 2 and 3 S.

Grimsdale William, paper carrier, 10th wd. 4 S. bet. 7 and 8 E.
Gritten Thomas, lab. 10th wd. 4 S. cor. 8 E.
Gritten William, lab. 10th wd. 4 S. cor. 8 E.
Groesbeck William, 14th wd. 1 W. bet. 1 and 2 S.
Groesbeck Nicholas, 17th wd. Crooked, bet. Currant and 1 N.
Groo Isaac, street commissioner and water master, 9th wd. 4 E. cor. 5 S.
Grow Henry, carpenter and builder, 19th wd. 3 N. cor. 3 W.
Guiver Benjamin G. lab. 15th wd. 1 S. bet. 5 and 6 W.
Gunn John, lab. 3d wd. 2 E. bet. 7 and 8 S.
Gunn John, tinner, 20th wd. High, cor. Oak
Gunn Benjamin, lab. 20th wd. cor. Locust and Wall

H

Hagell John, warehouseman at Naisbett & Hendley's, res. 20th wd. Spruce, cor. Wall
Hague James sr. gunsmith, ws. E. T. bet. 1 and 2 S. res. 7th wd, 3 S. bet. E. and W. T.
Hague James jr. gunsmith, ws. E. T. bet. 1 and 2 S. res. 7th wd. 3 S. bet. E. and W. T.
Hailstone William, butcher, meat market, res. 15th wd. 1 S. bet. 2 and 3 W.
Hair John, lab. 20th wd. Cedar, cor. Fruit
Halander John, lab. 9th wd. 3 E. bet. 5 and 6 S.
Hall T. C. groceries and provisions, E. T. bet. 2 and 3 S.
Hall John K. builder, 15th wd. 4 W. bet. 2 and 3 S.
Hall James R. lab. 15th wd. S. T. bet. 5 and 6 W.
Hall Timothy, lab. 7th wd. W. T. cor. 5 S.
Hallam James, lab. 9th wd. 3 S. bet. 5 and 6 E.
Hallet Samuel, lab. 20th wd. Garden, bet. Locust and Ash
Halther Lewis, tailor, 16th wd. 1 N. bet. 1 and 2 W.
Hamar Joseph, clerk in post office, res. 15th wd. S. T. bet. 3 and 4 W.
Hamlin George, painter, 19th wd. cor. Central and Plum
Hammer Martin, painter, 8th wd. 2 E. bet. 4 and 5 S.
Hammer Olof, lab. 8th wd. 2 E. bet. 4 and 5 S.
Hammer Edward, lab. 20th wd. Cherry, cor. Bluff
Hammer C. blacksmith, Railroad shops
Hammer Franklin, lab. 8th wd. 2 E. bet. 4 and 5 S.
Hammer Paul, painter, 10th wd. 9 E. bet. 4 and 5 S.
Hammerman William, lab. 1st wd. 9 E. bet. 8 and 9 S.
Hampton Benjamin, salesman, Tithing Store, res. 3 W. bet. N. T and 1 N.

Hampton B. Y. policeman, 15th wd. 2 S. bet. 3 and 4 W.
Hancock John, lab. 19th wd. 2 W. bet. 4 and 5 N.
Hanham Edward, bookkeeper, with H. Dinwoodey, res. 17th wd. cor.
Central and Currant
Hansen Hans, farmer, 10th wd. 5 S. bet. 8 and 9 E.
Hanson Frank, lab. 5th wd. 6 S. bet. 4 and 5 W.
Hanson Chris. miller, 2d wd. 6 S. bet. 5 and 6 E.
Hanson John, cabinetmaker, 2d wd. 6 E. cor. 7 S.
Hanson Hans, lab. 2d wd. 4 E. bet. 8 and 9 S.
Hanson Hans, shoemaker, 20th wd. Birch, cor. Fruit
Hanson William, machinist, 17th wd. Grape, bet. Currant and 1 N.
Hannibal Peter, lab. 11th wd. 6 E. cor. 2 S.
Harbach Adolph, watchmaker, 20th wd. Bluff, bet. Ash and Locust
Hardie James H. actor, 14th wd. 1 W. bet. 2 and 3 S.
Hardman George, lab. 17th wd. 1 N. cor. W. T.
Hardman George, lab. 4th wd. 2 W. bet. 6 and 7 S.
Hardman Abraham, lab. 4th wd. 2 W. bet. 6 and 7 S.
Hardman Isaac, lab. 4th wd. 2 W. cor. 7 S.
Hardy Leonard W. bishop, 12th wd. 4 E. cor. 2 S.
Hardy Josiah, carpenter, 12th wd. 1 S. bet. 5 and 6 E.
Harford Thomas, plasterer, 13th wd. 3 E. bet. 2 and 3 S.
Harkins Augustus, carpenter, 7th wd. 1 W. bet. 5 and 6 S.
Harman David, lab. 16th wd. N. T. bet. 7 and 8 W.
Harman William, lab. 16th wd. 6 W. bet. N. T. and 1 N.
Harman Edwin, lab. 16th wd. N. T. bet. 7 and 8 W.
Harman Charles, lab. 16th wd. 6 W. bet. N. T. and 1 N.
Harman Robert, lab. 15th wd. S. T. cor. 7 W.
Harman George, lab. 15th wd. S. T. cor. 7 W.
Harman Benjamin, shoemaker, 15th wd. 1 S. bet. 4 and 5 W.
Harman Charles, farrier, 16th wd. 7 W. bet. S. and N. T.
Harper William, lab. 5th wd. 7 S. bet. 3 and 4 W.
Harper Joseph S. joiner, 1st wd. 6 S. bet. 6 and 7 E.
Harrington Thomas, farmer, 7th wd. 4 S. bet. 1 and 2 W.
Harris John, baker, 10th wd. 6 E. bet. 3 and 4 S.
Harris William (H. & Son), groceries and provisions, 1 S. bet. E. T. and
1 E. res. 11th wd. S. T. bet. 7 and 8 E.
Harris Ed. (H. & Son). 1 S. bet. E. T. and 1 E.
Harrison Thomas, lab. 20th wd. S. T. bet. Ash and Beech
Harrison ——, tinner, with Pyper & Co. res. 8th wd.
Harrison E. L. T. editor, Utah Magazine, office at Exchange Bldgs. res.
13th wd. 3 E. cor. 2 S.
Harrison William, lab. 9th wd. 5 S. bet. 3 and 4 E.
Harrop Charles, lab. 19th wd. 4 N. bet. 1 and 2 W.
Hart William, lab. 2d wd. 5 F. cor. 7 S.

. Hart James, mason, 9th wd. 6 E. bet. 3 and 4 S.

Hart L. shoemaker, es. E. T. bet. S. T.' and 1 S. res. 19th wd. 2 W. bet. 3 and 4 N.

Harter John, gardener, 2d wd. 6 S. cor. 6 E.

Hartle John, lab. 9th wd. 4 E. bet. 3 and 4 S.

Hartog Herbert, wagon repa'rer, 13th wd. 1 E. bet. 1 and 2 S.

Hartwell Elliot, clerk to Secretary of Territory, res. 12th wd. 6 E. bet. 1 and 2 S.

Harvey Andrew, watchmaker, 1 S. bet. E. T. and 1 E. res. 14th wd. 1 W. bet. 1 and 2 S.

Harvey William, confectioner, 1 S. bet. E. T. and 1 E.

Haskins Thomas W. Rev. principal, St. Mark's School

Haslam John R. painter, 19th wd. 3 N. bet. 6 and 7 W.

Hasledon John, butcher, 5th wd. 2 W. bet. 6 and 7 S.

Haven John, farmer, 9th wd. 4 S. cor. 5 E.

Hawk William, lab. r. 19th wd. 2 W. cor. 4 N.

Hawkes Thomas, umbrella maker, 11th wd. 2 S. bet. 6 and 7 E.

Hawks Lewis, blacksmith, 9th wd. 4 E. bet. 3 and 4 S.

Hawkins Clayton, farmer, 1st wd. 7 S. bet. 6 and 7 E.

Hawkins Thomas, tinner, ws. E. T. bet. 1 and 2 S. res. 14th wd. W. T. bet. S. T. and 1 S.

Hawkins Henry, lab. 13th wd. 2 E. bet. 2 and 3 S.

Hayes Sarah A. wid. 16th wd. N. T. bet. 3 and 4 W.

Hays John, broommaker, 2d wd. 4 E. cor. 9 S.

Haystack William, shoemaker, 17th wd. 1 N. bet. 1 and 2 W.

Hayward Gammon, wagonmaker, 1 E. bet. 2 and 3 S. res. 16th wd. 1 N. bet. 5 and 6 W.

Head F. H. supt. Indian affairs, 12th wd. 5 E. bet. S. T. and 1 S.

Heagren John, lab. 15th wd. 2 W. bet. S. T. and 1 S.

Heath Frederick, farmer, 7th wd. 2 W. bet 4 and 5 S.

Heath Thomas, farmer, 15th wd. 3 S. bet. 2 and 3 W.

Heath Henry, farmer, 15th wd. 2 S. bet. 2 and 3 W.

Heath Orson O. lab. 16th wd. 2 W. bet. N. T. and 1 N.

Hedger George W. musician, 11th wd. 9 E. cor. S. T.

Hedgger James, shoemaker, 10th wd. 7 E. bet. 4 and 5 S.

Hefferman Mrs. wid. 9th wd. 5 E. bet. 4 and 5 S.

Helvorsen Peter O. cabinetmaker, 17th wd. W. T. bet. N. T. and 1 N.

Hellman & Co. clothing, es. E. T. bet. 1 and 2 S.

Hemar Jane, wid. 16th wd. 5 W. cor. 1 N.

Hemar John, blacksmith, 16th wd. 5 W. bet. 1 and 2 N.

Hemmenway L. S. nurseryman, 4th wd. 1 W. cor. 6 S.

Hemstead Charles H. attorney at law, office in Little's Row, 2 S. bet. E. and W. T. res. 13th wd. 3 S. bet. 2 and 3 E.

Henderson Peter, mason, 20th wd. Ash, bet. Wall and Garden

Henderson William, miner, 1st wd. 9 E. bet. 7 and 8 S.

Henderson David P. joiner, 8th wd. 6 S. bet. E. T. and 1 E.

Henderson John, minor, 2d wd. 3 E. bet. 6 and 7 S.

Henderson Thomas, lab. 11th wd. 10 E. bet. 2 and 3 S.

Hennesfer William, barber, ws. E. T. bet. 1 and 2 S. res. 3 E. bet. 3 and 4 S.

Hepworth John, butcher, meat market, res. 8th wd. 6 S. cor. E. T. ·

Herdman Joseph, gardener, 7th wd. W. bet. 5 and 6 S.

Hewlett Phillip, gardener, 12th wd. 3 E. bet. 1 and 2 S.

Hewett Thomas, shoemaker, 11th wd. 1 S. bet. 6 and 7 E.

Hexham Titus, lab. 16th wd. 2 N. cor. 6 W.

Heywood William, 14th wd. 1 S. bet. W. T. and 1 W.

Heywood Joseph L. farmer, 17th wd. 1 N. bet. E. T. and W. T.

Hickenlooper William, bishop, 6th wd. res. 2 W. bet. 4 and 5 S.

Hickenlooper John, farmer, 6th wd. 2 W. bet. 4 and 5 S.

Hicks Thomas, farmer, 2d wd. 5 E. cor. 9 S.

Hicks J. shoemaker, 16th wd. N. T. bet. 1 and 2 W.

Hicks William, teamster, 2d wd. 8 S. bet. 5 and 6 E.

Higgins Edwin, Territorial Secretary, office, Little's Row, 2 S. bet. E. and W. T.

Higgs Thomas, carpenter, 17th wd. N. T. bet. W. T. and 1 W.

Higley W. J. watchmaker, E. T. bet. 1 and 2 S.

Higson John, teamster, 1st wd. 7 E. bet. 6 and 7 S.

Hill Margaret, wid. 2d wd. 3 E. cor. 6 S.

Hill George, potter, 7th wd. 1 W. bet. 3 and 4 S.

Hill George, farmer, 1st wd. 8 S. bet. 6 and 7 E.

Hill Samuel H. clerk, 14th wd. 2 S. cor. W. T.

Hill Archibald N. clerk, 14th wd. 2 S. cor. W. T.

Hill Andrew, plasterer, 7th wd. S. T. cor. 2 W.

Hill James, lab. 16th wd. 3 W. bet. N. T. and 1 N.

Hillam Robert, mason, 10th wd. 5 S. bet. 6 and 7 E.

Hillam Rodney, tanner, 10th wd. 7 E. cor. 5 S.

Hillam Abram, tanner and currier, 10th wd. 5 S. bet. 8 and 9 E.

Hills L. S. land registrar, 14th wd. 1 W. bet. 1 and 2 S.

Hilton David, lab. 20th wd. cor. Oak and Garden

Hilton Allen, teamster, 20th wd. cor. Elm and Bluff

Hindley John (Naisbett & H.), general merchandise, ws. E. T. bet. 1 and and 2 S. res. 17th wd. S. T. bet. 1 and 2 W.

Hinds William, lab. 5 E. bet. 5 E. bet. 6 and 7 E.

Hingham Charles, lab. 4th wd. 6 S. cor. 2 W.

Hitesman David, farmer, 8th wd. 2 E. bet. 5 and 6 S.

Hoagland Abraham, bishop, 14th wd. 2 S. cor. 1 W.

Hoagland Lucas, freighter, 14th wd. 2 S. bet. 1 and 2 W.

Hobbs Leroy, carpenter, 14th wd. 1 S. bet. E. and W. T.

Hochstasser Rudolph, shoemaker, 9th wd. 5 S. cor. 4 E.
Hodden Frank, carpenter, 12th wd. 3 S. cor. 4 E.
Hodges William A. currier, 19th wd. 3 N. bet. 5 and 6 W.
Hodgson Henry, lab. 20th wd. Pine, cor. Prospect
Hoffman John W. lab. 20th wd. Locust, cor. Prospect
Hoge Enos D. associate justice, 11th wd. S. T. bet. 6 and 7 E.
Hoggan Walter, lab. 11th wd. 1 S. cor. 9 E.
Hoggan George, weaver, 11th wd. 1 S. bet. 8 and 9 E.
Holden Michael, wagonmaker, 2d wd. 6 E. cor. 5 S.
Holland Henry, lab. 8th wd. 3 E. cor. 3 S.
Holling Marcus, clerk, 11th wd. S. T. bet. 6 and 7 E.
Holmes John, farmer, 16th wd. 5 W. bet. N. T. and 1 N.
Holmes John, lab. 17th wd. 1 W. bet. 1 and 2 N.
Holt Robert, weaver, 9th wd. 5 S. bet. 4 and 5 E.
Holt Edward, lab. 12th wd. 3 S. bet. 5 and 6 E.
Holt Alfred, weaver, 8th wd. 1 E. bet. 5 and 6 S.
Holt William, carpenter, 11th wd. 2 S. cor. 7 E.
Homer Russel K. farmer, 7th wd. 1 W. bet. 5 and 6 S.
Hood Amelia, wid. 17th wd. 2 W. cor. 1 N.
Hook Louis, saddler, 12th wd. 5 E. bet. 2 and 3 S.
Hooper W. H. delegate for Utah, res. 19th wd. 1 W. bet. Currant and Plum
Hooper William J. bootmaker, ss. 2 S. bet. E. T. and 1 E. res. 12th wd. 3 E. bet. 2 and 3 S.
Hopper Abraham, Railroad Carriage Shops 2 E. bet. S. T. and 1 S. res. 13th wd. 2 E. bet. 1 and 2 S.
Hopwood William, tailor, 17th wd. bet. Currant and 1 N.
Horlick John, wheelwright, 7th wd. W. T. cor. 5 S.
Horne Thomas, lab. 17th wd. cor. W. and N. T.
Horne Joseph, distiller, 14th wd. 1 W. cor. 2 S.
Horner C. blacksmith, Railroad Shops
Hornick Frederick, lab. 6th wd. 5 W. bet. 5 and 6 S.
Horr John H. lab. 20th wd. cor. Fruit and Poplar
Horrocks Catherine, wid. 13th wd. 2 S. bet. 2 and 3 E.
Hosmer Josiah, U. S. marshall
Hostins Henry, wheelwright, 17th wd. 1 W. bet. 1 and 2 N.
Hostmark William, lab. 11th wd. 2 S. bet. 6 and 7 E.
Houghton Frederick, mason, 12th wd. 2 S. bet. 5 and 6 E.
Houtz Henry P. (Browning & H.), general merchandise, ns. 2 S. bet. E. T. and 1 E. res. 13th wd. 2 E. bet. 2 and 3 S.
Houtz John S. (Faust & H.) livery stables, ss. 2 S. bet. E. T. and 1 E.
Hovey O. D. physician, 19th wd. 5 N. cor. 1 W.
Howard John, clerk, 20th wd. Elm, cor. Wall
Howard John, lab. 3d wd. 2 E. cor. 7 S.

Howe Adam S. farmer, 9th wd. 3 E. bet. 4 and 5 S.
Howe Amos, freighter, 17th wd. 1 N. bet. W. T. and 1 W.
Howe Thomas, lab. 17th wd. 1 N. bet. W. T. and 1 W.
Howell Jefferson, lab. 12th wd. 1 S. bet. 4 and 5 E.
Howells William, lab. 9th wd. 5 S. bet. 4 and 5 E.
Howells Thomas, stonemason, 15th wd. 6 W. bet. S. T. and 1 S.
Howlett Robert, lab. 11th wd. 9 E. bet. S. T. and 1 S.
Hoy Charles, carpenter, 7th wd. 3 S. bet. E. and W. T.
Hucks George, mercantile agent, bds. with J. W. Stevens, 13th wd.
Hudson Thomas N. cabinetmaker, 17th wd. 2 N. bet. W. T. and 1 W.
Hughes John, lab. 15th wd. 6 W. bet. 1 and 2 S.
Hughes Francis, painter, 11th wd. 2 S. bet. 8 and 9 E.
Hughes John, tailor, 11th wd. 8 E. bet. 2 and 3 S.
Hulse James, woodturner, 20th wd. Spruce, cor. Prospect
Humes Nathan, cabinetmaker, 2d wd. 7 S. bet. 3 and 4 E.
Hunt William H. carpenter, 1st wd. 8 S. cor. 9 E.
Hunt Ralph H. carpenter, 14th wd. 3 S. bet. W. T. and 1 W.
Hunter Adam, quarryman. 11th wd. 1 S. cor. 7 E.
Hunter James, carpenter, 12th wd. 3 S. bet. 5 and 6 E.
Hunter Isaac, mason, 16th wd. N. T. bet. 5 and 6 W.
Hunter James, lab. 6th wd. 4 W. bet. 3 and 4 S.
Hunter Stephen, wellsinker, 7th wd. E. T. cor 4 S.
Huntington Dimick B., Indian interpreter, 16th wd. 2 N. cor. 3 W.
Hurd William, whitewasher, 10th wd. 8 E. bet. 4 and 5 S.
Huss John, blacksmith, 8th wd. 2 E. bet. 4 and 5 S.
Hussey Warren (Hussey, Dahler & Co.), banker, es. E. T. bet. 1
    and 2 S. res. 7th wd. 4 S. bet. E. and W. T.
Hutchings Eliza, wid. 16th wd. 1 N. bet. 4 and 5 W.
Hutchings Amanda, wid. 14th wd. W. T. bet. S. T. and 1 S.
Hutchins Joseph, lab. 19th wd. 2 N. cor. 2 W.
Hyam Thomas, gardener, 20th wd. Maple, cor. Garden
Hyde Heman, farmer, 13th wd. 1 E. bet. 2 and 3 S.
Hyde William, policeman, 13th wd. 1 S. bet. 1 and 2 E.
Hyde H. glovemaker, 1 E. bet. 2 and 3 S.
Hyde Orson, one of the twelve apostles, 17th wd. N. T. bet. E. and W. T.
Hyde Joseph E. actor, 15th wd. 2 S. bet. 3 and 4 W.
Hyde Charles W. 7th wd. 1 W. bet. 3 and 4 S.
Hyler M. R. physician, Bench, bet. 8 and 9 S.

ALL SORTS OF NOTIONS, CHEAP, AT H. E. PHELPS' VARIETY STORE.

SALT LAKE CITY DIRECTORY. 115

I

Idaho Corral, 3 S. bet. 1 and 2 E.

Independence Hall, 7th wd. 3 S. bet. E. and W. T.

Ingelineson Hendrick, farmer, 17th wd. 1 W. bet. N. and S. T.

Irish James E. provision dealer, ws. E. T. bet. S. T. and 1 S. res. 14th wd. W. T. bet. 1 and 2 S.

Irvin Robert, cabinetmaker, 14th wd. 1 W. bet. S. T. and 1 S.

Irvin James, bartender, Railroad saloon, res. at saloon

Irvine George, lab. 6th wd. 3 S. bet. 4 and 5 W.

Irvine Agnes, wid. 6th wd. 3 S. bet. 4 and 5 W.

Isaac John, mason, 16th wd. 1 N. cor. 7 W.

Isaacson Henry W. attorney at law, office, E. T. bet. 1 and 2 S. res. 17th wd. 1 W. bet. N. and S. T.

Iser J. gunsmith, 9th wd. 3 E. bet. 3 and 4 S.

Isherwood James, lab. 16th wd. 7 W. bet. 1 and 2 N.

Ivins Anthony, general merchandise, es. E. T. bet. S. T. and 1 S. res. 14th wd. 1 S. cor. 1 W.

Ivison Soren, lab. 2d wd. 7 S. bet. 3 and 4 E.

J .

Jack James, clerk in tithing office, res. 12th wd. 5 E. cor. 2 S.

Jack Thomas, farmer, 1st wd. 8 E. cor. 7 S.

Jackman Levi, saddletree maker, 16th wd. b W. cor. 1 N.

Jackman A. R. clerk, res. 14th wd. 2 W. bet. S. T. and 1 S.

Jacobs Andrew, cabinetmaker, 20th wd. Cherry, cor. Bluff

Jacobs Zebulon, clerk, 17th wd. N. T. bet. E. and W. T.

Jacobs Chauncey, carriagemaker, 9th wd. 3. S. bet. 5 and 6 E.

James Thomas J. carpenter, 10th wd. 7 E. bet. 3 and 4 S.

James Joseph, lab. 10th wd. 4 S. cor. 7 E.

James Isaac, lab. 1st wd. 7 E. bet. 8 and 9 S.

James Sylvester, farmer, 1st wd. 8 S. bet. 8 and 9 E.

Janney T. A. bookkeeper, with J. K. Trumbo

Jaques John, clerk. res. 12th wd. S. T. bet. 5 and 6 E.

Jenkins William, saddler, 17th wd. S. T. bet. 1 and 2 W.

Jenkins Thomas, bishop, 4th wd. 6 S. cor. E. T.

Jennings William (J. & Co.), general merchandise, cor. 1 S. and E. T. res. 16th wd. S. T. bet. 2 and 3 W.

Jensen Soren, carpenter, 1st wd. 9 E. bet. 7 and 8 S.

Views of the Overland Route, at Carter's Gallery, adjoin'g Wells, Fargo & Co.'s.

116   SALT LAKE CITY DIRECTORY.

Jensen Annie, wid. 2d wd. 3 E. bet. 8 and 9 S.   •
Jeremy Thomas E. farmer, 16th wd. S. T. cor. 6 W.
Jeremy Thomas, teamster, 16th wd. 6 W. bet. N. and S. T.
Jeremy David, farmer, 19th wd. 2 N. cor. 5 W.
Joel Samuel, auctioneer, es. E. T. bet. S. T. and 1 S. res. 14th wd. W.
    T. bet. 1 and 2 S.
John David, mason, 11th wd. 9 E. bet. 2 and 3 S.
Johnson Thomas, engaged at Revere House, res. 4th wd. 2 W. bet. 6
    and 7 S.
Johnson E. P. attorney at law, office, 2 S. bet. E. and W. T. res. 13th
    wd. 3 S. bet. 2 and 3 E.
Johnson Joseph W. mason, 14th wd. 3 S. cor. W. T.
Johnson Augustus, shoemaker, 20th wd. Pine, bet. High and Prospect
Johnson & Odell, boots and Shoes, 2 S. bet. E. T. and 1 E.
Johnson S. clerk, 19th wd.
Johnson Lucius L. trader, 15th wd. 3 S. bet. 3 and 4 W.
Johnson William D. trader, 15th wd. S. T. bet. 3 and 4 W.
Johnson Charles W. saddler, 12th wd. 2 S. bet. 4 and 5 E.
Johnson John W. teamster, 15th wd. 3 W. bet. S. T. and 1 S.
Johnson Andrew S. lab. 15th wd. 3 W. bet. 1 and 2 S.
Johnson Thomas, farmer, 5th wd. 2 W. bet. 6 and 7 S.
Johnson Samuel, glovemaker, 2 S. bet. E. T. and 1 E.
Johnson John, tinsmith, 9th wd. 5 S. bet. 3 and 4 E.
Johnson James, farmer, 2d wd. 3 E. bet. 7 and 8 S.
Johnson John P. farmer, 1st wd. 9 S. bet. 7 and 8 E.
Jones Mrs. wid. Bench, bet. 8 and 9 S.
Jones Rebecca, wid. 15th wd. 2 W. bet. 1 and 2 S.
Jones John R. lab. 10th wd. 6 E. cor. 7 S.
Jones Thomas J. farmer, 16th wd. 6 W. bet. N. and S. T.
Jones Charles C. lab. 16th wd. 1 N. bet. 6 and 7 W.
Jones Amos, stonemason, 15th wd. 2 S. bet. 4 and 5 W.
Jones Thomas, brushmaker, 1 N. bet. 2 and 3 W.
Jones William R. tailor, 15th wd. 2 S. cor. 3 W.
Jones Edward, tinner, 10th wd. 4 S. bet. 7 and 8 E.
Jones S. groceries and provisions, 1 S. bet. E. T. and 1 E.
Jones William, plasterer, 15th wd. S. T. bet. 5 and 6 W.
Jones George, lab. 15th wd. 1 S. bet. 6 and 7 W.
Jones Charles F. tinner, 15th wd. 2 W. bet. 2 and 3 S.
Jones Charles R. tailor, ns. 2 S. bet. E. T. and 1 E. res. 14th wd.
    2 S. bet. W. T. and 1 W.
Jones D. W. saddler, ss. 2 S. bet. E. T. and 1 E. res. 11th wd. 2 S. cor.
    3 E.
Jones S. L. stonecutter, 13th wd. 1 E. bet. 2 and 3 S.
Jones Edward, lab. 4th wd. 7 S. bet. 3 and 4 W.

Jones John T. miner, 20th wd. Maple, cor. Bluff
Jones Thomas, mason, 11th wd. 2 S. cor. 9 E.
Jones Henry, painter, 19th wd. Quince, bet. Apricot and Plum
Jones William, jeweler, ss. 1 S. bet. E. T. and 1 E. res. 19th wd. 4 N. bet. 5 and 6 W.
Jones John W. clerk, with Walker Bros. res. 19th wd. Grape, bet. Currant and 1 N.
Jordan Thomas, lab. 15th wd. 1 S. bet. 6 and 7 W.
Jordan James, cooper, 10th wd. 8 E. cor. 4 S.
Jorgensen Ole, carpenter, 14th wd. S. T. bet. W. T. and 1 W.
Jorgensen Christina, wid. 20th wd. Beech, cor. Garden
Jorgenson Peter, lab. 11th wd. 1 S. bet. 6 and 7 E.
Jorgesen C. F. gunsmith, 6th wd. 6 S. bet. 4 and 5 W.
Judd Thomas, lab. 15th wd. 4 W. bet. 1 and 2 S.

K

Kahn Samuel (K. Bros.), dry goods and groceries, Commerce bldg. es- E. T. bet. 1 and 2 S. res. 8th wd. 5 S. bet. E. T. and 1 E.
Kahn Emanuel (K. Bros.), dry goods and groceries, res. at store
Kammerle Fritz, carpenter, 1st wd. 8 E. cor. 8 S.
Kay Susan, wid. 12th wd. 4 E. cor. S. T.
Keaton George D. clerk, Daily Telegraph office, res. 6th wd. 4 W. bet. 5 and 6 S.
Keats James, clerk, res. 8th wd. 6 S. bet. E. T. and 1 E.
Keddington William, butcher, 10th wd. 8 E. bet. 4 and 5 S.
Keeler S. saddler, 19th wd. 2 N. cor. 3 W.
Keep James J. mason, 8th wd. E. T. bet. 3 and 4 S.
Keir David, plasterer, 7th wd. 6 S. cor. 2 W.
Kelly John B. bookbinder, Deseret News office, and actor, res. 7th wd. 1 W. bet. 4 and 5 S.
Kelly John J. stonemason, 7th wd. 1 W. bet. 4 and 5 S.
Kelsen John H. (K. & Field), bakers and confectioners, E. T. bet. 1 and 2 S. and 1 S. bet. E. T. and 1 E.
Kempster Charles O. lab. 15th wd. 7 W. bet. S. T. and 1 S.
Kendall James, carpenter, 16th wd. N. T. bet. 6 and 7 W.
Kennedy Washington, lab. 9th wd. 3 S. bet. 5 and 6 E.
Kenner Scipio A. compositor, Telegraph office, res. 7th wd.
Kenner Robert H. physician, 7th wd. 5 S. bet. E. and W. T.
Kerr John W. cashier, Miners' National Bank
Kesler Frederick, bishop, 16th wd. res. N. T. cor. 3 W.
Keysor Guy, mason, 8th wd. 3 E. bet. 4 and 5 S.
Kidd William, carpenter, 19th wd. bet. 4 and 5 N.

Views of Echo Kanyon, at Carter's Gallery, adjoining Wells, Fargo & Co.'s.

118   SALT LAKE CITY DIRECTORY.

Kidgell Charles, sr. jeweler, 2 S. bet. E. and 1 E. res. 10th wd. 5 E. bet.
  5 and 6 S.

Kidgell Charles jr. machinist, 10th wd. 5 E. bet. 5 and 6 S.

Kimball & Lawrence, general merchandise, E. T. cor. 1 S.

Kimball John B. (K. & Lawrence), merchant, cor. E. T. and 1 S. res. 8th
  wd. E. T. cor. 4 S.

Kimball Sarah M. wid. 15th wd. 2 W. cor. 1 S.

Kimball Hiram, clerk, with Kahn Bros. res. 15th wd. 2 S. bet. 2 and
  3 W.

Kimball Amanda, wid. 17th wd. 1 W. bet. 1 and 2 N.

Kimball Charles S. freighter, 17th wd. E. T. bet. N. T. and 1 N.

Kimball David P. freighter and rancher, 17th wd. 1 N, e. of E. T.

Kimball Heber, freighter and rancher, 17th wd. 1 N. bet. E. and W. T.

Kimmersley Henry, lab. 19th wd. cor. Central and Plum

King Thomas, basketmaker, 10th wd. 8 E. bet. 3 and 4 S.

King Charles, contractor and builder, office at res. 8th wd. 3 S. bet. E.
  and 1 E.

King Thomas H. farmer, 17th wd. 1 N. bet. 1 and 2 W.

Kingsbury Joseph, clerk, 12th wd. 2 S. cor. 3 E.

Kirby William, barkeeper, res. 13th wd. 2 S. bet. 2 and 3 E.

Kirkendall Isaac, hostler, 7th wd. W. T. cor. 5 S.

Kirkham William, carpenter, 8th wd. 6 S. bet. E. T. and 1 E.

Kirkwood Robert C. (Stubbs & K.), City Bakery, res. 14th wd. W. T.
  bet. 2 and 3 S.

Kiskadden J., Miners' National Bank

Knight William, bootcloser, 20th wd. Spruce, cor. Mountain

Knight Robert, bootcloser, 20th wd. High, cor. Spruce

Knight Maria, wid. 6th wd. 4 S. bet. 4 and 5 W.

Knight Oswald, farmer, 6th wd. 4 S. bet. 4 and 5 W.

Knowlden Thomas B. carpenter, 12th wd. 4 E. bet. 1 and 2 S.

Knowlton J. Q. freighter, 19th wd. 3 N. cor. 5 W.

Knowlton Frank, farmer, 19th wd. 3 N. bet. 1 and 2 W.

L

Ladd Samuel G. general dealer, 7th wd. W. T. bet. 5 and 6 S.

Lake William, lab. 19th wd. 2 W. bet. 4 and 5 N.

Lambert Charles, builder, 7th wd. 1 W. bet. 3 and 4 S.

Lambert George, compositor, Juvenile Instructor office, res. 7th wd. 1
  W. bet. 3 and 4 S.

Lambourne William, paperhanger, 20th wd. Wall, cor. Fir

Lambourne Alfred, painter, 20th wd. Wall, cor. Fir

Lambson Alfred B. 17th wd. 1 N. cor. 1 W.

Lamorn Stewart, blacksmith, 12th wd. 3 S. cor. 4 E.

Lancaster William, millwright, 8th wd. 3 S. bet. 2 and 3 E.

Lane Thomas A. tailor, 20th wd. Locust, cor. Garden

Laney Isaac, farmer, 10th wd. 6 S. cor. 9 E.

Langfield Samuel, shoemaker, 16th wd. 1 N. bet. 6 and 7 W.

Lanham Thomas, woodturner, 11th wd. 1 S. bet. 7 and 8 E.

Lank William, shoemaker, 1st wd. 8 S. bet. 6 and 7 E.

Lark John, lab. 19th wd. cor. Central and Cane

Larkin Elijah, shepherd, 11th wd. 1 S. bet. 6 and 7 E.

Larson Hans, lab. 2d wd. 8 S. bet. 3 and 4 E.

Larsen Christian, farmer, 2d wd. 4 E. bet. 7 and 8 S.

Lashbrook C. H. general trader, 1 S. bet. E. T. and W. T.

Latey John H. (Godbe & Co.), drugs, medicines, etc. Exchange bldgs. cor. 1 S. and E. T. res. 7th wd. 3 S. bet. E. and W. T.

Latey William, trader, res. 7th wd. 3 S. bet. E. and W. T.

Latham James, lab. 6th wd. 3 S. bet. 4 and 5 W.

Latimer Thomas, sash and door maker, 14th wd. 2 S. bet. E. and W. T.

Lawrence H. W. (Kimball & L.), merchant, cor. E. T. and 1 S. res. 8th wd. 3 S. bet. E. and 1 E.

Lawrence Nelson, agent and clerk in Kimball & Lawrence's, res. 8th wd. 3 S. bet. E. and 1 E.

Lawrence George, bootmaker and provision dealer, ns. 2 S. bet. E. T. and 1 E. res. 12th wd. 3 E. cor. 3 S.

Lawson James, machinist, 16th wd. 2 W. bet. N. T. and 1 N.

Lawson Charles, clerk, 11th wd. 2 S. bet. 6 and 7 E.

Lawson Julius, lab. 11th wd. 2 S. bet. 6 and 7th

Lawson Lars, lab. 20th wd. Pine cor. Mountain

Leach James, farmer, 2d wd. 5 E. cor. 7 S.

Leach Joseph, Boise Stage office, 2 S. bet. E. T. and 1 E.

Leaker David W. blacksmith, 11th wd. 1 S. bet. 6 and 7 E.

Leaver Samuel H. bookkeeper, 8th wd. 1 E. bet. 3 and 4 S.

Leavett William, lab. 1st wd. 9 E. cor. 7 S.

Le Barron David, lab. 15th wd. 2 S. bet. 3 and 4 W.

Lee Ezekiel, physician, 19th wd. 3 N. cor. 2 W.

Lee Henry, groceries and provisions, E. T. bet. S. T. and 1 S.

Lee Stephen, boarding house, 13th wd. 1 S. cor. 3 E.

Lee Alfred, gardener, 19th wd. 3 W. cor. 4 N.

Lees John, Sr. lab. 19th wd. 4 N. cor. 5 W.

Lees John, Jr. butcher, 19th wd. 4 N. cor. 5 W.

Lees Josiah, teamster, 19th wd. 4 N. cor. 5 W.

Leitz Thomas, cabinetmaker at H. Dinwoodey's, res. 15th wd. 2 S. bet. 2 and 3 W.

Lenzi Martin, salesman with Kimball & Lawrence, r. 14th wd. 1 W. bet. 1 and 2 S.

The largest assortment of views, at Carter's Gallery, adj'g Wells, Fargo & Co.'s.

120   SALT LAKE CITY DIRECTORY.

Leonard Lyman, farmer, 7th wd. E. T. bet. 3 and 4 S.
Leonard Bradford, 16th wd. N. T. bet. 2 and 3 W.
Lesser Bros. dry goods and clothing, ws. E. T. bet. 1 and 2 S.
Lester Feargus, farmer, 11th wd. 10 E. bet. 2 and 3 S.
Leventhall A. auctioneer, E. T. bet. 1 and 2 S.
Levy Lewis, auctioneer, es. E. T. bet. S. T. and 1 S. res. 14th wd. S. T. bet. E. and W. T.
Lewis John W. lab. 19th wd. 4 W. bet. 2 and 3 N.
Lewis Henry, Sr. blacksmith, 20th wd. cor. Pine and Garden
Lewis Henry, Jr. teamster, 20th wd. Elm, cor. Wall
Lewis John B. carpenter, 20th wd. Spruce, cor. Fruit
Lewis James B. carpenter, 20th wd. Spruce, cor. Garden
Lewis John A. lab. 20th wd. cor. Locust and Bluff
Lewis T. R. telegraph operator, Utah Telegraph office
Lewis John, lab. 16th wd. 7 W. bet. N. T. and 1 N.
Lewis William, stonemason, 16th wd. S. T. bet. 6 and 7 W.
Lewis James S. shoemaker, 15th wd. 1 S. bet. 5 and 6 W.
Lewis John, lab. 5th wd. 2 W. bet. 7 and 8 S.
Liddell Andrew, with A. C. Pyper & Co.
Liddell John C. (A. C. Pyper & Co.), groceries and general merchandise, es. E. T. bet. S. T. and 1 S. res. 13th wd. 2 S. bet. S. T. and 1 S.
Lichtenburg Paul, teacher, 19th wd. 5 W. bet. 2 and 3 N.
Liljenstrom Wm. tailor, 20th wd. Birch, cor. Fruit
Limb William, lab. 11th wd. 3 S. bet. 8 and 9 E.
Lindsay Gilbert, carpenter, 17th wd. W. T. bet. N. T. and 1 N.
Lindsay John S. actor, 8th wd. E. bet. 5 and 6 S.
Lindsay Mark, gardener, 20th wd. cor. Beech and Fruit
Linroot Peter, lab. 19th wd. 2 W. cor. 3 N.
Lipper Henry, bartender, res. 7th wd. 3 S. bet. W. T. and W.
Little Feramorz, propr. Salt Lake House, res. 13th wd. 1 S. cor. 2 E.
Little Jesse C. carriage, wagon and sleigh manufacturer, 13th wd. 2 E. cor. 1 S.
Littlefield Lyman O. compositor, Daily Telegraph office, res. 13th wd. 2 S. cor. 2 E.
Livingston James, foreman, Sharp & Young, res. 20th wd. Elm, cor. Fruit
Livingston Charles M. trader, 7th wd. 1 W. cor. 5 S.
Livingston Archibald, lab. 15th wd. S. T. bet. 2 and 3 W.
Livingston Charles, policeman, 11th wd. 7 E. bet. 1 and 2 S.
Livsdale P. cabinetmaker, 17th wd. W. T. bet. N. T. and 1 N.
Livsey John, lab. 10th wd. 5 S. bet. 9 and 10 E.
Lloyd William, shoemaker, 15th wd. 1 S. bet. 4 and 5 W.
Lloyd Thomas, lab. 20th wd. cor. Poplar and Wall

Buck Skins and Deer Skins Bought and Sold at H. E. PHELPS' VARIETY STORE.

SALT LAKE CITY DIRECTORY. 121

Lloyd John, carpenter, 10th wd. 9 E. bet. 3 and 4 S.

Lollin John, Railroad saloon, es. E. T. bet. 1 and 2 S. bds. Salt Lake House

Long John V. attorney at law and collector, 13th wd. 2 E. bet. 1 and 2 S.

Longmore William, tailor, 20th wd. cor. S. T. and Larch

Longstroth Ann, wid. 14th wd. 1 S. bet. E. and W. T.

Loren G. B. railroad boardinghouse, 14th wd. 2 S. bet. E. and W. T.

Lorimer William, barber, 12th wd. 2 S. bet. 3 and 4 E.

Lovandalk John, carpenter, 11th wd. 7 E. bet. 1 and 2 S.

Love David, lab. 6th wd. 4 S. bet. 4 and 5 W.

Lovering Benjamin, farmer, 12th wd. 3 S. cor. 4 E

Lovesey Henry, lab. 9th wd. 4 E. bet. 4 and 5 S.

Lovesey Edward, lab. 10th wd. 6 E. bet. 3 and 4 S.

Lowe Richard, tailor, 15th wd. 7 W. bet. S. T. and 1 S.

Lowe William, blacksmith, 11th wd. 2 S. bet. 7 and 8 E.

Lowe John O. teamster, 19th wd. 2 W. cor. 5 N.

Luce Wilford, freighter, 14th wd. 1 W. bet. 2 and 3 S.

Luce Martin, lab. 6th wd. 2 W. bet. 4 and 5 S.

Luddington Elam, gardener, 12th wd. 4 E. bet. S. T. and 1 S.

Luff Harry, carpenter, 20th wd. Fir, cor. Bluff

Luff George, carpenter, 20th wd. Oak, cor. Wall

Lunbeck Charles J. carpenter, 14th wd. S. T. bet. W. T. and 1 W.

Lundegreen Sven N. shoemaker, 2d wd. 6 S. bet. 3 and 4 E.

Lutz Charles, shoemaker, 12th wd. 2 S. bet. 3 and 4 E.

Lutz Albert, lab. 12th wd. 3 E. cor. 2 S.

Lutz Frederick, coach dispatcher, Wells, Fargo & Co.'s office

Lynch William, gunsmith, 3d wd. 2 E. bet. 6 and 7 S.

Lynch Patrick, notary public and clerk district court, 3d district, r. 20th wd. Pine, cor. Garden

Lyne T. A. dramatic teacher, 12th wd. 1 S. bet. 4 and 5 E.

Lyon John sr. librarian, 20th wd. Oak, cor. Garden

Lyon John jr. carpenter, 20th wd. Spruce, cor. Bluff

Lyon Mathew, teamster, 20th wd. Elm, cor. Wall

Lyon Thomas, lab. 2d wd. 4 E. cor. 6 S.

Lyons Albert, farmer, 16th wd. 1 N. bet. 2 and 3 W.

Lyons Joseph, plasterer, 12th wd. 5 E. bet. 2 and 3 S.

Lyungburg Charles, machinist, 9th wd. 5 S. bet. 3 and 4 E.

M

Mackey John, farmer, 20th wd. cor. Pine and Fruit

Madison James T. shoemaker, 11th wd. 3 S. cor. 9 E.

Madson Peter, lab. 1st wd. 6 S. cor. 6 E.

Maeser Karl G. teacher, 20th wd. Elm, cor. Fruit

Maiben John B. dry goods and groceries, cor. E. T. and 1 S. res. 7th wd. W. T. bet. 3 and 4 S.

Mair James, clerk for J. A. Young, S. T. bet. E. and W. T. res. 9th wd. 4 E. cor. 5 S.

Makin William, teamster, 4th wd. W. T. cor. 7 S.

Malin John, farmer, 12th wd. 3 S. bet. 3 and 4 E.

Malin Samuel, lab. 12th wd. 4 E. bet. 2 and 3 S.

Malin James, farmer, 10th wd. 6 S. cor. 8 E.

Mallet Phillip, lab. 14th wd. 2 S. bet. 1 and 2 W.

Maltese S. groceries and provisions, E. T. bet. 2 and 3 S.

Mansion House, cor. 3 S. and 1 E.

Manning John, tailor, 2 S. bet. E. T. and 1 E.

Marchbanks James lab. 12th wd. 5 E. cor. 2 S.

Marcroft John, weaver, 4th wd. 8 S. bet. 2 and 3 W.

Margetts Richard B. blacksmith, 19th wd. 2 N. bet. 2 and 3 W.

Margetts Phillip, actor, 17th wd. 1 W. bet. N. and S. T.

Margetts Henry, blacksmith, 17th wd. 1 N. bet. W. T. and 1 W.

Marsden William, lab. 16th wd. 7 W. cor. N. T.

Marsden James, lab. 5th wd. 3 W. bet. 8 and 9 S.

Marsden James, lab. 4th wd. 3 W. cor. 8 S.

Marshall Thomas (M. & Carter), attorney at law, office, ws. E. T. bet. 1 and 2 S. res. 7th wd. W. T. bet. 3 and 4 S.

Martin Andrew F. lab. 12th wd. 6 E. bet. 1 and 2 S.

Martin James, carpenter, 13th wd. 1 E. bet. 2 and 3 S.

Martin Ezra, bootmaker, 13th wd. 3 S. bet. 1 and 2 E.

Masters Joseph, quarryman, 8th wd. 4 S. cor. 3 E.

Matthews John, carriage painter, ss. 2 S. bet. E. T. and 1 E. res. 20th wd. Bluff, cor. Maple

Matthews William, gardener, 20th wd. Birch, cor. Fruit

Matthews Joseph, mason, 19th wd. 4 W. bet. 2 and 3 N.

Matthews Richard, pressman, Deseret News office, res. 17th wd. 1 N. cor. 1 W.

Maxwell John, gardener, 14th wd. S. T. bet. W. T. and 1 W.

Maycock Thomas, lab. 3d wd. 3 E. bet. 6 and 7 S.

McAllister John D. T., Territorial marshal, office and res. 8th wd.

McAllister Richard, deputy marshal, 8th wd. 1 E. bet. 3 and 4 S.

McAllister Duncan, clerk at Post Office, res. 14th wd. 1 W. bet. 2 and 3 S.

McAvoy John (Tullidge & McA.), 2 S. bet. E. T. and 1 E. res. 20th wd. Birch, cor. Fruit

McClelland Thomas, bishop, 7th wd. res. W. T. bet. 3 and 4 S.

McCloy John, miner, 2d wd. 6 S. cor. 4 E.

300 different views of Utah, at Carter's Gallery, adjoining Wells, Fargo & Co's.

SALT LAKE CITY DIRECTORY. 123

McComie Peter, carpenter, 5 E. bet. 5 and 6 S.

McComie John, bootmaker, 13th wd. 1 E. bet. 1 and 2 S.

McComie John, carpenter, 6 E. bet. 6 and 7 S.

McComins Annie, wid. 2 wd. 8 S. bet. 4 and 5 E.

McCullough Alexander, lab. 20th wd. Maple, cor. Fruit

McDonald John, wagonmaker, 13th wd. 1 S. bet. 1 and 2 E.

McDonald Edward, minor, 20th wd. cor. Oak and High

McDonald John, groceries and provisions, E. T. bet. 2 and 3 S.

McDuff & Sons, limeburners, E. T. bet. 2 and 3 S.

McEwan Henry, foreman, Daily Telegraph, res. 12th wd. 1 S. bet. 3 and 4 E.

McFall John, plasterer, 13th wd. 3 S. bet. 1 and 2 E.

McGregor William, stonemason, 2d wd. 4 E. cor. 8 S.

McIntyre Thomas, compositor, Deseret News office, res. 20th wd. Locust, cor. Fruit

KcKay Joseph, lab. 3d wd. 6 S. cor. 3 E.

McKay Samuel, lab. 11th wd. 2 S. cor. 10 E.

KcKay Robert, weaver, 20th wd. cor. S. T. and Hickory

McKean Theodore, Territorial road com. 16th wd. 4 W. cor. 1 N.

McKeller Angus, blacksmith, 3d wd. 2 E. bet. 6 and 7 S.

McKennion Peter, shoemaker, 14th wd. 3 S. cor. W. T.

McKenzie David, engraver, 7th wd. 6 S. cor. W. T.

McKenzie George G. clerk with Pyper & Co.

McKinney Elizabeth, wid. 13th wd. 3 S. bet. E. T. and 1 E.

McKinnon Archibald, saddler, res. 8th wd. 5 S. bet. E. T. and 1 E.

McKnight James, compositor, 12th wd. 1 S. cor. 5 E.

McLaughlan William, carpenter, 7th wd. W. T. bet. 4 and 5 S.

McLean Albert, teacher, 14th wd. 1 S. bet. E. and W. T.

McMaster William, ropemaker, 11th wd. 9 E. bet. S. T. and 1 S.

McMinn John A. gardener, 4th wd. 1 W. bet. 7 and 8 S.

McMurrin Joseph, cooper, with C. Donelson, res. 8th wd. 6 S. cor. 1 E.

McRae Alexander, bishop, 11th wd. 6 E. cor. 2 S.

McRae Joseph, blacksmith, 11th wd. 6 E. bet. 1 and 2 S.

Meads Nathan, lab. 11th wd. 8 E. bet. 2 and 3 S.

Meeks John, pioneer jewelry store, es. E. T. bet. 1 and 2 S. res. 8th wd. 4 S. cor. E. T.

Mercroft John, lab. 5th wd. 8 S. bet. 2 and 3 W.

Merkley Christopher, farmer, 17th wd. N. T. bet. 1 and 2 W.

Merrill Samuel, farmer, 19th wd. 2 W. bet. 3 and 4 N.

Merrill Albert, hatter, 17th wd. 1 W. bet. 1 and 2 N.

Meyer M. drygoods, boots and shoes, ws. E. T. bet. 1 and 2 S.

Micheal Thomas, cabinetmaker, 19th wd. Central, bet. Currant and Apricot

Michealson William, cabinetmaker, 10th wd. 3 S. bet. 6 and 7 E.

Middlemas Edward, shoemaker, 6th wd. 5 S. bet. 2 and 3 W.

Midgeley Joshua (M. & Evans), painter, 2 S. bet. E. and W. T. res. 12th wd. 5 E. bet. 2 and 3 S.

Mikesell Hyrum, lab. 5 E. bet. 8 and 9 S.

Milam Elizabeth, wid. 17th wd. 1 W. bet. N. and S. T.

Miles Orson, clerk, in Kimball & Lawrence's, res. 8th wd. 3 S. bet. E. T. and 1 E.

Millard Charles, property-man at theatre, res. 8th wd. 1 E. cor. 5 S.

Millard William, shoemaker, 20th wd. Chesnut, cor. Garden

Miller Charles W. salesman, with A. Ivins

Miller John, shoemaker, 11th wd. S. T. bet. 7 and 8 E.

Miller William, lab. 11th wd. 3 S. cor. 7 E.

Miller Thomas, teamster, 19th wd. cor. Peach and 1 W.

Miller John, lab. 12th wd. 5 E. cor. 2 S.

Miller John, lab. 4th wd. 7 S. cor. 3 W.

Miller Eben, carpenter, 11th wd. 3 S. bet. 10 E. and Bench

Miller Elijah, lab. 11th wd. 2 S. bet. 9 and 10 E.

Miller Eleazer, nurseryman, 12th wd. 2 S. bet. 4 and 5 E.

Miller Francis, blacksmith, 15th wd. 7 W. bet. S. T. and 1 S.

Milner F. blacksmith, Railroad shops

Mineer Andrew, violinist, 10th wd. 3 S. bet. 6 and 7 E.

Miner Aurelius, attorney at law, 14th wd. 2 S. bet. W. T. and 1 W.

Minker Mary A. wid. 16th wd. S. T. bet. 4 and 5 W.

Misener Alfred, teamster, 8th wd. 5 S. bet. 2 and 3 E.

Mitchell Hezekiah, salesman at F. A. Mitchell's, res. 1st. wd. 7 E. cor. 6 S.

Mitchell B. F. stonecutter, 15th wd. 1 S. bet. 2 and 3 W.

Mitchell F. A. general merchandise, Exchange bldgs. 1 S. cor. E. T. res. 13th wd. 2 S. bet. 2 and 3 E.

Moffat David, miner, 3d wd. 2 E. bet. 7 and 8 S.

Molten James, farmer, 3d wd. 1 E. bet. 6 and 7 S.

Monken Peter, blacksmith, 9th wd. 5 E. bet. 5 and 6 S.

Montana Corral, W. H. Alma, propr. 1 E. bet. 1 and 2 S.

Montana Restaurant, Broy & Woodworth, proprs. 2 S. bet. E. T. and 1 E.

Moon Hugh, farmer, 1st wd. 7 S. cor. 7 E.

Moon Henry, Bishop, 1st wd. 7 S. bet. 7 and 8 E.

Moore William, shoemaker, 20th wd. cor. Larch and Fruit

More Henry, lab. 15th wd. 6 W. cor. 2 S.

Morf T. M. clerk, Wells, Fargo & Co.'s office, res. 12th wd. 3 E. bet. 2 and 3 S.

Morgan William, plasterer, 15th wd. 6 W. cor. 1 S.

Morgan John R. lab. 15th wd. 5 W. bet. 1 and 2 S.

Morgan John, principal, commercial college, E. T. bet. 2 and 3 S. res. 17th wd.

Morris Isidore, trader, 17th wd 1 N. bet. 1 and 2 W.

Morris William, painter, 15th wd. 4 W. bet. S. T. and 1 S.
Morris William V. painter, 15th wd. 1 S. bet. 4 and 5 W.
Morris John, mason, 6th wd. 4 W. bet. 4 and 5 S.
Morris Hugh, mason, 15th wd. 3 W. bet. 2 and 3 S.
Morris Thomas, mason, 16th wd. 7 W. bet. N. T. and 1 N.
Morris George, mason, 17th wd. 2 N. cor. 1 W.
Morris Charles, lab. 11th wd. 3 S. cor. 9 E.
Morris Richard V. assistant assessor, internal revenue, 19th wd. cor.
    Quince and Currant
Morris B. tailor, E. T. bet. 2 and 3 S.
Morris Elias, mason, 15th wd.
Morris John T. boatbuilder, 12th wd. 2 S. bet. 4 and 5 E.
Morris Joseph, provision dealer, 2 S. cor. 1 E. res. 13th wd. 2 S. bet. 2
    and 3 E.
Morrow William, painter, 19th wd. cor. Quince and Plum
Mortimer A. M. carpenter and builder, E. T. bet. 2 and 3 S.
Moss William I. saddler, 11th wd. 9 E. bet. S. T. and 1 S.
Moss Thomas, cook, 20th wd. S. T. cor. Cedar
Moss W. I. harnessmaker, Railroad Shops
Moss F. William, clerk with D. Day, 15th wd. 3 W. bet. 7 and 8 S.
Moulding William H. butcher, Meat Market, res. 3d wd. 6 S.
    bet. 1 and 2 E.
Mousley Elizabeth, wid. 16th wd. 4 W. bet. N. T. and 1 N.
Moyle James, stonecutter, 15th wd. 5 W. bet. 1 and 2 S.
Muir Thomas, limeburner, 20th wd. Garden, cor. Maple
Muir James, shoemaker, 9th wd. 5 S. bet. 4 and 5 E.
Mulvey John, contractor, 18th wd. 2 S. bet. 2 and 3 E.
Mumford Edward T. carpenter, 14th wd. 3 S. bet. E. and W. T.
Murdock U. farmer, 7th wd. 4 S. bet. E. and W. T.
Murray George, miner, 1st wd. 7 S. cor. 7 E.
Music Hall, 14th wd. 1 S. bet. 1 and 2 W.
Musser A. Milton, superintendent, Deseret Telegraph Line, res. 13th wd.
    2 E. bet. S. T. and 1 S.
Mutch Lewis F. school teacher, 17th wd. W. T. bet. N. T. and 1 N.
Muzell John, lab. 14th wd. 1 W. bet. 2 and 3 S.
Myers Charles, lab. 14th wd. 3 S. bet. 1 and 2 W.
Myers John W. trader, 20th wd. Spruce, cor. Wall
Myers Ann, wid. 9th wd. 4 E. cor. 4 S.
Myrick George L. freighter, 17th wd. 1 N. bet. W. T. and 1 W.

Those splendid gem portraits, at Carter's Gallery, adjoining Wells, Fargo & Co.'s.

126   SALT LAKE CITY DIRECTORY.

N

Naisbitt Henry W. (N. & Hindley), purchasing agent for Zion's Wholesale Co-operative Institution, res. 20th wd. cor. Fruit and Walnut
Napper John, sawyer, 20th wd. Fir, cor. Wall
Nash John, shoemaker, 4th wd. 6 S. cor. 3 W.
Nash John, lab. 5th wd. 3 W. bet. 6 and 7 S.
Naylor William, Wells, Fargo & Co.'s messenger, 13th wd. 2 S. cor. 3 E.
Naylor Thomas, blacksmith, 13th wd. 3 E. bet. 1 and 2 S.
Naylor George, blacksmith, 13th wd. 2 E. bet. 1 and 2 S.
Neal William C. proprietor of saw mill, res. 19th wd. cor. Currant and Plum
Neal George, farmer, 17th wd. 1 N. cor. 1 W.
Nebeker Harry, teamster, 19th wd. 3 N. bet. 4 and 5 W.
Nebeker George, farmer, 19th wd. 4 W. cor. 3 N.
Nebeker Peter, farmer, 19th wd. 2 N. cor. 3 W.
Nebeker John, farmer, 19th wd. 2 N. cor. 4 W.
Nebeker Aaron, lab. 16th wd. 2 N. cor. 6 W.
Needham James, 7th wd. W. T. bet. 3 and 4 S.
Needham John (J. Needham & Co.), commission merchants, res. 8th wd. 1 E. bet. 3 and 4 S.
Needham Jonathan, lab. 19th wd. 4 N. bet. 5 and 6 W.
Needham A. S. music teacher, 7th wd. W. T. bet. 3 and 4 S.
Neibaur H. match factory, 13th wd. 2 E. bet. 2 and 3 S.
Neibaur Isaac, freighter, 13th wd. 2 E. bet. 2 and 3 S.
Neil William, miner, 1st wd. 6 S. cor. 6 E.
Neil S. wid. 1st wd. 6 S. cor. 9 E.
Neilson Olef, lab. 2d wd. 4 E. bet. 6 and 7 S.
Neimeyer William, plasterer, 2d wd. 3 S. bet. 5 and 6 E.
Neslen Samuel, carpenter, 20th wd. S. T. cor. Walnut
Neslen Robert, costumer at theatre, res. 20th wd. S. T. cor. Chesnut
Neve Peter, upholsterer, es. E. T. bet. 2 and 3 S. res. 20th wd. Beech, cor. Bluff
Newman William J. lab. 16th wd. N. T. bet. 6 and 7 W.
Newman Henry, lab. 15th wd. 3 W. bet. 2 and 3 S.
Newton S. E. physician, 12th wd. 2 S. bet. 3 and 4 E.
Newton James, distiller, 10th wd. 3 S. cor. 7 E.
Newton John, currier, 19th wd. 3 N. cor. 2 W.
Nichols Henry W. carpenter, 15th wd. 1 S. bet. 2 and 3 W.
Nichols Robert F. carpenter, 8th wd. E. T. bet. 5 and 6 S.
Nichollson Louis, carpenter, 20th wd. Cherry, cor. Bluff .
Nicholson John, agent, Deseret News, res. 20th wd. Pine, cor. Fruit

H. E. PHELPS BUYS AND SELLS PISTOLS, REVOLVERS, SKINS, FURS, ETC.

SALT LAKE CITY DIRECTORY. 127

Ninde Albert, tailor, ns. 2 S. bet. E. T. and 1 E. res. 8th wd. 3 S. bet. E. T. and 1 E.

Nineteenth Ward Assembly Room, ws. 2 W. cor. 4 N.

Nixon Thomas, lab. 14th wd. 1 W. bet. 2 and 3 S.

Nixon Jane, wid. 14th wd. W. T. bet. 1 and 2 S.

Noals Simon, carpenter, 19th wd. 4 W. cor. 4 N.

Noon Alonzo, farmer, 9 E. bet. 8 and 9 S.

Norman Henry, gardener, 15th wd, 4 W. cor. S. T.

Norman Saul, carpenter, 12th wd. 3 S. cor. 4 E.

Norris David, lab. 20th wd. Pine, cor. Bluff

Nounnan Joseph E. contractor, U. P. R. R. 13th wd. 1 E. bet. 2 and 3 S.

Nowell William, plasterer, 12th wd. 2 S. bet. 3 and 4 E.

Nutt James, plasterer, 6th wd. 4 S. bet. 3 and 4 W.

O

Oakey Thomas, carpenter, 9th wd. 3 E. cor. 5 S.

Oakley Ezra, gardener, 7th wd. 3 S. bet. W. T. and 1 W.

Old Elephant Corrall, J. Wickel, propr. 2 E. bet. 3 and 4 S.

Oblad John, blacksmith, 9th wd. 4 E. bet. 5 and 6 S.

Oglesby William H. bookbinder, 12th wd. 3 S. bet. 3 and 4 E.

Olfer Nancy, wid. 16th wd. 4 W. bet. N. and S. T.

Olsen John, photographer, ns. 1 S. bet. E. and W. T. res. 17th wd. 1 W. bet. N. and S. T.

Olsen Olse, clerk, with Pyper & Co.

Olsen James P. carpenter, 2d wd. 4 E. bet. 7 and 8 S.

Olsen Shure, carpenter, 15th wd. 4 W. cor. 1 S.

Olstrein John, shoemaker, 9th wd. 5 S. bet. 3 and 4 E.

Ordidge William, lab. 19th wd. 5 W. cor. 3 N.

Ornstein Jacob (Ornstein & Popper), soap mnfr. and butcher, office, 1 S. bet. E. and 1 E. res. 8th wd. 3 S. bet. E. and 1 E.

Osborne Lewis, blacksmith, 19th wd. 5 N. cor. 2 W.

Ostler Oliver, carpenter, 10th wd. 9 E. bet. 3 and 4 S.

Ostler William, shoemaker, 10th wd. 3 S. cor. 9 E.

Oswald John, moulder, 12th wd. S. T. cor. 6 E.

Ott Mary J. wid. 14th wd. 1 W. bet. S. T. and 1 S.

Ottinger George (Savage & O.), artist, ws. E. T. bet. S. T. and 1 S. res. 20th wd. Fir, cor. Bluff

Oughton Adam, chairmaker, 16th wd. N. T. bet. 6 and 7 W.

Owens J. M. carpenter, 7th wd. 3 S. bet. E. and W. T.

Large number of Indian photographs, at Carter's, adj'g Wells, Fargo & Co.'s.

128   SALT LAKE CITY DIRECTORY.

P

Pacific House, F. Reich, propr. E. T. bet. 2 and 3 S.
Pack Ward E. teamster, 17th wd. 1 N. bet. W. T. and 1 W.
Pack George C. freighter, 15th wd. 1 S. bet. 2 and 3 W.
Pack John, farmer, 17th wd. W. T. cor. 1 N.
Page John, lab. 5th wd. 6 S. bet. 2 and 3 W.
Page John, tailor, 4th wd. 6 S. bet. 2 and 3 W.
Palmer Morris, blacksmith, 8th wd. 5 S. cor. 1 E.
Palmer Edmund F. farmer, 8th wd. 3 E. cor. 5 S.
Palmer Joseph, farmer, 8th wd. 3 E. cor. 5 S.
Palmer A. B. blacksmith, 12th wd. 1 S. bet. 5 and 6 E.
Palmer William, teamster, 6th wd. 2 W. bet. 5 and 6 S.
Palmer F. cook, 19th wd. 2 W. cor. 3 N.
Palmers James, farmer, 7th wd. 2 W. bet. 5 and 6 S.
Palmquist Helis D. shoemaker, 2d wd. 4 E. bet. 6 and 7 S.
Palmquist Daniel E. tailor, 2d wd. 4 E. bet. 6 and 7 S.
Papworth James, butcher, 20th wd. cor. Quaking Asp and Fruit
Paramore George, mason, 8th wd. 1 E. cor. 5 S.
Parker Joshua, carpenter, 16th wd. N. T. bet. 2 and 3 W.
Parker William K. lab. 15th wd. 3 W. cor. 1 S.
Parker David B. lab. 19th wd. 2 W. bet. 4 and 5 N.
Parkington Ralph, carpenter, 7th wd. 5 S. bet. 1 and 2 W.
Parkman George, shoemaker, 10th wd. 7 E. bet. 5 and 6 S.
Parks Hamilton D. business agent, res. 13th wd. 3 S. bet. 1 and 2 E.
Parratt George, cabinetmaker, res. 4th wd. 6 S. bet. 4 and 5 W.
Perry Edward W. mason, 15th wd. 5 W. bet. S. T. and 1 S.
Perry Thomas, mason, 15th wd. 1 S. cor. 5 W.
Parry Joseph, mason, 15th wd. 1 S. bet. 5 and 6 W.
Parry Harriet, wid. 16th wd. S. T. cor. 5 W.
Parry John, gardener, 16th wd. N. T. bet. 5 and 6 W.
Parry John, mason, 16th wd. 5 W. bet. N. and S. T.
Parson Elijah, lab. 10th wd. 8 E. bet. 5 and 6 S.
Parsons T. F. groceries and provisions, 1 S. bet. E. T. and 1 E.
Pasby Andrew, plasterer, 10th wd. 7 E. bet. 5 and 6 S.
Pascoe J. F. P. practical chemist and lime burner, 19th wd. N. T. bet.
    1 and 2 W.
Patrick Robert, carpenter, 20th wd. cor. Chesnut and Wall
Patten Thomas, tanner, 15th wd. bet. 2 and 3 S.
Patten Henry, saddler, 8th wd. W. T. bet. 5 and 6 S.
Patty Edward, lab. 11th wd. 2 S. bet. 6 and 7 E.
Paul Adam, lab. 8th wd. 6 S. bet. E. and W. T.

Paul Walter, carpenter, 20th wd. Fruit, cor. Maple

Paul William, architect and builder, 20th wd. Garden, cor. Locust

Paul John (Jennings & P.), butcher, meat market, res. 20th wd. S. T. cor. Poplar

Payne James, boot and shoemaker, ns. 2 S. bet. E. and 1 E. res. 12th wd. S. T. bet. 5 and 6 E.

Pea John, blacksmith, 17th wd. 2 N. cor. 1 W.

Peacock James, lab. 11th wd. 1 S. bet. 6 and 7 E.

Pearl George, carpenter, 14th wd. 3 S. cor. W. T.

Pearl Benjamin, carpenter, 14th wd. 3 S. cor. W. T.

Pearl Jacob, mason, 14th wd. 3 S. cor. W. T.

Peck Joseph, blacksmith, 17th wd. 1 W. cor. N. T.

Peck Martin H. blacksmith, 17th wd. 1 W. bet. N. T. and 1 N.

Peirce Frank, carpenter, 15th wd. 5 W. bet. S. T. and 1 S.

Pembroke James L. watchmaker, 7th wd. 1 W. cor. 5 S.

Pendleton Andrew J. blacksmith, 2d wd. 6 S. bet. 4 and 5 E.

Pendleton Benjamin, blacksmith, 2d wd. 6 S. bet. 4 and 5 E.

Pendleton & Vanwoltenberg, blacksmiths, 2 S. bet. E. and W. T.

Peppers William, blacksmith, 17th wd. N. T. bet. 1 and 2 W.

Perkes Henry, cooper, ws. E. T. bet. 2 and 3 S. res. 11th wd. S. T. cor. 7 E.

Perkes William H. clerk, Deseret News office, res. 11th wd. 1 W. bet. 2 and 3 S.

Perkins Washington, teamster, 16th wd. 7 W. bet. 1 and 2 N.

Perkins Levi, lab. 19th wd. 4 N. bet. 4 and 5 W.

Perkins John, lab. 10th wd. 4 S. cor. 8 E.

Perkins William L. mason, 19th wd. 4 N. bet. 4 and 5 W.

Perris Frederick T. (Cronyn & P.), general merchandise, ws. E. T. bet. 1 and 2 S. res. 7th wd. 1 W. bet. 3 and 4 S.

Perry Benjamin, shoemaker, 7 E. cor. 9 S.

Perry William, clerk, 7th wd. W. T. bet. 3 and 4 S.

Perry E. & A. general merchandise, 2 S. bet. 1 and 2 S.

Peterson Andrew, tailor, 17th wd. 1 W. cor. N. T.

Peterson C. shoemaker, 11th wd. 3 S. cor. 6 E.

Peterson Charles, cabinetmaker, 11th wd. 7 E. bet. 1 and 2 S.

Peterson Mrs. wid. 9th wd. 5 E. bet. 4 and 5 S.

Peterson Andrew, lab. 6th wd. 6 S. bet. 4 and 5 W.

Peterson Samuel P. farmer, 2d wd. 4 E. cor. 7 S.

Peterson Hendric, carpenter, 16th wd. 2 W. cor. N. T.

Peterson Frederick, potter, 2d wd. 3 E. bet. 6 and 7 S.

Peterson Eric, woodturner, 10th wd. 5 S. cor. 8 E.

Peterson James, lab. 19th wd. 4 N. bet. 2 and 3 W.

Pettigrew Caroline, wid. 10th wd. 8 E. bet. 5 and 6 S.

Pettit Edward, teamster, 14th wd. 2 W. bet. 2 and 3 S.

Best Bread, Pies and Crackers, by CLIVE & REID, 2d South St., Salt Lake City.

130   SALT LAKE CITY DIRECTORY.

Pettit Brower, carpenter, 15th wd. 1 S. cor. 4 W.

Pettit Ezra, lab. 15th wd. 4 W. bet. 1 and 2 S.

Pettit Richard, carpenter, 16th wd. N. T. bet. 4 and 5 W.

Phelps W. W. notary public, 14th wd. W. T. bet. S. T. and 1 S.

Phelps Henry E. variety store, ws. E. T. bet. S. T. and 1 S. res. 14th wd. W. T. bet. S. T. and 1 S.

Phillips William G. policeman, 20th wd. Elm, cor. Bluff

Phillips James, clerk with Jennings & Co. res. 10th wd. 8 E. cor. 3 S.

Phillips William J. shoemaker, 9th wd. 5 S. cor. 5 E.

Phippon James W. saddler, 16th wd. S. T. bet. 4 and 5 W.

Pickering William, lab. 3d wd. 6 S. bet. 2 and 3 E.

Pickering John, painter, 20th wd. lives with Simeon Pickering

Pickering Simeon, miller, 20th wd. cor. Locust and Garden

Picknell John H. butcher, Meat Market, res. 20th wd. Fruit, bet. Poplar and Willow

Pickwick Henry, lab. 19th wd. bet. Central and Quince

Pierce Isaac R. farmer, 10th wd. 9 E. cor. 5 S.

Pierce Joseph, farmer, 10th wd. 9 E. cor. 5 S.

Pierpoint Thomas, machinist, 14th wd. 1 S. cor. 1 W.

Piggot George W. painter, 8th wd. 6 S. bet. 2 and 3 E.

Pine Horace A. joiner, 12th wd. 3 S. cor. 4 E.

Pinney William, carpenter, 19th wd. 4 W. cor. 3 N.

Pinnock William, clerk, res. 10th wd. 9 E. cor. 4 S.

Pioneer Corral, J. G. Brooks, proprietor, 3 S. bet. 2 and 3 E.

Pitman Frank, lab. 14th wd. 3 S. bet. 1 and 2 W.

Pitt Thomas D. freighter, 13th wd. 1 S. bet. 2 and 3 E.

Pitt Moroni, painter, 19th wd. cor. Central and Peach

Pitt William, painter, 17th wd. N. T. cor. 1 W.

Pitts William, veterinary surgeon, 6th wd. 4 W. bet. 4 and 5 S.

Pitts William H. salesman with Godbe & Co. res. 8th wd. E. T. bet. 5 and 6 S.

Plant Charles M. blacksmith, 19th wd. Beet, bet. Cane and Pear

Platt Francis, saddler, ss. 2 S. bet. E. T. and 1 E. res. 13th wd. 3 E. bet. 1 and 2 S.

Platts John, mason, 19th wd. cor. Quince and Apricot

Player Charles W. stonecutter, 19th wd. 2 N. bet. 6 and 7 W.

Player William, blacksmith, 16th wd. 2 N. cor. 5 W.

Player William W. stonecutter, 17th wd. 1 W. bet. N. T. and 1 N.

Poll James, carpenter, 10th wd. 9 E. bet. 5 and 6 S.

Pollard Joseph, carpenter, 15th wd. 6 W. bet. S. T. and 1 S.

Pollock Sarah A. wid. 15th wd. S. T. bet. 2 and 3 W.

Pomeroy Francis M. farmer, 12th wd. 3 S. bet. 3 and 4 E.

Pomeroy Charles E. corresponding clerk with Hussey, Dahler & Co.

Pool John, lab. 14th wd. S. T. bet. W. T. and 1 W.

ALL SORTS OF NOTIONS, CHEAP, AT H. E. PHELPS' VARIETY STORE.

SALT LAKE CITY DIRECTORY. 131

Pope George, teamster, 2d wd. 4 E. cor. 8 S.

Porcher Thomas, lab. 20th wd. cor. Quakenasp and Fruit

Porcher James, lab. 12th wd. 3 S. bet. 5 and 6 E.

Poulton James, shoemaker, 6th wd. 4 S. bet. 3 and 4 W.

Powell Daniel, carriagemaker, 2d wd. 4 E. bet. 6 and 7 S.

Powell Abraham, lab. 6th wd. 4 S. bet. 2 and 3 W.

Powell Thomas S. lab. 17th wd. 2 W. bet. 1 and 2 N.

Prag Conrad (Ransohoff & Co.), dry goods and general merchandise, 13th wd. res. 1 E. bet. 2 and 3 S.

Pratt Mary, wid. 15th wd. 3 S. bet. 3 and 4 W.

Pratt H. O. telegraph operator

Pratt E. W. oyster dealer, 2 S. near 1 S.

Pratt Parley P. farmer, 12th wd. 2 S. bet. 5 and 6 E.

Pratt Belinda M. wid. 14th wd. S. T. bet. E. and W. T.

Pratt Laren, compositor

Pratt Orson, Sr. one of the 12 apostles, 14th wd. W. T. bet. S. T. and 1 S.

Pratt Orson, Jr. music teacher, 14th wd. W. T. bet. S. T. and 1 S.

Pratt Abinadi, compositor, S. T. bet. E. and W. T.

Pratt Eleanor, wid. 14th wd. 1 S. bet. E. and W. T.

Pratt Elizabeth, wid. 19th wd. 3 N. cor. 3 W.

Preece John, farmer, 4th wd. 7 S. cor. W. T.

Price Robert, farmer, 19th wd. 2 W. bet. 5 and 6 N.

Price William, shoemaker, 19th wd. 2 N. bet. 1 and 2 W.

Price William, farmer, 7th wd. 5 S. bet. 1 and 2 W.

Price L. William, compositor, 6th wd. 3 W. bet. 5 and 6 S.

Price George W. carpenter, 15th wd. 5 W. bet. S. T. and 1 S.

Priestley John, compositor, Deseret News office, 6th wd. 4 W. bet. 5 and 6 S.

Priestley William H. teacher, 14th wd. 1 S. bet. W. T. and 1 W.

Priscott James, canvasser, 16th wd. 4 W. bet. N. and S. T.

Priday Thomas, stonecutter, 5th wd. 7 S. bet. 2 and 3 W.

Proctor John, bishop, 10th wd. 9 E. bet. 4 and 5 S.

Provis Richard, farmer, 6 E. bet. 6 and 7 S.

Prydie Samuel, stonecutter, 4th wd. 7 S. bet. 2 and 3 W.

Pugmire Jonathan, blacksmith, 7th wd. 3 S. bet. W. T. and 1 W.

Pugsley Phillip, flouring mill and tannery, 19th wd. 2 W. cor. 5 N.

Pusey H. wagonmaker, Railroad shop

Pyper A. C. (Pyper & Co.), E. T. bet. S. T. and 1 S. res. Sugar House wd.

Clothing, Wholesale and Retail, at HELLMAN & CO.'S, Salt Lake City.

132   SALT LAKE CITY DIRECTORY.

Q

Quayle Thomas, farmer, 7th wd. 4 S. bet. W. T. and 1 W.
Quin George, woodcarver, 12th wd. 6 E. bet. S. T. and 1 S.

R

Raddon Henry, carpenter, 14th wd. 2 S. bet. 1 and 2 W.
Raffle Thomas, stonecutter, 11th wd. 8 E. bet. 1 and 2 S.
Rager H. teacher, 13th wd. 2 S. bet. 1 and 2 E.
Railroad Shops, 2 E. bet. S. T. and 1 S.
Raleigh Alonzo H. bishop, 19th wd. 2 N. cor. 1 W.
Ramsay Ralph, woodcarver, 20th wd. cor. Fruit and Fir
Ramsey Mary, wid. 14th wd. 2 S. bet. 1 and 2 W.
Rance Samuel, pressman in Telegraph office, res. 10th wd. 5 S. bet. 6
    and 7 E.
Randall Alfred, Ogden Woolen Mills and freighter, 17th wd. bet. 1 and
    2 N.
Randers George, cook, res. 8th wd. 5 S. bet. E. T. and 1 E.
Rands Joseph, shoemaker, 17th wd. S. T. bet. W. T. and 1 W.
Rankin Richard, weaver, 9th wd. 4 E. bet. 3 and 4 S.
Ransohoff N. S., E. T. bet. 1 and 2 S.
Ransohoff Eli, E. T. bet. 1 and 2 S.
Ransohoff & Co. general merchandise, ws. E. T. bet. 1 and 2 S.
Rasmus N. P. lab. 11th wd. 3 S. bet. 9 and 10 E.
Rasmussen Carl, jeweler, E. T. bet. 1 and 2 S.
Rasmussen Annie C. wid. 2d wd. 3 E. bet. 7 and 8 S.
Rawley Edwin, carpenter, 19th wd. bet. Quince and Central
Rawlins Richard, lab. 8th wd. 6 S.
Rawlings Joseph, shoemaker, 20th wd. Elm, cor. Wall
Ray David, shoemaker, 14th wd. S. T. bet. W. T. and 1 W.
Raybould Benjamin, bookkeeper, at Walker Bros. res. 8th wd. W. T.
    bet. 5 and 6 S.
Raybould William, foreman, at Dinwoodey's furniture factory, res. 17th
    wd. 2 N. cor. W. T.
Raybould Charles, painter, 7th wd. W. T. bet. 5 and 6 S.
Read John, mason, 20th wd. Wall, bet. Chesnut and Pine
Reading John, nurseryman, 13th wd. 2 S. cor. 2 E.
Reamer William E. jobwagon, 14th wd. 1 S. bet. E. and W. T.
Reed George, clerk, 20th wd. cor. Ash and Garden
Reed Ervin D. lab. 16th wd. 7 W. bet. S. and N. T.

THE IDAHO BAKERY, SECOND SOUTH STREET, IS THE PLACE TO GO TO.

SALT LAKE CITY DIRECTORY. 133

Rees Joseph, lab. 15th wd. 7 W. cor. 1 S.
Rees Elizabeth, wid. 15th wd. 1 S. bet. 6 and 7 W.
Rees Albert, smelter, 16th wd. 1 N. bet. 3 and 4 W.
Rees William, smelter, 16th wd. 1 N. bet. 3 and 4 W.
Reese John, agent, 14th wd. 1 S. bet. 1 and 2 W.
Reese Enoch, freighter and trader, 17th wd. E. T. bet. N. T. and 1 N.
Reggel L. dry goods, ws. E. T. bet. 1 and 2 S.
Reich F. propr. Pacific House. E. T. bet. 2 and 3 S.
Reid George, plasterer, 16th wd. 6 W. bet. N. and S. T.
Reid John, baker, 16th wd. N. T. bet. 4 and 5 W.
Reid Peter, machinist at theatre, res. 16th wd. N. T. cor. 3 W.
Reid Samuel, bookkeeper, 17th wd. 1 W. bet. N. and S. T.
Reinder John, cook, Salt Lake House
Reinsimer Peter H. blacksmith, 9th wd. 3 E. bet. 5 and 6 S.
Revere House, 2 S. near 1 E.
Reynolds George, clerk, 20th wd. Spruce, cor. Wall
Reynolds John, lab. 8th wd. 6 S. cor. E. T.
Rheinbold Felix (Diehl & R.), hairdresser, below Salt Lake House
Rice Robert, carpenter, 17th wd. Crooked, bet. Currant and 1 N.
Rich Charles C. one of the 12 apostles, 17th wd. 2 N. cor. 1 W.
Rich Charles, lab. 5th wd. 7 S. bet. 4 and 5 W.
Rich Adam, lab. 9th wd. 4 E. bet. 5 and 6 S.
Richards Alexander, carpenter, 1st wd. 9 E. cor. 7 S.
Richards Samuel W. contractor, 14th wd. 2 S. bet. E. and W. T.
Richards Phineas, gilder and painter, 14th wd. W. T. bet. 2 and 3 S.
Richards Henry P. salesman with Kimball & Lawrence, res. 14th wd. W. T. bet. 2 and 3 S.
Richards Franklin D. one of the 12 apostles, 14th wd. W. T. bet. 2 and 3 S.
Richards Samuel, clerk with Jno. B. Maiben, res. 8th wd. 3 S. bet. E. T. and 1 E.
Richardson Andrew, lab. 20th wd. cor. Fruit and Poplar
Richardson Jeremiah, freighter, 14th wd. S. T. cor. 1 W.
Richardson Solon, farmer, 14th wd. 2 S. cor. W. T.
Ricketts George, blacksmith, 2d wd. 6 S. bet. 3 and 4 E.
Ricketts John, farmer, 6 E. bet. 3 and 4 S.
Ridges Joseph, organbuilder, 19th wd. 3 N. bet. 3 and 4 W.
Ridout Samuel, teamster, 19th wd. 2 N. cor. 6 W.
Rigby William, farmer, 4 S. 7th wd. bet. W. T. and 1 W.
Rigby Barnet, farmer, 7th wd. W. T. bet. 4 and 5 S.
Rigby Seth, lab. 7th wd. 4 S. bet. W. T. and 1 W.
Ringwood Charles, policeman, 20th wd. S. T. bet. Maple and Elm

Riser George C. shoemaker, ws. E. T. bet. S. T. and 1 S. res. 16th wd. N. T. bet. 2 and 3 W.

Riser Henry, watchmaker, ws. E. T. bet. 1 and 2 S. res. 6th wd. 3 W. bet. 3 and 4 S.

Risley Joseph P. farmer, 17th wd. E. T. bet. N. T. and 1 N.

Ritchey John, lab. 8th wd. 3 E. bet. 3 and 4 S.

Riter Levi, farmer, 9th wd. 3 E. cor. 4 S.

Ritter William C. logger, 9th wd. 5 S. bet. 5 and 6 E.

Roberts Bolivar, (Bassett & R.) general merchandise, ws. E. T. bet. 1 and 2 S. res. 13th wd. 1 S. bet. 2 and 3 E.

Roberts Samuel, foreman at Deseret News office, res. 19th wd. 4 W. cor. 3 N.

Roberts Owen, lab. 15th wd. 1 S. bet. 5 and 6 W.

Roberts Griffith, tailor, 15th wd. 6 W. bet. S. T. and 1 S.

Robertson W. H. (A. C. Pyper & Co.), general merchant, E. T. bet. S. T. and 1 S.

Robertson R. H. attorney at law and register in bankruptcy office, ss. E. T. bet. 1 and 2 S. bds. with Judge Strickland

Robins John R. lumberman, 17th wd. 2 W. bet. N. and S. T.

Robins Franklin, lab. 9th wd. 4 S. cor. 5 E.

Robinson Joseph, barber, 8th wd. 3 E. cor. 3 S.

Robinson William, carpenter, 20th wd. Pine, cor. Wall

Robinson Lewis, farmer, 8th wd. 4 S. bet. E. and 1 E.

Robson William, currier, 15th wd. 2 S. bet. 2 and 3 W.

Rockwell O. Porter, rancheman, 12th wd. 3 E. bet. 1 and 2 S.

Rockwood A. P. warden at penitentiary, 1 E. bet. 1 and 2 S.

Rodford George, bookkeeper in Hussey, Dahler & Co.'s bank

Rodway George, lab. 8th wd. E. cor. 5 S.

Rogers Charles, carpenter, 20th wd. cor. Beech and Garden

Rogers William, lab. 20th wd. Beech, cor. Garden

Roland Benjamin, lab. 15th wd. 2 S. bet. 4 and 5 W.

Rolfe Benjamin, carpenter, 16th wd. 3 W. bet. 1 and 2 N.

Romney George, builder and contractor, 20th wd. Spruce, cor. Bluff

Rose George, teamster, 12th wd. 3 S. bet. 3 and 4 E.

Rose William F. carpenter, 7th wd. 1 W. bet. 5 and 6 S.

Rose Stephen B. salesman with Jennings & Co. res. 17th wd. S. T. bet. W. T. and 1 W.

Rosengreen Neils, lab. 2d wd. 8 S. bet. 4 and 5 E.

Rosequist Andrew, lab. 3d wd. 3 E. bet. 6 and 7 S.

Ross James D. commission agent, 20th wd. Elm, cor. Fruit

Ross R. T. (R. & Barratt), general merchandise, res. 12th wd. 4 E. bet. 1 and 2 S.

Rossiter Solomon, mason, 20th wd. Wall, cor. Fir

Rossiter William, lab. 10th wd. 8 E. bet. 5 and 6 S.

Gent's Furnishing Goods, cheap, at HELLMAN & CO.'S, Salt Lake City.

SALT LAKE CITY DIRECTORY.   135

Roundy Shadrach, farmer, 16th wd. 3 W. bet. 1 and 2 N.
Rowe William P. butcher, 14th wd. 1 S. bet. E. and W. T.
Ruben Jaques, shoemaker, 20th wd. Oak, cor. Fruit
Rubin H. tobacco and cigars, es. E. T. bet. 1 and 2 S.
Rudd Joshua, lab. 20th wd. Beech, cor. Wall
Ruhling J. C. bookkeeper with Ransohoff & Co.
Rumell Nicholas, plasterer, 11th wd. 2 S. bet. 6 and 7 E.
Ruse George, lab. 2d wd. 4 E. bet. 7 and 8 S.
Rushton Edward, lab. 6th wd. 4 S. bet. 2 and 3 W.
Rushton Edwin, farmer, 6th wd. 5 S. bet. 2 and 3 W.
Russell Robert, Sr. barber, ns. 2 S. bet. E. T. and 1 E. res. 8th wd. E.
       T. bet. 4 and 5 S.
Russell Robert, Jr. lab. 8th wd. E. T. bet. 4 and 5 S.
Russell Samuel, farmer, 15th wd. 4 W. cor. S. T.
Russell J. E. S. painter, 8th wd. E. T. bet. 4 and 5 S.
Russell William, hostler, 13th wd. 2 E. bet. 1 and 2 S.
Rutherford John, blacksmith, 15th wd. 1 S. cor. 6 W.

S

Sackett Theo. N. blacksmith, 12th wd. 2 S. cor. 5 E.
Saddler Henry (Jennings & Co.), merchant, cor. E. T. and 1 S. res. 8th
       wd. E. T. bet. 3 and 4 S.
Saddler William, shoemaker, 16th wd. N. T. bet. 6 and 7 W.
Salsbury Joseph, gardener, 11th wd. 7 E. cor. S. T.
Salsbury Joseph, carpenter, 7th wd. W. T. bet. 4 and 5 S.
Salsbury William, carpenter, 13th wd. 3 S. cor. 3 E.
Salsbury Henry, carpenter, 13th wd. 3 S. cor. 3 E.
Salt Lake Corral, J. C. Orem, propr. 1 S. bet. E. T. and 1 E.
Salt Lake House, E. T. bet. 1 and 2 S.
Sandberg John C. carpenter, 19th wd. Central, cor. Plum
Sanders Thomas, lab. 17th wd. 2 W. bet. N. and S. T.
Sands Robert, porter at Wells, Fargo & Co.'s office, res. 14th wd. 1 S.
       bet. W. T. and 1 W.
Sansom Charles, clerk, with Jennings & Co. res. 20th wd. Oak, bet. Bluff
       and Garden
Saulsbury Benjamin, tailor and glovemaker, ns. 2 S. bet. E. T. and 1 E.
       res. 15th wd. 2 W. bet. 1 and 2 S.
Saunders James, clerk, with D. H. Wells, res. 16th wd. 5 W. bet. N. and
       S. T.
Saunders William, clerk, with Jennings & Co. res. 16th wd. 5 W. bet.
       N. and S. T.

Ice Cream, and the et cetras in the Season, at the Idaho Bakery, 2d South St.

136   SALT LAKE CITY DIRECTORY.

Saunders J. trader, E. T. bet. S. T. and 1 S.

Savage C. R. (S. & Ottinger), photographer and artist, ws. E. T. bet. S. T. and 1 S. res. 20th wd. Spruce, cor. Garden

Savage Levi, farmer, 6th wd. 4 S. bet. 3 and 4 W.

Savage George N. trader, 12th wd. 3 E. bet. 1 and 2 S.

Savill George, bootmaker, 14th wd. 1 S. bet. E. and W. T.

Sawdon William, machinist, 9th wd. 5 E. cor. 4 S.

Sawyer Edwin, farmer, 7th wd. W. T. bet. 4 and 5 S.

Sayers Thomas, shoemaker, 17th wd. S. T. bet. W. T. and 1 W.

Scheib John P. cabinetmaker, 12th wd. S. T. bet. 3 and 4 E.

Schereur Daniel, whipmaker, 13th wd. 2 S. bet. 1 and 2 E.

Schettler Bernard H. clerk, Pres. Young, res. 20th wd. S. T. cor. Pine

Schettler Paul A. city treasurer, 12th wd. 1 S. cor. 4 E.

Schonfieldt Edward, clerk, with Kimball & Lawrence, res. 16th wd. N. T. bet. 4 and 5 W.

Scofield Joseph, joiner, 13th wd. 1 S. bet. 1 and 2 E.

Scott W. H. compositor, Telegraph office, res. 19th wd. cor. Apricot and Central

Scroggie Archibald, farmer, 8th wd. 6 S. cor. 3 E.

Scully Daniel T. carpenter, 11th wd. 3 S. bet. 9 and 10 E.

Seaman ——, wid. 9th wd. 4 E. bet. 5 and 6 S.

Seaman John, lime burner, 9th wd.

Sears Septimus (John Needham & Co.), comission merchant, res. 8th wd. 1 E. bet. 3 and 4 S.

Sedon Richard, miner, 1st wd. 6 S. cor. 6 E.

Sedon Caroline, wid. 5th wd. 2 W. bet. 6 and 7 S.

Senior Edwin, barber, res. 16th wd. S. T. cor. 7 W.

Sessions Perigrine, farmer, 16th wd. N. T. cor. 4 W.

Sessions Patty, wid. 16th wd. N. T. bet. 3 and 4 W.

Seventeenth Ward School House, 1 N. bet. W. T. and 1 W.

Seventh Ward School House, 5 S. bet. W. T. and 1 W.

Seventies' Hall, 1 E. bet. 1 and 2 S.

Sewell James, miner, 19th wd. cor. Peach and 1 W.

Shanks James, tailor, 9th wd. 4 E. bet. 4 and 5 S.

Sharkey Emma, wid. 12th wd. 1 S. bet. 3 and 4 E.

Sharp Adam, freighter, 20th wd. cor. S. T. and Fir

Sharp James, freighter, 20th wd. cor. S. T. and Oak

Sharp William H. dentist, S. T. bet. E. T. and 1 E. res. 17th wd. 1 W. bet. N. and S. T.

Sharp John sr. bishop, 20th wd. S. T. cor. Spruce

Sharp John jr. freighter, 20th wd. Spruce, cor. Fruit

Sharp Margaret, wid. 20th wd. S. T. cor. Oak

Shaw Osmond, painter, 17th wd. N. T. bet. 1 and 2 W.

Shaw Luke, lab. 16th wd. 1 N. bet. 5 and 6 W.

Shaw Joseph, lab. 19th wd. 5 W. cor. 3 N.
Shaw R. P. farmer, 19th wd. 2 N. bet. 2 and 3 W.
Shelton Robert, shoemaker, 15th wd. 4 W. bet. 2 and 3 S.
Sheets Elijah T. bishop, 8th wd. 2 E. bet. 3 and 4 S.
Shelmerdine James, hat factory, 8th wd. 3 S. bet. 2 and 3 E.
Sherman ——, blacksmith, Railroad shops
Shipp Austin (A. S. & Co.), boots and shoes, ws. E. T. bet. 1 and 2 S. res. 13th wd. 2 E. bet. 2 and 3 S.
Shipp M. B. (A. S. & Co.), boots, shoes and hats, 11th wd. 7 E. bet. S. and 1 S.
Shires William, clerk, with Kimball & Lawrence, res. 8th wd. 5 S. bet. E. T. and 1 E.
Shore James, lab. 20th wd. Prospect, cor. Ash
Short William, teamster, 8th wd. E. T. cor. 5 S.
Showell George, trader, es. E. T. bet. 2 and 3 S. res. 8th wd. 3 S. bet. E. and W. T.
Showell James, lab. 7th wd. 1 W. cor. 3 S.
Showell William, provisions and groceries, cor. 2 S. and E. T. res. 8th wd. 3 E. bet. 4 and 5 S.
Showell Thomas, horse dealer, ss. 2 S. bet. E. T. and 1 E. res. 13th wd. 1 E. bet. 2 and 3 S.
Siegel Bros. Sol. clothing, es. E. T. bet. 1 and 2 S.
Silva Louis, teamster, 9th wd. 3 E. bet. 3 and 4 S.
Silver William J. machinist, 19th wd. cor. Central and Beach
Silver Joseph, provision dealer, es. E. T. bet. 1 and 2 S. res. 11th wd. 2 S. bet. 7 and 8 E.
Simmons Nathaniel, lab. 5th wd. 7 S. bet. 4 and 5 W.
Simmons Joseph M. clerk, 13th wd. 1 S. bet. 1 and 2 E.
Simpson Francis, lab. 4th wd. 4 W. bet. 6 and 7 S.
Simpson Frank, lab. 5th wd. 4 W. bet. 6 and 7 S.
Simpson Thurston, farmer, 15th wd. 4 W. cor. 2 S.
Sims Isabella, wid. 20th wd. cor. Pine and Fruit
Sinclair Peter, millwright, 3d wd. 1 E. cor. 7 S.
Singleton William S. lab. 16th wd. 7 W. bet. N. T. and 1 N.
Singleton Stephen, lab. 6th wd. 3 W. bet. 3 and 4 S.
Sirrine Samuel D. clerk at Salt Lake House, res. 14th wd. W. T. bet. 2 and 3 S.
Sixteenth Ward School House, 4 W. cor. 1 N.
Sixth Ward School House, 3 W. bet. 4 and 5 S.
Skidmore Samuel, cabinetmaker, 14th wd. 1 S. bet. W. T. and 1 W.
Slade George W. shoemaker, 12th wd. 5 E. bet. 2 and 3 S.
Slade Henry H. stonemason, 7th wd. 5 S. bet. 1 and 2 W.
Slade Henry S. blacksmith, 10th wd. 3 S. bet. 8 and 9 E.
Slater Frederick, shoemaker, 19th wd. bet. Quince and Central

Views of the Overland Route, at Carter's Gallery, adjoin'g Wells, Fargo & Co.'s.

138   SALT LAKE CITY DIRECTORY.

Slaughter Samuel, turner, 19th wd. cor. Beet and Short

Sleater R. G. traveling agent, Telegraph office, res. 17th wd.

Sloan William, boot and shoe factory (big boot), ws. E. T. bet. 1 and 2 S. res. 8th wd.

Sloan Edward L. phonographer, 20th wd. S. T. cor. Elm

Sloane Thomas, farmer, 10th wd. 9 E. cor. 5 S.

Smart Hezekiah, farmer, 2 S. bet. 1 and 2 W.

Smart Thomas, tanner, 15th wd. 3 W. cor. 1 S.

Smedly S. carpenter, 9th wd. 3 S. cor. 3 E.

Smith George A. territorial historian, office and res. 13th wd. S. T. bet. E. T. and 1 E.

Smith George, painter, 20th wd. Maple, cor. Garden

Smith James, carpenter, 4th wd. 3 W. bet. 6 and 7 S.

Smith J. Fewson, civil engineer, 20th wd. cor. Locust and Garden

Smith Frederick, 20th wd. Oak, cor. Prospect

Smith Charles, accountant, Walker Bros. res. 17th wd. cor. Central and Cross

Smith John, patriarch, Church of J. C. of L. D. S. 14th wd. 3 S. cor. 1 W.

Smith Thomas, lab. 13th wd. 3 S. bet. E. T. and 1 E.

Smith S. H. B. teamster, 17th wd. 1 W. bet. N. and S. T.

Smith Andrew, miner, 8th wd. 6 S. bet. E. T. and 1 E.

Smith Alma, farmer, 12th wd. 1 S. bet. 4 and 5 E.

Smith Charles F. auditor, Overland Express, Wells, Fargo & Co.'s office, bds. with J. W. Stevens, 13th wd.

Smith William J. cabinetmaker, 11th wd. 6 E. bet. S. T. and 1 S.

Smith Theodore A. compositor, Deseret News office, res. 6th wd. 5 S. bet. 3 and 4 W.

Smith Joseph (Smith Bros.), carpenter, 8th wd. 1 E. bet. 3 and 4 S. res. 4 S. bet. E. and 1 E.

Smith Thomas (Smith Bros.), carpenter, 8th wd. 1 E. bet. 3 and 4 S. res. 4 S. bet. E. and 1 E.

Smith John, carpenter, 9th wd. 5 E. bet. 4 and 5 S.

Smith Robert, butcher, 16th wd. S. T. cor. 7 W.

Smith John, stonemason, 3d wd. 3 E. cor. 6 S.

Smith Joseph F. one of the 12 apostles, 16th wd. 1 N. bet. 2 and 3 W.

Smith Elias, probate judge, Salt Lake county, res. 17th wd. N. T. bet. W. T. and 1 W.

Smith Leonard I. mail contractor, 17th wd. S. T. bet. W. T. and 1 W

Smith Robert Y. miner, 3d wd. 7 S. cor. 3 E.

Smith Job, millinery and basketmaking, ws. E. T. bet. 2 and 3 S. res. 7th wd. 2 W. cor. 4 S.

Smith Henry, stonemason, 1st wd. 8 E. bet. 7 and 8 S.

Smith George, carpenter, 7th wd. 1 W. bet. 3 and 4 S.

Clive & Reid, Idaho Bakery, aim at obtaining customers and then retain them.

SALT LAKE CITY DIRECTORY. 139

Smith John Y. miner, 3d wd. 2 E. cor. 6 S.

Smith Robert, city prisoners' guard, 19th wd. 5 N. bet. 2 and 3 W.

Smith John P. carpenter, 7th wd. 1 W. bet. 3 and 4 S.

Smith Louis W. farmer, 3d wd. 2 E. bet. 6 and 7 S.

Smith Albert, carpenter, 7th wd. 1 W. bet. 3 and 4 S.

Smith William S. shoemaker, 3 E. bet. 6 and 7 S.

Smith James, mason, 19th wd. 3 N. bet. 6 and 7 W.

Smoot A. O. farmer, 20th wd. S. T. cor. Spruce

Snarr James, lab. 6th wd. 6 S. bet. 2 and 3 W.

Snedden Robert, miner, 20th, wd. Locust, cor. Fruit

Snedeker Morris, saltboiler, 2 S. bet. E. T. and 1 E. res. 9th wd. 4 S. bet. 4 and 5 E.

Snelgrove Edward, bootmaker, ns. 2 S. bet. E. T. and 1 E. res. 12th wd. 2 S. bet. 3 and 4 E.

Snell John, freighter, 9th wd. 3 S. bet. 3 and 4 E.

Snell Henry, accountant with Eldredge & Clawson, bds. with H. B. Clawson

Snider John, Jr. mason, 17th wd. 1 W. bet. N. T. and 1 N.

Snider John, Sr. mason, 17th wd. 1 W. bet. N. T. and 1 N.

Snow George, miner, 3d wd. 2 E. cor. 8 S.

Snow Zerubbabel, territorial attorney gen. res. 13th wd. 1 E. cor. 2 S.

Snowball John, teamster, 20th wd. Garden, bet. Spruce and Pine

Snowball Ralph, teamster, 20th wd. Maple, bet. Garden and Bluff

Snyder Charles, miller, 9 E. bet. 8 and 9 S.

Snyder Benjamin F. clerk with Perry & Co. res. 13th wd. 2 S. bet. 1 and 2 E.

Snyder Maria, wid. 6th wd. 2 W. bet. 4 and 5 S.

Social Hall, 13th wd. es. 1 E. bet. S. T. and 1 S.

Solomon William H. shoemaker, 5th wd. 3 W. bet. 8 and 9 S.

Solomon James, shoemaker, 19th wd. 3 N. bet. 4 and 5 W.

Sorenson Niels, sawyer, 2d wd. 5 E. cor. 8 S.

Sorenson Peter, lab. 2d wd. 3 E. bet. 7 and 8 S.

South Charles, cooper, 17th wd. 2 N. bet. W. T. and 1 W.

Speed William, mason, 4th wd. 8 S. bet 2 and 3 W.

Speed James, lab. 5th wd. 8 S. bet. 2 and 3 W.

Spence —— painter, 12th wd. 3 E. bet. 2 and 3 S.

Spencer John, groceries and provisions, E. T. bet. 2 and 3 S.

Spencer Howard O. farmer, 8th wd. 1 E. bet. 5 and 6 S. .

Spencer Claudius V. lab. 13th wd. 1 E. bet. 2 and 3 S.

Spencer Martha, wid. 13th wd. 3 S. bet. E. T. and 1 E.

Spencer Almon, farmer, 8th wd. 2 E. bet. 4 and 5 S.

Sperry Harrison, farmer, 4th wd. 6 S. bet. 1 and 2 W.

Spicer William, farmer, 19th wd. 2 N. bet. 5 and 6 W.

Spiers Thomas, blacksmith, 10th wd. 6 S. cor. 8 E.

Clothing, Wholesale and Retail, at HELLMAN & CO.'S, Salt Lake City.

140   SALT LAKE CITY DIRECTORY.

Spiers Orson, lab. 10th wd. 6 S. cor. 7 E.

Spiers George, teamster, 10th wd. 7 E. cor. 5 S.

Spiers Adam, blacksmith, 10th wd. 5 S. bet. 7 and 8 E.

Spiring William, lab. 14th wd. S. T. bet. W. T. and 1 W.

Sprague A. C. proprietor, California Stables, cor. 2 S. and W. T.

Sprague S. L. physician, 13th wd. 1 E. bet. S. T. and 1 S.

'Spring A. blacksmith, Railroad Shops

Sproat Christopher, tailor, 1 S. bet. E. T. and 1 E. res. 17th wd. 2 N. cor. Melon

Sprouce Sarah, wid. 14th wd. 2 S. bet. 1 and 2 W.

Sproul Andrew, plasterer, 20th wd. S. T. cor. Ash

Sproul Francis, weaver, 11th wd. 1 S. bet. 8 and 9 E.

Squires John, barber, ws. E. T. bet. S. T. and 1 S. res. 20th wd. cor. Fir and Garden

Squires William, blacksmith, 19th wd. 4 W. bet. 4 and 5 N.

Stackdale Michael, stonecutter, 6th wd. 4 W. bet. 4 and 5 S.

Stahl D. W. wagonmaker, Railroad Shops

Staines W. C. gardener, res. 12th wd. S. T. cor. 5 E.

Standing James, stonecarver, 12th wd. 1 S. cor. 4 E.

Standish Henry, blacksmith, 14th wd. 2 S. bet. E. and W. T.

Staples James A. mason, 15th wd. 1 S. bet. 2 and 3 W.

Starkey William, shoemaker, 2d wd. 6 S. bet. 3 and 4 E.'

Starr Anna, wid. 8th wd. 3 E. cor. 4 S.

Startup William, clerk with Jennings & Co. res. 20th wd. Oak, cor. Bluff

Stayner Thomas J. general merchandise, res. 7th wd. 5 S. bet. W. T. and 1 W.

Stayner Charles W. clerk, 7th wd. E. T. bet. 3 and 4 S.

St. Clair George, miner, 14th wd. 2 S. bet. 1 and 2 W.

Steeder Henry, stonemason, 7th wd. 4 S. cor. 2 W.

Steel Archibald, telegraph constructionist, 20th wd. Maple, cor. High

Steel Edward, joiner, 8th wd. 2 E. bet. 4 and 5 S.

Steele Alexander, weaver, 1st wd. 8 S. bet. 8 and 9 E.

Steers William, mason, 20th wd. Pine, cor. Wall

Stein Aaron, cashier, Wells, Fargo & Co.'s Overland Express Co. res. 1 S. near Theatre

Stein Nat. bookkeeper in Hussey, Dahler & Co.'s Bank

Stelfox Thomas, lab. 11th wd. 1 S. cor. 9 E.

Stenhouse T. B. H. editor and proprietor, Daily Telegraph, 1 S. bet. E. and W. T. res. 17th wd. cor. Vine and 1 N.

Stephens William, carpenter, 12th wd. 4 E. cor. 2 S.

Stephens Jacob, engineer, 13th wd. S. T. cor. 2 E.

Stephens Thomas, lab. 7th wd. 5 S. bet. 1 and 2 W.

Stephens Charles, lab. 2d wd. 3 E. bet. 6 and 7 S.

Stephenson Charles, engineer, 14th wd. W. T. bet. 1 and 2 S.

Gent's Furnishing Goods, cheap, at HELLMAN & CO.'S, Salt Lake City.

SALT LAKE CITY DIRECTORY.   141

Stevens James W. carpenter, 13th wd. 1 E. bet. 1 and 2 S.

Stevenson Edward, tinner, ns. 1 S. bet. E. and W. T. res. 14th wd. 1 W. bet. 1 and 2 S.

Stevenson William D. lab. 19th wd. 2 N. cor. 2 W.

Stewart William, lab. 19th wd. 3 N. bet. 5 and 6 W.

Stewart George, trader, 8th wd. 1 E. bet. 5 and 6 S.

Stewart Samuel D. lab. 15th wd. 5 W. bet. 1 and 2 S.

Stewart Hannah R. wid. 7th wd. 1 W. bet. 4 and 5 S.

Stickells Richard, engineer, 16th wd. S. T. bet. 6 and 7 W.

Stickells James, lab. 16th wd. S. T. bet. 6 and 7 W.

St. Mark's School, 7th wd. 3 S. bet. E. and W. T., Rev. Thos. W. Haskins, principal

Stockdale William, lab. 16th wd. S. T. cor. 7 W.

Stockdale Michael, stonecutter, 6th wd. 4 S. bet. 4 and 5 W.

Stockdale William, stonecutter, 6th wd. 4 W. bet. 5 and 6 S.

Stoffers C. T. cabinetmaker, 1 S. bet. E. T. and & E.

Stokes George, lab. 4th wd. 2 W. bet. 6 and 7 S.

Stokes George, lab. 5th wd. 2 W. bet. 6 and 7 S.

Stokes Christopher, teamster, 19th wd. 2 W. bet. 5 and 6 N.

Stokes Jane, wd. 5th wd. 7 S. bet. 2 and 3 W.

Stout Hosea, city attorney, office at City Hall, res. 13th wd. 2 E. bet. S. T. and 1 S.

Strickland Obed F. (S. & Robertson), conselor, office es. E. T. bet. 1 and 2 S. res. 8th wd. E. T. bet. 4 and 5 S.

Strickland Alvin, teacher, 9th wd. 5 E. bet. 4 and 5 S.

Stringfellow Bros. groceries and provisions, E. T. bet. 1 and 2 S.

Stringam George, freighter, 8th wd. E. T. bet. 4 and 5 S.

Stringam Bryant, county pound keeper, 13th wd. S. T. bet. 2 and 3 E.

Strong James T. farmer, 10th wd. 4 S. bet. 8 and 9 E.

Strong William, farmer, 10th wd. 4 S. bet. 8 and 9 E.

Strong Hyram, farmer, 10th wd. 8 E. cor. 4 S.

Strong Jacob, farmer, 10th wd. 8 E. cor. 4 S.

Stuart D. & Son, groceries and provisions, E. T. bet. S. T. and 1 S.

Suhrke Ludwig, carpenter, 14th wd. S. T. cor. 1 W.

Summers Henry, farmer, 3d wd. 2 E. cor. 8 S.

Suter F. W. tailor, 2 S. bet. E. T. and 1 E.

Sutton John A. blacksmith, 16th wd. 1 N. bet. 4 and 5 W.

Swain Robert, mason, 11th wd. 2 S. bet. 8 and 9 E.

Swan George, bookkeeper at F. A. Mitchell's, res. 15th wd. 5 W. cor. S. T.

Swenson John, shoemaker, ss. 2 S. bet. E. and W. T. res. 7th wd. 4 S. bet. E. and W. T.

Swetland Andrew, lab. 6th wd. 8 W. bet. 3 and 4 S.

Symons J. pressman, Telegraph office, res. 5th wd.

Symons Charles W. photographer, res. 10th wd. 5 S. bet. 6 and 7 E.
Symons B. mailing clerk, Telegraph office, res. 5th wd.

T

Taft Mrs. wid. 9th wd. 3 S. bet. 4 and 5 E.
Tait William, M. D., M. R. C. S. L. surgeon and physician, office
 at Bauman's & Co.'s es. E. T. bet. 1 and 2 S. res. 3 S. bet. E. and
 W. T.
Tall George, blacksmith, 16th wd. N. T. cor. 6 W.
Tame Alfred, harnessmaker, 20th wd. cor. Chesnut and Wall
Tanner William, lab. 14th wd. 3 S. bet. 1 and 2 W.
Tappets John H. farmer, 19th wd. 4 N. bet. 1 and 2 W.
Tavey Peter, tailor, ss. 2 S. bet. E. T. and 1 E.
Taylor Edward, lab. 10th wd. 7 E. bet. 3 and 4 S.
Taylor G. E. G. tailor, 12th wd. 3 S. cor. 5 E.
Taylor Elizabeth, wid. 5th wd. 3 W. bet. 7 and 8 S.
Taylor Thomas E. cooper, 17th wd. S. T. bet. W. T. and 1 W.
Taylor Mrs. wid. 6th wd. 4 S. bet. 2 and 3 W.
Taylor William, teamster, 11th wd. 8 E. cor. 1 S.
Taylor Joshua, tanner, 15th wd. 2 S. bet. 2 and 3 W.
Taylor John (T. Bros.), merchant tailor, ss. 1 S. bet. E. T. and 1 E
 res. 9th wd. 5 E. bet. 3 and 4 N.
Taylor Joseph (T. & Bros.), merchant tailor, ss. 1 S. bet. E. T. and
 1 E. res. 10th wd. 6 E. bet. 4 and 5 S.
Taylor Joseph E. city sexton, 13th wd. 1 S. bet. 2 and 3 E.
Taylor William, farmer, 14th wd. 1 S. cor. 1 W.
Taylor John, one of the 12 apostles, 14th wd. 1 S. cor. 1 W.
Taylor Thomas (T. & W. Taylor), general merchandise, ws. E. T. bet.
 1 and 2 S. res. 14th wd. 2 W. bet. 1 and 2 S.
Taylor Charles B. butcher, meat market, res. 20th wd. Fruit, bet. Poplar
 and Willow
Taylor John, lab. 14th wd. 3 S. bet. 1 and 2 W.
Taylor Joseph H. weaver, 19th wd. Pear, bet. Central and Beet
Taylor James, 14th wd. S. T. cor. 1 W.
Taylor Joseph, salesman, with Bassett & Roberts, res. 14th wd. 1 S. bet.
 W. T. and 1 W.
Taylor George J. teacher, of grammer in Deseret University, res. 14th
 wd. 1 S. cor. 1 W.
Taylor George H. sash and doormaker, works, S. T. bet. 1 and 2 W.
 res. 14th wd. 3 S. bet. W. T. and 1 W.
Taylor Jabez, joiner, 20th wd. Mountain, cor. Fir

Tayson Nathaniel, mason, 17th wd. S. T. bet. 1 and 2 W.

Taysum Andrew J. plasterer, 20th wd. Oak, cor. Garden

Teasdale George, clerk, 20th wd. S. T. cor. Elm

Teasdel Samuel (Jennings & Co.), general merchandise, whol. and ret. res. 20th wd. S. T. cor. Elm

Telegraph Office, Western Union, es. E. T. bet. S. T. and 1 S.

Tempest Henry, farmer, 20th wd. cor. Locust and Bluff

Terry Henry, lab. 10th wd. 4 S. bet. 6 and 7 E.

Tester Charles, lab. 19th wd. bet. Quince and Currant

Thatcher George W. contractor, 18th wd.

Theatre, cor. 1 S. and 1 E.

Thirkill Charles (T. & Earl), tailor, 20th wd. Ash, cor. Fruit

Thirteenth Ward Assembly Rooms, 2 S. bet. 1 and 2 E.

Thomas Richard K. clerk with Jennings & Co. res. 13th wd. 1 S. bet. 1 and 2 E.

Thomas John, mason, 20th wd. cor. S. T. and Box Elder

Thomas Thomas F. miner, 20th wd. cor. Fir and Garden

Thomas Joseph, lab. 7th wd. 1 W. bet. 4 and 5 S.

Thomas William, lab. 7th wd. 1 W. bet. 5 and 6 S.

Thomas Elizabeth, wid. 7th wd. 1 W. bet. 4 and 5 S.

Thomas David G. machinist, 9th wd. 6 E. cor. 4 S.

Thomas Samuel, lab. 15th wd. S. T. cor. 6 W.

Thomas Thomas, shoemaker, 15th wd. 1 S. bet. 6 and 7 W.

Thomas Edwin H. teamster, 15th wd. 3 W. bet. S. T. and 1 S.

Thomas Chauncey R. 7th wd. 4 S. bet. 1 and 2 W.

Thomasson Peter, clerk, 20th wd. Chesnut, cor. High

Thompson Ralph, salesman in Godbe's drug store, res. 6th wd. 3 W. bet. 4 and 5 S.

Thompson James A. compositor, Deseret News office, res. 6th wd. 5 S. bet. 3 and 4 W.

Thompson Mercy R. wid. 16th wd. 2 W. cor. N. T.

Thompson John P. tailor, 2 S. bet. E. T. and 1 E. res. 11th wd. 3 S. cor. 8 E.

Thompson Willian, shoemaker, 10th wd. 3 S. cor. 7 E.

Thornburg Frederick, upholsterer, 4 E. cor. 5 S.

Thorne William, farmer, 7th wd. 6 S. bet. W. T. and 1 W.

Thorpe Thomas, papercarrier, Daily Telegraph office

Thorpe Theodore, saddletree maker, Pine, bet. High and Prospect

Thorpe Joseph, pressman, Deseret News office

Thorpe Charles, papercarrier, Deseret News office

Thurgood John, agent, 9th wd. 4 E. bet. 5 and 6 S.

Thurgood J. papercarrier, Telegraph office

Thurrygood Thomas, lab. 15th wd. 3 S. bet. 2 and 3 W.

Thurston Moses, farmer, 7th wd. E. T. bet. 3 and 4 S

Boys' Clothing, in any quantity, low, sold by HELLMAN & CO, Salt Lake City.

144   SALT LAKE CITY DIRECTORY.

Tibbets William, machinist, 2d wd. 5 E. cor. 7 S.

Tillison Alonzo, brickmaker, 13th wd. 1 S. bet. 2 and 3 E.

Tilt Richard, salesman, with Savage & Ottinger, 20th wd. Cedar. cor. Fruit

Timmins Thomas, lab. 5th wd. 7 S. bet. 3 and 4 W.

Tingey John, shoemaker, 17th wd. 2 W. bet. N. T. and 1 N.

Todd Joseph, shoemaker, 14th wd. 3 S. cor. W. T.

Tomlinson George, lab. 6th wd. 5 W. bet. 4 and 5 S.

Tomlinson Alfred, miner, 20th wd. Oak, cor. Garden

Toms James, gun and locksmith, ws. E. T. bet. 2 and 3 S. res. 8th wd. 5 S. bet. E. T. and 1 E.

Tomson John, tailor, 6th wd. 5 S. bet. 3 and 4 W.

Tomson James, tailor, 6th wd. 5 S. bet. 3 and 4 w.

Tompson John J. H. bookkeeper, Godbe & Co. res. 13th wd. 3 E. bet. 2 and 3 S.

Toone John, painter, 20th wd. Spruce, cor. Garden

Torbet A, soapmaker, 5th wd. 3 W. bet. 7 and 8 S.

Toronto Joseph, owner of herd ground, 20th wd. cor. Fruit and Walnut

Towler Daniel, steward, Salt Lake House, res. 13th wd. 1 S. bet. 1 and 2 E.

Townsend House, 14th wd. cor. W. T. and 1 S.

Townsend James, proprietor, Townsend House

Townsend John, turner, 6th wd. 5 W. bet. 5 and 6 S.

Tracy Theodore F. resident agent, Wells, Fargo & Co. res. Townsend House

Treherne William, lab. 15th wd. 6 W. bet. 1 and 2 S.

Tremaine William H. machinist, 12th wd. S. T. bet. 5 and 6 E.

Treseder Richard M. cabinetmaker, 14th wd. W. T. bet. 2 and 3 S.

Treseder Charles M. tailor, res. 17th wd. N. T. bet. W. and 1 W.

Treseder Richard, tailor, 12th wd. 6 E. bet. S. and 1 S.

Tribe Henry, clerk with Eldredge & Clawson, res. 16th wd. 2 W. bet. N. T. and 1 N.

Trickey J. M. tobacco and cigars, E. T. bet. 1 and 2 S.

Tripp Enoch B. tanner, 16th wd. N. T. cor. 2 W.

Tripp Bartlett, teacher in Rager's Seminary, res. 16th wd. N. T. cor. 2 W.

Trotter William, 16th wd. 5 W. cor. N. T.

Trowbridge Charles, bds. at Salt Lake House

Trump A. embroiderer, 2 S. bet. E. T. and 1 E.

Trumbo J. K. auctioneer and commission merchant, es. E. T. bet. 1 and 2 S.

Truscott Wesley S. tanner, 17th wd. W. T. bet. N. T. and 1 N.

Trucker Stephen, lab. 8 S. bet. 4 and 5 E.

Tuckett Henry, harnessmaker, 11th wd. 1 S. cor. 10 E.

Tuckett William, gardener, 17th wd. Crooked

Best Bread, Pies and Crackers, by Clive & Reid, 2d South St., Salt Lake City.

SALT LAKE CITY DIRECTORY. 145

Tuckfield Joseph W. machinist, 20th wd. Elm, cor. Bluff
Tuckfield James C. boatbuilder, 20th wd. Garden, bet. Locust and Maple
Tuckfield James R. boatbuilder, 20th wd. Garden, bet. Locust and Maple
Tuddenham John, bricklayer, 20th wd. cor. Ash and Garden
Tufts Elbridge, proprietor, Mansion House, 8th wd. cor. 1 E an
    3 S.
Tufts Emira, Mansion House, 8th wd. cor. 1 E. and 3 S.
Tufts Josiah, farmer, 8th wd. 1 E. bet. 5 and 6 S.
Tullidge John, Sr. music teacher, 13th wd.
Tullidge John, Jr. (Tullidge & MacAvoy), painter, 13th wd.
Tullidge Edward, literateur, 13th wd.
Turnbow Samuel, farmer, 14th wd. 2 W. bet. 1 and 2 S.
Turnbow Samuel, lab. 14th wd. 1 S. bet. 1 and 2 W.
Turnbow Frank, teamster, 14th wd. 2 W. bet. 1 and 2 S.
Turnbow Milton, lab. 14th wd. 2 W. bet. 1 and 2 S.
Turnbull James, lab. 11th wd. 3 S. bet. 8 and 9 E.
Turner Henry, painter, 20th wd. Wall, bet. Spruce and Fir
Turner William, carpenter, 20th wd. High, cor. Locust
Tuttle Elanson, lab. 19th wd. 4 N. bet. 4 and 5 W.
Twede C. F. boot and shoemaker, 2 S. bet. E. T. and 1 E.
Twells Mathew, lab. 20th wd. Maple, cor. Prospect
Twentieth Ward School House and Square, bet. Spruce,
    Fir, Garden and Bluff
Twigg John, farmer, 7th wd. 4 S. bet. 1 and 2 W.
Twigg Esther, wid. 7th wd. 4 S. bet. 1 and 2 W.
Twitchell Luther, carpenter, 19th wd. 3 N. bet. 1 and 2 W.
Tyson William, mason, 12th wd. 4 E. cor. S. T.

U

Union Pacific Railroad Stables, H. W. Willard, propr. 2 S. bet.
    E. and W. T.
Ure James, lab. 15th wd. S. T. cor. 6 W.
Ure James W. carpenter, 15th wd. 6 W. bet. S. T. and 1 S.
Utah Magazine, office, Exchange Buildings, cor. 1 S. and E. T.

V

Valentine James, porter, Salt Lake House, res. 14th wd. W. T. bet. 1
    and 2 S.
Van Cott John, farmer, 14th wd. W. T. cor. 1 S.

7

Vanloenen C. L. lab. 16th wd. N. T. bet. 3 and 4 W.
Van Natta James H. cooper, 19th wd. cor. Central and Pear
Varney Samuel, gardener, 15th wd. 4 W. bet. S. T. and 1 S.
Vanschoonhoven Gilbert H. contractor, 7th wd. 4 S. bet. E. and W. T.
Vantassell Henry, drayman, 1st wd. 8 S. cor. 7 E.
Vantassell James, carpenter, 1st wd. 6 S. cor. 9 E.
Vaughan Phillip, lab. 12th wd. 5 E. bet. 2 and 3 S.
Vincent Thomas, watchman, res. 15th wd. 3 S. bet. 4 and 5 W.
Vincent John, farmer, 16th wd. 2 N. cor. 4 W.
Vincent James, Sr. lab. 10th wd. 3 S. bet. 6 and 7 E.
Vincent James, Jr. lab. 12th wd. 3 S. bet. 3 and 4 E.

W

Wade Moses, broommaker, 15th wd. 3 W. bet. 2 and 3 S.
Wagstaff William, nurseryman, 3d wd. E. cor. 6 S.
Wakeham John A. shoemaker, 16th wd. 2 W. bet. N. T. and 1 N.
Walker Charles, wheelwright, 2d wd. 7 S. bet. 3 and 4 E.
Walker Edwin, shoemaker, 9th wd. 5 S. bet. 3 and 4 E.
Walker D. F. (W. Bros.), general merchandise whol. es. E. T. bet. 1 and 2 S. res. 7th wd. W. T. cor. 5 S.
Walker J. R. (W. Bros.), general merchandise, es. E. T. bet. 1 and 2 S. res. 7th wd. E. T. bet. 4 and 5 S.
Walker S. S. (W. Bros.), general merchandise, es. E. T. bet. 1 and 2 S. res. 7th wd. E. T. bet. 4 and 5 S.
Walker William H. farmer, 16th wd. 4 W. bet. 1 and 2 N.
Walker George, tanner, 16th wd. S. T. cor. 2 W.
Walker David, lab. 10th wd. 4 S. cor. 6 E.
Walker Walter, lab. 11th wd. 2 S. cor. 10 E.
Walker David, carpenter, 11th wd. 3 S. cor. 7 E.
Walker William, cutler, 20th wd. cor. Chesnut and Wall
Wall John, lab. 13th wd. 2 E. cor. 2 S.
Wallace Henry (W. & Evans), confectionery, fancy groceries, bakery, etc. es. E. T. bet. 1 and 2 S. res. 8th wd. 1 E. bet. 5 and 6 S.
Wallace George B. nurseryman, 17th wd. 2 W. cor. 1 N.
Walsh Henry, lab. 16th wd. 5 W. bet. N. T. and 1 N.
Walstrom Nels, blacksmith, 17th wd. bet. Grape and Crooked
Walters Henry, carpenter, 14th wd. 3 S. bet. E. and W. T.
Walters Henry, shoemaker, 16th wd. 4 W. bet. N. and S. T.
Warburton Joseph, brickmaker, 1st wd. 7 E. cor. 7 S.
Wardrobe John, carpenter, 13th wd. 1 S. bet. 1 and 2 E.
Waring George, bootcloser, 20th wd. Pine, cor. Bluff
Warren William S. contractor, 7th wd. 4 S. bet. W. T. and 1 W.

Warren A. blacksmith, Railroad shops
Wartemer James, mason, 20th wd. High, cor. Elm
Waterfall James, shoemaker, 7th wd. 3 S. bet. W. T. and 1 W.
Watmough William, watchmaker, 19th wd. Quince, cor. Apricot
Watson Margaret, wid. 14th wd. 2 S. bet. 1 and 2 W.
Watson James & Joseph, masons, 19th wd. Quince, bet. Apricot and Currant
Watson James, lab. 5th wd. 5 S. bet. 4 and 5 W.
Watson John, lab. 8th wd. 2 E. bet. 3 and 4 S.
Watson Alexander, miner, 6th wd. 5 S. bet. 3 and 4 W.
Watson Robert, miner, 6th wd. 5 S. bet. 3 and 4 W.
Watt G. D. commission merchant, 20th wd. Fruit, facing Walnut
Watt, Sleater & Ajax, commission merchants, 1 S. bet. E. and W. T.
Watts Richard A. baker, 20th wd. cor. Fruit and Larch
Watters I. jeweler, E. T. bet. 1 and 2 S.
Watters A. jeweler, E. T. bet. 1 and 2 S.
Wayman John, farmer, 3d wd. E. T. cor. 6 S.
Webb Chauncey, carpenter, 12th wd. 2 S. bet. 3 and 4 E.
Webb Charles M. shoemaker, 12th wd. 6 E. bet. 1 and 2 S.
Webb Gilbert, freighter, 9th wd. 3 S. cor. 4 E.
Webb William, shoemaker, 14th wd. 3 S. bet. 1 and 2 W.
Webber Thomas G. clerk, 14th wd. 2 S. cor. W. T.
Webster Thomas, machinist, 9th wd. 5 E. cor. 4 S.
Weggeland Dan. artist, 2d wd. 4 E. cor. 6 S.
Weiler Jacob, bishop, 3d wd. res. 7 S. bet. 1 and 2 E.
Weiler Joseph, farmer, 4th wd. 7 S. cor. E. T.
Weinel John, miller, 14th wd. 2 S. bet. 1 and 2 W.
Wells Daniel H. superintendent public works, 2d counselor to president Young, res. 13th wd. cor. S. T. and E. T.
Wells, Fargo & Co. office, es. E. T. bet. 1 and 2 S.
Wells Phares, teamster, 11th wd. 6 E. cor. 1 S.
Wells Phares, millwright, 12th wd. S. T. bet. 4 and 5 E.
Wells James, cutler, E. T. bet. 2 and 3 S.
Wells William R. baker, 20th wd. High, bet. Fir and Oak
Wesley John, lab. 3d wd. 6 S. bet. 2 and 3 E.
West Jesse, stonemason, 6th wd. 5 S. bet. 2 and 3 W.
West William L. bartender, Salt Lake Billiard Rooms, res. 14th wd. 2 2 S. bet. W. T. and 1 W.
Weston John, lab. 13th wd. 3 S. bet. 1 and 2 E.
Weston George, tinner, 15th wd. 2 S. bet. 6 and 7 W.
Westwood Thomas, lab. 16th wd. 1 N. bet. 5 and 6 W.
Wheeler Edward, cooper, 20th wd. Oak, cor. Prospect
Whipple Nelson W. carpenter, 19th wd. 5 W. cor. 3 N.

White John, weaver, 10th wd. 3 S. cor. 7 E.
White A. W. cashier, Wells, Fargo & Co.'s Banking dept.
White Jesse, lab. 11th wd. 3 S. bet. 8 and 9 E.
White George, Sr. harnessmaker, 15th wd. 3 E. bet. 1 and 2 S.
White George, Jr. carpenter, 20th wd. cor. Ash and Garden
Whitehead James, weaver, 19th wd. 4 N. bet. 5 and 6 W.
Whitelock James, engine driver, 7th wd. 3 E. bet. 5 and 6 S.
Whiting John, stonemason, 3 E. bet. 3 and 4 S.
Whitemore & Alt, gunsmiths, ns. 2 S. bet. E. T. and 1 E.
Whitney Isaac E. teamster, 20th wd. Mountain, bet. Oak and Elm.
Whitney H. K. clerk, 18th wd.
Whitney John S. teamster, 18th wd.
Whittaker George, stonemason, 7th wd. 3 S. bet. W. T. and 1 W.
Whittaker Isaac, farmer, 16th wd. 1 N. bet. 3 and 4 W.
Whitworth Jeffrey, lab. 19th wd. Beet, bet. Peach and Pear
Whitworth Atkinson, lab. 19th wd. Beet, bet. Peach and Pear
Whytock James, engineer, 7th wd. 3 S. bet. W. T. and 1 W.
Widdison Thomas, file cutter, 19th wd. 6 W. cor. 3 N.
Wight James, farmer, 14th wd. 3 S. bet. 1 and 2 W.
Wilber Milson, lastmaker, 8th wd. 2 E. cor. 5 S.
Wilcox William, sawyer, 19th wd. 1 W. bet. 4 and 5 N.
Wilcox Walter E. sawyer, 19th wd. 2 W. bet. 5 N. and city wall
Wild Eliza, wid. 8th wd. 3 E. cor. 3 S.
Wiler William, gardener, 2 wd. 7 S. bet. 5 and 6 E.
Wilkie Samuel, peddler, 14th wd. S. T. cor. 1 W.
Wilkins Charles, miller, 20th wd. Maple, cor. Bluff
Wilkins Stephen, gardener, 4th wd. W. T. bet. 7 and 8 S.
Wilkinson W. B. provisions and groceries, ws. E. T. bet. 1 and 2 S. res.
    14th wd. 2 S. cor. W. T.
Wilkinson Moses, woodturner, 11th wd. 9 E. cor. S. T.
Willard H. W. proprietor, Union Pacific Railroad Stables, 2 S. bet. E.
    and W. T.
Willard James, lab. 20th wd. Fruit, cor. Cedar
Willes William, teacher, 12th wd. 4 E. bet. S. T. and 1 S.
Williams Thomas, treasurer at Theatre, res. 14th wd. 2 W. bet. S. T.
    and 1 S.
Williams Thomas, salesman with F. A. Mitchell, res. 13th wd. 2 E. bet.
    1 and 2 S.
Williams Samuel, farmer, 20th wd. cor. Fir and Garden
Williams P. L. attorney at law, 20th wd. cor. Fir and Garden
Williams Robert, tailor, 20th wd. S. T. cor. Beech
Williams Neils, logger, 17th wd. Vine, bet. Currant and 1 N.
Williams Charles, painter, 4th wd. 1 W. bet. 7 and 8 S.
William Evan, lab. 16th wd. 6 W. bet. N. T. and 1 N.

Williams Charles W. cabinet maker, 8th wd. 5 S. bet. 2 and 3 E.

Williams William, lab. 8th wd. 3 E. bet. 3 and 4 S.

Williams John, lab. 1st wd. 6 E. bet. 7 and 8 S.

Williams Christopher, farmer, 3d wd. 2 E. cor. 7 S.

Williams M. teamster, 16th wd. 4 W. bet. 1 and 2 N.

Williams Mary, wid. 7th wd. 1 W. bet. 4 and 5 S.

Williams David, lab. 9th wd. 3 S. bet. 5 and 6 E.

Williams Theophilus, mason, 15th wd. 2 S. cor. 5 W.

Williams William D. salesman at Kimball & Lawrence's, res. 15th wd. 3 W. cor. 1 S.

Willingbeck C. P. bootmaker, 2 S. bet. E. T. and 1 E.

Willock David, clerk at Ross & Barrett's, res. 14th wd. 2 S. bet. W. T. and 1 W.

Wilson James F. lab. 20th wd. Oak, cor. Bluff

Wilson John, lab. 11th wd. 1 S. bet. 9 and 10 E.

Wilson James M. G. weaver, 1st wd. 7 E. cor. 7 S.

Wilson Frank, lab. 15th wd. 2 S. bet. 5 and 6 E.

Wilson James, gardener, 2d wd. 6 E. bet. 7 and 8 S.

Wilson William, stonemason, 9th wd. 4 S. bet. 5 and 6 E.

Wilson James, carpenter, 15th wd. 1 S. bet. 4 and 5 W.

Wilson Edward, stonemason, 9th wd. 4 S. bet. 5 and 6 E.

Wilson William D. clerk, 7th wd. 5 S. cor. 2 W.

Winchester Stephen, lab. 17th wd. 2 W. bet. 1 and 2 N.

Winegar Alvin, stonecutter, 16th wd. N. T. cor. 4 W.

Winklers Joseph, lab. 4th wd. 6 S. cor. 2 W.

Winter Thomas W. gardener, 4th wd. 4 W. cor. 7 S.

Winter Thomas, lab. 6th wd. 5 S. bet. 2 and 3 W.

Winter T. W. farmer, 5th wd. 4 W. bet. 7 and 8 S.

Wiscombe George, lab. 11th wd. 3 S. bet. 8 and 9 E.

Witch Joseph, lab. 19th wd. cor. 4 N. and 1 W.

Wittenberg Charles P. carpenter, 20th wd. Maple, cor. High

Witzel Morgan, carpenter, 6th wd. 6 S. bet. 3 and 4 W.

Wixey John, lab. 15th wd. 1 S. bet. 6 and 7 W.

Wolce Louis, shoemaker, 16th wd. N. T. bet. 4 and 5 W.

Wolstenholme William, syrup mnfr. 16th wd. 6 W. bet. 1 and 2 N.

Wood H. coach trimmer, 12th wd. 3 S. bet. 4 and 5 E.

Woodbury Thomas, agriculturalist, 7th wd. 6 S. cor. 1 W.

Woodbury Jeremiah, farmer, 7th wd. 1 W. bet. 5 and 6 E.

Woodford E. clerk, 12th wd. 2 S. bet. 5 and 6 E.

Woodmansee Joseph (W. Bros.), general merchandise, es. E. T. bet. 1 and 2 S. res. 14th wd. W. T. bet. 2 and 3 S.

Woodruff Wilford, one of the 12 apostles, res. 14th wd. S. T. cor. W. T.

Woodruff Samuel, farmer, 10th wd. 6 S. bet. 7 and 8 E.

Woods James D. teamster, 8th wd. W. T. bet. 5 and 6 S.

THE IDAHO BAKERY, SECOND SOUTH STREET, IS THE PLACE TO GO TO.

SALT LAKE CITY DIRECTORY. 151

Woods James, clerk, 3d wd. 3 E. cor. 6 S.
Woods N. Park, salesman at Big Boot, res. 13th wd. 2 E. bet. 2 and 3 S.
Woods James, shoemaker, 10th wd. 4 S. cor. 8 E.
Woods William, painter, 7th wd. W. T. bet. 5 and 6 S.
Woodward Charles, farmer, 2d wd. 7 S. bet. 4 and 5 E.
Woodward Henry, teamster, 2d wd. 8 S. bet. 3 and 4 E.
Wollcott Henry, stonemason, 14th wd. 1 W. bet. 2 and 3 S.
Woolley Edwin D. bishop, 13th wd. 1 E. bet. S. T. and 1 S.
Woolley Samuel A. bishop, 9th wd. res. 3 E. cor. 4 S.
Woolley Caroline, wid. 9th wd. 3 S. bet. 4 and 5 E
Woolridge Silas, lab. 13th wd. 2 S. bet. 1 and 2 E.
Workman Joseph, tinner, 5th wd. 6 S. cor. 3 W.
Workman James, tinner, 5th wd. 3 W. bet. 6 and 7 S.
Workman H. P. lab. 12th wd. 2 S. bet. 5 and 6 E.
Works John, shoemaker, 7th wd. 1 W. bet. 4 and 5 S.
Worley John M. freighter, 4th wd. 6 S. cor. W. T.
Worley B. freighter, 7th wd. 2 W. bet. 3 and 4 S.
Worley Kleber, leather dresser, 7th wd. 2 W. bet. 3 and 4 S.
Worstledine Mary, wid. 15th wd. 3 S. bet. 2 and 3 W.
Worthing John, builder, 13th wd. 3 E. bet. 1 and 2 S.
Wryde Kichard, sawyer, 9th wd. 3 S. bet. 5 and 6 E.
Wright Caleb, farmer, 3d wd. 1 E. cor. 6 S.
Wright A. R. salesman with O. H. Elliot, res. 14th wd. 2 W. cor. 1 S.
Wright W. B. clerk with Bassett & Roberts, res. 14th wd. 1 W. bet. 1
   and 2 S.
Wright Robert, lab. 9th wd. 6 E. cor. 5 S.
Wright Abram, carpenter, 20th wd. Spruce, cor. Bluff
Wright Thomas, barber, ss. 1 S. bet. E. T. and 1 E. res. 11th wd. 2 S.
   bet. 9 and 10 E.
Wylie H. carpenter, 12th wd. 3 S. bet. 5 and 6 E.

Y

.

Yates John, farmer, 11th wd. 3 S. cor. 7 E.
Yeager Hyram, blacksmith, 2d wd. 7 S. bet. 3 and 4 E.
Yeates William, lab. 16th wd. S. T. cor. 5 W.
Young Brigham, president of Church of J. C. of L. D. Saints,
   res. 18th wd.
Young Joseph A. proprietor of saw mills and lumber merchant, S. T
   cor. E. T. res. 13th wd. 1 E. bet. S. T. and 1 S.
Young Brigham, Jr. one of the 12 apostles, 13th wd. 1 S. bet. 1 and 2 E
Young Brigham H. trader, 13th wd. 3 E. cor. 1 S.

Young Joseph, Sr. 13th wd. cor. S. T. and 1 E.

Young Phineas H. bishop, 2d wd. res. 5 E. bet. 6 and 7 S.

Young Le Grand, superintendent Salt Lake City and Wasatch wagon road, res. 17th wd. 2 W. bet. N. and S. T.

Young Andrew, carpenter, 10th wd. 3 S. bet. 6 and 7 E.

Young Seymour B. surgical student, 13th wd. 1 E. bet. 1 and 2 S. rear of Society Hall

Young Lorenzo D. bishop, 18th wd. res. mouth of City Creek Canon

Young John W. contractor, 18th wd. S. T.

Young John, job wagon, 10th wd.

Z

Zetton Charles E. cabinetmaker, 17th wd. W. T. bet. N. T. and 1 N.

Zuber Joseph, lab. 16th wd. 1 N. bet. 3 and 4 W.

SALT LAKE CITY
BUSINESS DIRECTORY,

EMBRACING

A Classified List of all Trades and Professions, in Salt Lake City, for the Year 1869, arranged Alphabetically for each Trade, thus exhibiting, at a glance, the full address and Special Business of the Citizens.

Accountants and Copyists.

Clayton William. office at Eldredge & Clawson's
Foster William, at theatre
Snell Henry, with Eldredge & Clawson

Agricultural Implements.

MITCHELL F. A.
1 S. near E. T.

CRONYN & PERRIS,
E. T. bet. 1 and 2 S.

WATTS, SLEATER & CO.
1 S. bet. E. & W. T.

ZION'S WHOLESALE CO-OP-
ERATIVE MERCANTILE INSTITUTION, E. T.

Agents.
(General.)

AUERBACH & BROS.
ws. E. T.

DWYER JAMES,
Post Office Building

MITCHELL F. A.
1 S. nr. E. T.
Parks H. D. 3 S. bet. 1 and 2 E.
Ross J. D., Elm, cor. Fruit
Reese Col. John, nw. cor. Court House Block
Young LeGrand.

(United States Postal.)

Clampitt John W. ws. E. T. office, Marshall & Carter

(Insurance.)

BASSETT & ROBERTS,
E. T. bet. 1 and 2 S.

CRONYN & PERRIS,
E. T. opp. Salt Lake House

CALLAHAN M. B.
ws. E. T.

MITCHELL F. A.
1 S. nr. E.. T.

GODBE & CO.
E. T. cor. 1 S.
Walker Bros., E. T. bet. 1 and 2 S.
Woods N. P. with William Sloan & Co.

(Mercantile.)

Hucks George, with J. W. Stevens, 18th wd.

Apothecaries.

(See Drugs and Medicines.)

Architects.

Albion James, 15th wd. 1 S. bet. 4 and 5 W.
Angell T. O. 1st wd.
Cram Charles S. 7th wd. 5 S. cor. 1 W.
Evans S. S. 4 W. bet. 4 and 5 S.

FOLSOM W. H.
S. T. cor. 1 W.
Paul William, Garden, cor. Locust
Walling Warren, "Sugar House Ward," County road.

Attorneys and Counsellors.

APPLEBY WILLIAM I.
14th wd. 1 S. bet. W. T. and 1 W.
Clayton William, N. T. 1 block west T. Block
Baskin R. N. ws. E. T. near 2 S.
Blair S. M. 1st wd.
De Wolfe S., E. T. bet. 1 and 2 S.

HEMPSTEAD C. H.
2 S. west of E. T.

CHAS. H. HEMPSTEAD,
ATTORNEY AT LAW

AND

UNITED STATES ATTORNEY

FOR UTAH.

**OFFICE--East end of LITTLE'S ROW,
Second South Street, half block west of
Main Street.**

Isaacson H. W., E. T. bet. 1 and 2 S.
Johnson E. P. 2 S. bet. E. and W. T.

LONG J. V.
13th wd. 2 E. bet. 1 and 2 S.

LYNCH PATRICK,
office, E. T. bet. 1 and 2 S.

MARSHALL & CARTER,
ws. E. T.

CALL AND EXAMINE OUR STOCK.   DUNFORD & SONS.

MARSHALL & CARTER,
COUNSELORS
AND
ATTORNEYS AT LAW.
OFFICE:
WEST SIDE OF EAST TEMPLE ST.,
SALT LAKE CITY.

Miner A. 2 S. bet. W. T. and 1 W.
STOUT HOSEA,
City Hall
STRICKLAND & ROBERTSON,
E. T. bet. 1 and 2 S.

O. F. STRICKLAND.   R. M. ROBERTSON.

STRICKLAND & ROBERTSON.

ATTORNEYS AT LAW,
AND
SOLICITORS IN CHANCERY,
Salt Lake City, - - - Utah Territory.

SNOW Z.
1 E. bet. 1 and 2 S.

Z. SNOW,
COUNSELOR
AND
ATTORNEY AT LAW.
OFFICE:
Snow's Corner,
First East and Second South Sts.
SALT LAKE CITY.
Business Promptly Attended to.

Williams P. L. cor. Fir and Garden

Artists' Materials.
Weggeland D. 4 E. cor. 6 S.
SAVAGE & OTTINGER,
E. T. bet. S. T. and 1 S.

Auctioneers.
Adair I. S. at Trumbo's, es. E. T.
Britner Charles. es. E. T. below 2d S.
Joel Samuel, E. T. above 1 S.
Levy Lewis, E. T. bet. S. T. and 1 S.
TRUMBO J. K.
E. T. nr. 2 S.

Auction and Commission.
BRITNER & FRIEDMAN,
es. F. T. bet. 1 and 2 S.

LEVENTHALL A.
Salt Lake City
TRUMBO J. K.
E. T. nr. 2 S.

Bakers.
Ames John, 13 wd.
CLIVE & REID,
2 S. bet. 1 E. and E. T.
Field & Dawson, ss. 2 S. nr. E. T.
GRENIG DANIEL,
es. E. T. nr. 2 S.
GOLIGHTLY R.
E. T. bet. S. T. and 1 S.
KELSON & FIELD,
E. T. opp. Salt Lake House
STUBBS & KIRKWOOD,
E. T. bet. 1 and 2 S.
WALLACE & EVANS,
E. T. bet. 1 and 2 S.
Banks and Bankers.
HUSSEY, DAHLER & CO.
es. E. T. bet. 1 and 2 S.
WELLS, FARGO & CO.
es. E. T. bet. 1 and 2 S.
Basket Manufacturer.
JOB SMITH,
E. T. bet. 2 and 3 S.

JOB SMITH,
MANUFACTURER AND DEALER
In all kinds of
BASKETS.
SIGN OF THE BIG BASKET,
East Temple, bet. 2d and 3d South Sts.,
Salt Lake City.

Baths.
ARNOLD HENRY,
19th wd. at Warm Spring Baths
CLAWSON JOHN R.
1 S. nr. E. T.

Beer Manufacturers.
California Brewery, office, Merchants' Exchange
Eddins John, es. E. T. below 2 S.

Blacksmiths.
Burnswood I., S. T. bet. 1 and 2 W.
Bowman Thomas, 11th wd. 9 E. bet. S. T. and 1 S.
Beck M. H. 1 W. bet. 1 and 2 S.
Crane A. 2 E. bet. 1 and 2 S.
Douglass Wm. S S., n. of Washington Square
Frost Burr, 3 S. cor. 2 E.
Hawkins ——, E. T. bet. 2 and 3 S.
Hopper A. railroad shops
Hamer John
Liddle James, rear ns. 2 S. nr. E. T.

Lawson James, ¼ block s. of Union Square
Lowe W. M. 1 E. bet. 1 and 2 S.
Margetts Henry, 1 N. bet. W. T. and 1 W.

NAYLOR & BRO.
1 E. bet. 1 and 2 S.
Peck Joseph, 1 W. cor. N. T.
Palmer A. B. 1 S. bet. 5 and 6 E.
Palmer M. 5 S. cor. 1 E.
Pendleton & Vannoltenberg, 2 S. nr. 1 E.
Pearpont H.
Peck M. H. 1 W. bet. N. T. and 1 N.
Pugmire J. 3 S. bet. W. T. and 1 W.
Railroad Shops, 2 E. above 1 S.
Reinsimer P. H. 3 E. bet. 5 and 6 S.
Sutton John A. 1 N. bet. 4 and 5 W.
Standish Henry, 2 S. bet. E. and W. T.
Spiers Thomas, 6 S. cor. 8 E.
Spiers Adam, 5 S. bet. 7 and 8 E.

Bookkeepers.
Addoms John, at L. Reggel's
Armstrong T. E. with Kimball & Lawrence
Browning James, 7th wd.
Decker R. 12th wd. 2 S. bet. 4 and 5 E.
Dunford Wm. 16th wd.
Hanham Edward, with H. Dinwoodey
Janney T. A. Trumbo's auction house
Raybould B. with Walker Bros.
Ruhling J. C, with Ransohoff & Co.
Reid Samuel, 1 W. bet. N. and S. T.
Swan George, at F. A. Mitchell's
Tompson J. J. with Godbe & Co.

Bookbinders.
KELLY J. B.
Deseret News office
Oglesby W. H. *Telegraph* office, 3 S. bet. 3 and 4 E.

Boarding Houses.
BROOKS J. G.
cor. 4th S. and 2 E.
Colwell Robert, 1 S. nr. E. T.
Douglass I. 1 S. nr. E. T.
LaCande, es. E. T. bel. 2 S.
Loren G. B. 2 S. bet. E. and W. T.
Reamer W. 1 S. bet. E. and W. T.
OCHILTREE M.
1 S. bet. E. and W. T.
SOUTHWORTH H. L.
ss. 1 S.

Book Sellers and Publishers.
(*See also Newspapers and Periodicals.*)
Brown T. D. & Sons, es. E. T.
Cannon Geo. Q., cor. E. T. and S. T.
Calder D. O. cor. S. T. and E. T.
Dwyer James, E. T. bet. S. T. and 1 S.
Elliott O. H., E. T. bet. S. T. and 1 S.

Boots and Shoes.
(*Wholesale.*)
AUERBACH & BROS. F.
ws. E. T.
BARTH & BRO. WM.
ns. 2 S. nr. E. T.
BASSETT & ROBERTS,
E. T. bet. 1 and 2 S.
Cohn & Co. Louis, ws. E. T.
DUNFORD & SONS,
E. T. bet. 1 and 2 S.
KAHN BROS.
es. E. T. bet. 1 and 2 S.
KIMBALL & LAWRENCE,
cor. E. T. and 1 S.
SLOAN & CO. WM.
E. T. nr. 2 S.

SHIPP & CO. A.
E. T. bet. 1 and 2 S.

A. SHIPP & CO.
Wholesale and Retail Dealers in
BOOTS, SHOES & HATS.
Also, Agents for Singer's New
FAMILY SEWING MACHINE.
East Temple Street,
SALT LAKE CITY.

Walker Bros., E. T. bet. 1 and 2 S.
WOODMANSEE BROS.
E. T. bet. 1 and 2 S.
ZION'S WHOLESALE CO-OP-
ERATIVE MERCANTILE INSTITUTION, E. T.
Boots and Shoes.
(*Retail.*)
AUERBACH & BROS. F.
ws. E. T.
BARTH & BRO. WM.
ns. 2 S. nr. E. T.
BASSETT & ROBERTS,
E. T. nr. 1 S.
Brown & Sons T. D. es. E. T.
BUNTING JAMES L.
E. T. bet. S. T. and 1 S.

JAMES L. BUNTING.
Custom Made
BOOTS & SHOES,
Warrented of the Best Make and Material.
North of Kimball & Lawrence's,
East Temple St. - - Salt Lake City.

COHN LOUIS & CO.
ws. E. T.
DUNFORD, GEORGE & SONS,
E. T. bet. 1 and 2 S.
DAVIS & COHN,
E. T. bet. 1 and 2 S.
Hooper W. J. & Co. 2 S. bet. 1 E. and E. T.
IVINS A.
E. T. bet. S. T. and 1 S.
Johnson & Odell, 2 S. bet. 1st E. and E. T.
KAHN BROS.
es. E. T. bet. 1 and 2 S.
KIMBALL & LAWRENCE,
cor. E. T. and 1 S.
Lesser S. & Bro., E. T. opp. Salt Lake House
Meyer M. ws. E. T.
MITCHELL F. A.
1 S. near E. T.

Clive & Reid, Idaho Bakery, aim at obtaining customers, and then retain them.

BOO   156   CIG

MAIBEN JOHN B.
cor. E. T. and 1 S.
Reggel L., E. T. bet. 1 and 2 S.
SLOAN WILLIAM & CO.
E. T. near 2 S.
SHIPP A. & CO.
E. T. below 1 S.
WOODMANSEE BROS.
E. T. bet. 1 and 2 S.
Walker Bros. E. T. bet. 1 and 2 S.

Boot and Shoe Makers and Repairers.
Cleary James F. 2 W. bet. N. and S. T.
Coberstrom O. ss. 1 S.
CUSHING HENRY,
1 S. bet. E. T. and 1 E.
Debenham H. ss. 2 S. near E. T.
Golding R. J. 2 W., North Union Square
Hart L., E. T. bet. S. T. and 1 S.
Hooper W. J. & Co. 2 S. bet. 1 E. and E. T.
JOHNSON & ODELL,
2 S. bet. 1 E. and E. T.
Nelson & Derstrom, es. E. T. bet. 2 and 3 S.
Lowe John. ns. 2 S.
Lawrence G. ns. 2 S.
Martin Ezra, 3 S. bet. 1 and 2 E.
Payne James, ns. 2 S.
Riser George C., E. T. bet. S. T. and 1 S.
RUBEN JACQUES,
E. T. bet. S. T. and 1 S.
Snelgrove F. ns. 2 S.
Slade G. W. ns. 2 S.
Shelton Robert, es. E. T. below 2 S.
Swenson I. 2 S. west of E. T.
SLOAN WILLIAM & CO.
E. T. near 2 S.
Thompson William, ss. 2 S. near E. T.
Twede C. T. ss. 2 S. bet. E. T. and 1 E.
Walters H. 1 E. bet. 2 and 8 S.
Wilingbeck C. P. ss. 2 S. near E. T.
Waterfall F. 3 S. cor. W. T.

Boot and Shoe Findings.
KAHN BROS.
es. E. T. bet. 1 and 2 S.
SLOAN WILLIAM & CO.
E. T. near 2 S.
ZION'S WHOLESALE CO-OPE-
RATIVE MERCANTILE INSTITUTE, E. T.

Brewers.
California Brewery, Wagner & Co., Merchant's Exchange
Eddins John, es. E. T. below 2 S.

Butchers.
(City Market House, 1 S. bet. E. T. and 1 W. T.)
Bicknell L. H. meat market
Chandler George, meat market
GARRETT L. & CO.
meat market
Hallstone Wm. meat market
Hepworth John, meat market
JENNINGS & PAUL,
meat market
MOULDING W. H.
meat market
Ornstein & Popper, meat market, office, 1 S. bet. E. and 1 E.
Picknell J. H. meat market
TAYLOR C. B.
meat market

Cabinet Makers.
ALLEN W. L. N.
20th wd.

Bird James, ss. 2 S.
Bell Wm. 20th wd. S. T. cor. Walnut
Capener Wm. 1 S. bet. 1 and 2 E.
Caste E. M. 1 E. bet. 2 and 3 S.
DINWOODEY HENRY,
E. T. bet. S. T. and 1 S.
Engstrom John, ss. 1 S.
Foster W. H. es. E. T. bel. 2 S.
Fallon H., S. T. cor. 2 E.
Jonson & Larson, es. E. T. bel. 2 S.
Parratt G. & Sons, ws. E. T. bel. 2 S.
Price ——, es. E. T. bel. 2 S.
Smith Wm. J. 6 E. bet. S. T. and 1 S.
Stoffers C. F. 1 S. bet. E. T. & 1 E.
Winegar A., N. T. bet. 3 and 4 W.
Wells James, es. E. T. bet. 2 and 3 S.
Zetton Charles, W. T. bet. N. T. and 1 N.

Carpenters and Builders.
(See also Contractors and Builders.)
Bolsen I. 1 blk. W. of 15th wd. school house
FOLSOM, ROMNEY & CO.
S. T. bet. 1 and 2 W.
Grow Henry, 3 N. cor. 3 W. 19th wd.
King Charles, 8 S. bet. E. T. and 1 E.
Mortimer A. M. es. E. T. bel. 2 S.
Oakey Thomas, 3 E. cor. 5 W.
Price G. W. 1 blk. W. of 15th wd. school house
SALSBURY WM.
3 S. cor. 3 E.
SMITH BROS.
1 E. bet. 3 and 4 S.
Stevens J. W. 1 E. bet. 1 and 2 S.
Walling Warren, Sugar House wd. county rd.
Wright A., Spruce, cor. Bluff

Carriage Builders.
(See also Wagon Makers.)
Bringhurst S. 3 S. bet. E. and 1 E.
Jacobs C. 3 S. bet. 5 and 6 E.
Little J. C. 2 E. cor. 1 S. 13th wd.
Railroad shops, 3 E. above 1 S.

Carriage Smiths.
(See also Blacksmiths.)
Railroad shops, 2 E. above 1 S.

Carriage Trimmers.
Wood H. at Railroad shops, 2 E. above 1 S.

Cigars and Tobacco.
Dunn T. C. es. E. T. near Salt Lake House
Ganz A., E. T. bet. 1 and 2 S.
GODBE & CO.
cor. E. T. and 1 S.
PYPER A. C. & CO.
E. T. bet. S. T. and 1 S.
Trickey J. M., E. T. bet. 1 and 2 S.
RUBIN H.
es. E. T. near Salt Lake House

Walker Bros. E. T. bet. 1 and 2 S.

Civil Engineers and Surveyors.

FOX JESSE W.
1 S. bet. 1 and 2 W.
Smith J. Fewson, cor. Locust and Garden

Clocks.

(See Watches.)

Clothing.

AUERBACH F. & BROS.
ws. E. T.
Brown T. D. & Sons, es. E. T. bet. 1 and 2 S.

BASSETT & ROBERTS,
E. T. near 1 S.

COHN LOUIS & CO.
ws. E. T.

DAVIS & COHN,
E. T. bet. 1 and 2 S.

HELLMAN B. & J. & CO.
E. T. near 2 S.

KAHN BROS.
es. E. T. bet. 1 and 2 S.

KIMBALL & LAWRENCE,
cor. E. T. and 1 E.
Lesser S. & Bro. E. T. opp. Salt Lake House
Meyer M. ws. E. T.

MITCHELL F. A.
1 S. near E. T.

MAIBEN JOHN B.
cor. E. T. and 1 S.
Reggel L. ws. E. T.
Siegel Bros., E. T. near Salt Lake House

WALKER BROS.
near Salt Lake House

WOODMANSEE BROS.
E. T. bet. 1 and 2 S.

ZION'S WHOLESALE CO-OPE-
RATIVE MERCANTILE INSTITUTION, E. T.

Clothes Cleaners.

Cowley William, E. T. in alley opp. Salt Lake House

Commission Merchants.

Beeston James, 14th wd. 1 S. cor. 1 W.

CRONYN & PERRIS,
E. T. bet. 1 and 2 S.

MITCHELL F. A.
1 S. near E. T.
Needham J. & Co.

TRUMBO J. K.
E. T. bet. 1 and 2 S.

WATT, SLEATER & AJAX,
1 S. west of Market

Corrals.

CALAFORNIA CORRAL,
cor. 2 S and W. T.
Colorado Corral, 2 S. nr. E. Temple
Elephant Corrall, Charles C. Hart, propr. ns. 2 S. nr. E. T.

EMIGRATION CORRALL,
Charles Davey, propr. Washington Square
Idaho Corrall, J. S. Davis, propr. 4 S. bet. 1 and 2 E.
Montana Corrall, W. Halma, propr. 1 E. bet. 1 and 2 S.

OLD ELEPHANT CORRALL,
J. Wickel, propr. 2 E. bet. 3 and 4 S.

Pioneer Corrall, J. G. Brooks, propr. 3 S. bet. 2 and 3 E.
Salt Lake Corrall, J. C. Orem, propr. 1 S. bet. E. T. and 1 E.

U. P. RAILROAD,
H. W. Willard, propr. 2 S. nr. 1 E.

Colleges.

Commercial College, cor. S. T. and E. T.
Commercial College, E. T. bet. 2 and 3 S.

Collector.

LONG J. V.
13th wd. 2 E. bet. 1 and 2 E.

Confectioners.

Brown John, E. T. bet. S. T. and 1 S.
Brown James, 1 S. next to Theatre
Camp James, ws. E. T. below 2 S.
Harvey Wm. ss. 1 S.
McDonald John, ws. E. T. below 2 S.

KELSON & FIELD,
E. T. opp. Salt Lake House
Saunders J., E. T. bet. S. T. and 1 S.

WALACE & EVANS,
E. T. bet. 1 and 2 S.

Contractors and Builders.

Armstrong Frank, 11th wd.
Cram Charles S., 5 S. cor. 1 W.
Brain Ed. 20th wd. Pine, cor. Garden
Empy N. 1 S. bet. 3 and 4 E.

FOLSOM & ROMNEY,
S. T. cor. 1 W.
King Charles, 3 S. bet. E. and 1 E.
Mulvey John, 2 S. bet. 2 and 3 E.
Morris J. T. 2 S. bet. 4 and 5 E.
Nounnan J. E., & Co.
Paul William, Garden, cor. Locust
Thatcher G. W. 18th wd.
Van Schoonhoven G. H. 4 S. bet. E. and W. T.
Worthing J. 3 E. bet. 1 and 2 S.
Warren William S. 4 S. bet. W. T. and 1 W.
Zomig John W. 18th wd.

Coopers.

Atley S. W. 1 E. bet. 2 and 3 S.

DONELSON C. M.
ns. E. T. bet. S. T. and 1 S.
Forman J. 2 S. near 1 E.
Jordan James, 8 E. cor. 4
Lang N. 1 E. bet. 2 and 3 S.
Perkes H., E. T. bet. 2 and 3 S.
Vanatta J. H. cor. Central and Pear
Wheeler E., Oak, cor. Prospect

Crockery.

KAHN BROS.
es. E. T. bet. 1 and 2 S.

MITCHELL F. A.
1 S. near E. T.

ZION'S WHOLESALE CO-OPE-
RATIVE MERCANTILE INSTITUTION, E. T.

Cutlers.

BARKER & WELLS,
ns. 2 S. bet. E. T. and 1 E.
Clayton John, E. T. bet. 2 and 3 S.

Dentists.

Barlow J. M. 1 S. cor. 3 W.
Groves W. H. ns. 2 S.
Sharp William H., S. T. bet. E. T. and 1 E.

Distillers.

Horne Joseph, 1 W. cor. 2 S.
Newton James, 3 S. cor. 7 E.

Best Bread, Pies and Crackers, by Clive & Reid, 2d South St., Salt Lake City.

DOO 159 FRE

Doors, Sash and Blinds.

FOLSOM, ROMNEY & CO.
S. T. bet. 1 and 2 W.

Dry Goods.

AUERBACH F. & BROS.
ws. E. T.
Auerbach & Levy, ws. E. T. opp. Salt Lake House

BASSETT & ROBERTS,
E. T. near 1 S.

BROWNING & HOUTZ,
ns. 2 S.

COHN LOUIS & CO.
ws. E. T.
Cunnington John, cor. E. T. and 2 S.
Chislett John & Co., E. T. bet. 1 and 2 S.

CRONYN & PERRIS,
E. T. opp. Salt Lake House
Daft A. ns. 2 S. near 1 E.

IVINS A.
E. T. bet. S. T. and 1 S.

KAHN BROS.
es. E. T. bet. 1 and 2 S.

KIMBALL & LAWRENCE,
cor. E. T. and 1 S.
Lesser S. & Bro. E. T. opp. Salt Lake House

MITCHELL F. A.
1 S near E. T.

MAIBEN J. B.
cor. E. T. and 1 S.

ESTABLISHED IN 1856.

J. B. MAIBEN
DEALER IN
DRY GOODS,
GROCERIES,
BOOTS & SHOES, CLOTHING
And General Merchandise.
HOOPER'S CORNER,
Opposite Kimball & Lawrence's, Salt Lake City.

Meyer M. ws. E. T.
Reggel L. ws. E. T.

WALKER BROS.
E. T. bet. 1 and 2 S.

WOODMANSEE & BRO.
E. T. bet. 1 and 2 S.

WATTS, SLEATER & CO.
1 S. bet. E. and W. T.

ZION'S WHOLESALE CO-OPE-
RATIVE INSTITUTION, E. T.

Druggists.

Bauman J. & Co. E. T. near 2 E.
Clinton Jeter, cor. E. T. and 2 S.

GODBE & CO.
cor. E. T. and 1 S.

Dyer and Scourer.
Bond George, ws. E. T.

Embroidering.
Trump A. ns. 2 S.

Engraver and Embroidery Stamper.
Druce H. ns. 2 S.

Engravers.
Druce H. ns. 2 S. bet. E. T. and 1 E.
McKenzie David, cor. W. T.
Quin George, 6 E. bet. S T. and 1 S.

Engineers.
Brown M. 12th wd. 5 E. bet. 2 and 3 W.
Bedell E. 18th wd. 1 S. bet. 2 and 3 E.
Bennett R. 20th wd. bet. Fir and Oak
Bratton H. 13th wd. 1 E. bet. 2 and 3 S.
Dyer William, 17th wd.
Derrick Z. 13th wd. 6 E. cor. 2 S.
Faraday John, E. T. bet. 7 and 8 S.
Stickells R., S. T. bet. 6 and 7 W.
Stephens Jacob, S. T. cor. 2 E.
Whitlock I., S. E. bet. 5 and 6 S.

Fancy and Millinery Goods.

AUERBACH F. & BROS.
ws. E. T.
Auerbach & Levy, ws. E. T. opp. Salt Lake House

COHN LOUIS & CO.
ws. E. T.
Ivins A., E. T. bet. S. T. and 1 S.

KAHN BROS.
es. E. T. bet. 1 and 2 S.

KIMBALL & LAWRENCE,
E. T. cor. 1 S.
Meyer M. ws. E. T.
Phelps H. E., E. T. bet. S. T. and 1 S.
Reggel L., E. T.

MRS. ADELAIDE SMITH,
STRAW AND FANCY
MILLINER,
Keeps on hand and sells at small prof-
its a full stock of Goods in her line.
E. Temple, bet. Second and Third S.,
SALT LAKE CITY.

Strickley John, es. E. T. below 2 S.

WOODMANSEE & BRO.
E. T. bet. 2 and 3 S.

ZION'S WHOLESALE CO OPE-
RATIVE INSTITUTION, E. T.

Freighters.
Alpine John, 18th wd.
Box Thomas, 17th wd. 1 N. cor. 1 W.
Booth Thomas, 7th wd. 2 W. bet. 5 and 6 S.
Brewer William, 20th wd. Birch, cor. S. T.
Crismon Chs. 14th wd. 1 W. cor. 2 S.
Crismon George, 14th wd. 1 W. bet. 1 and 2 S.
Green John Y. 2 S. bet. 4 and 5 E.
Hoagland L. 14th wd. 2 S. bet. 1 and 2 W.
Howe Amos, 1 N. bet. W. T. and 1 W.
Kimball C. S., E. T. bet. N. T. and 1 N.
Kimball Heber, 1 N. bet. E. and W. T.
Kimball D. P. 1 N. east of E. T.
Knowlton J. Q. 3 N. cor. 5 W.
Luce Wilford, 1 W. bet. 2 and 3 S.
Myrick George L. 1 N. bet. W. T. and 1 W.

NAISBITT & HINDLEY,
es. E. T.

Nelbaur Isaac, 2 E. bet. 2 and 8 S.
Pack George C. 1 S. bet. 2 and 8 W.
Reese Enoch, E. T. bet. N. T. and 1 N.
Richardson J., S. T. cor. 1 W.
Randall A. 1 W. bet. 1 and 2 N.
Stringam George, E. T. bet. 4 and 5 S.
Sharp Adam, cor. S. T. and Fir
Sharp James, cor. S. T. and Oak
Sharp John, Spruce, cor. Fruit
Webb Gilbert, 3 S. cor. 4 E.
Worley B. 2 W. bet. 3 and 4 S.
Worley J. M. 6 S. cor. W. T.

Flour and Grain.
(*See Produce and Grain.*)

Flour Mills.

Empire Flour Mills, Brigham Young, propr.
Jennings Wm. & Co. cor. E. T. and 1 S.
Flour Mills, executors of H. C. Keinball

PYPER A. C. & CO.
E. T. bet. S. T. and 1 S.
Pugsley Phillip, 2 W. cor. 5 N.

Furniture.

Doolittle John, 7th wd. 2 S. bet. 1 and 2 E.

DINWOODEY HENRY,
E. T. bet. S. T. and 1 S.
Capener William, 1 S. bet. 2 and 3 E.
Caste E. M. 1 E. bet. 2 and 3 S.

Furriers.

Anderson A. ns. 2 S.

AUERBACH F. & BROS.
ws. E. T.
Loser Lewis, E. T. bet. 1 and 2 S.

Gents' Furnishing Goods.

AUERBACH F. & BROS.
ws. E. T.
Anderson A. ns. 2 S.
Cunnington John, cor. E. T. and 2 S.

COHN LOUIS & CO.
ws. E. T.

DAVIS & COHN,
E. T. bet. 1 and 2 S.

HELLMAN B. & J. & CO.
E. T. near 2 S.

KAHN S. & BRO.
E. T. bet. 1 and 2 S.
Meyer M. ws. E. T.
Reggel L. ws. E. T.
Siegel Bros. E. T. near Salt Lake House

General Merchandise.

BROWNING & HOUTZ,
ns. 2 S.

BASSETT & ROBERTS,
E. T. bet. 1 and 2 S.
Brown T. D. & Sons, E. T.
Barrows E. ns. 2 S.
Cunnington John, cor. E. T. and 2 S.

CRONYN & PERRIS,
E. T. opp. Salt Lake House
Cooper Samuel & Bro. es. E. T. near 2 S.
Chislett John & Co. E. T. bet. 1 and 2 S.
Day David, E. T. bet. 1 and 2 S.
Gray John, E. T. bet. 2 and 3 S.
Gilbert & Sons, ws. E. T. near 2 S.

IRISH J. E.
E. T. bet. 1 S. and S. T.

KIMBALL & LAWRENCE,
E. T. cor. 1 S.

NAISBITT & HINDLEY,
E. T. opp. Salt Lake House
McAllister R. W., E. bet. 2 and 3 S.
Morgan O. J. ws. E. T.

MITCHELL F. A.
1 S. near E. T.
Morris & Bro. 2 S. near 1 E.

MAIBEN JOHN B.
cor. E. T. and 1 S.
Needham S. A. 1 E. bet. 2 and 3 S.

PYPER A. C. & CO.
E. T. bet. S. T. and 1 S.
Perry E. & A. 2 S. bet. E. T. and 1 E.
Stubbs & Kirkwood, ws. E. T.
Showell Thomas, ss. 2 S. near E. T.
Showell Wm. & James, cor. E. T. and 2 S.

TRUMBO J. K.
E. T. near 2 S.
Taylor T. & W., E. T. opp. Salt Lake House
Wilkinson W. B., E. T. near 2 S.
Walker Bros. E. T. bet. 1 and 2 S.

WATT, SLEATER & CO.
1 S. bet. E. and W. T.

WOODMANSEE BROS.
E. T. bet. 1 and 2 S.

ZION'S WHOLESALE CO-OPE-
RATIVE INSTITUTION, E. T.

Gilders of Picture Frames, Etc.

Richards P., W. T. bet. 2 and 3 S.
Gregg W. C. 13th wd.

Gloves and Mittens.

Andres Frantzen, ss. 1 S.
Anderson A. ns. 2 S.
Bjorkman P. E., S. T. bet. 1 and 2 W.
Frantz A., ns. 2 S.
Hyde H., E. T. bet. 2 and 3 S.
Johnson Samuel, ns. 2 S.
McAllister R. W., E. T. bet. 2 and 3 S.
Stoffers C. F. ss. 1 S.
Wood Mrs. C. ns. 2 S.

Groceries and Provisions.

Barrows E. ns. 2 S.
Brazer George, ss. 1 S.
Brown T. D. & Sons, es. E. T.

BASSETT & ROBERTS,
E. T. near 1 S.
Camp James, ws. E. T. bet. 2 and 3 S.
Childs T. W. ns. 2 S
Chislett J. & Co. E. T. bet. 1 and 2 S.

CRONYN & PERRIS,
E. T.
Cunnington John, cor. E. T. and 2 S.

DAVIS G. W.
E. T. bet. S. and 1 S.
Davis J. S. 4 S. bet. 1 and 2 E.
Dunbar W. C. ws. E. T.
Day David, E. T. bet. 1 and 2 S.

GRENIG DANIEL,
es. E. T. near 2 S.

| GUN | 161 | HOT |

HARRIS W. T. & SON,
1 S. bet. E. T. and 1 E.
Hall T. C., E. T. below 2 S.

IVINS A.
E. T. bet. S. T. and 1 S.
Johnson William, S. T. bet. 3 and 4 W.
Jones S. ss. 1 S.

KIMBALL & LAWRENCE,
E. T. cor. 1 S.
Lee Henry, E. T. bet. S. T. and 1 S.
Lashbrook C. H. es. 1 S.
McDonald John, ws. E. T. below 2 S.
Maltese S., E. T. near 2 S.

MITCHELL F. A.
1 S. near E. T.

MAIBEN J. B.
cor. E. T. and 1 S.

NAISBITT & HINDLEY,
E. T. bet. 1 and 2 S.
Parsons T. F. ss. 1 S.

PYPER A. C & CO.
E. T. bet. S. T. and 1 S.
Perry E. & A. 2 S. bet. E. T. and 1 E.
Reggel L., E. T.
Spencer John, ws. E. T. below 2 S.

STUART D. & SON,
E. T. bet. S. T. and 1 S.

STUBBS & KIRKWOOD,
E. T.
Stringfellow & Bro. E. T. below 1 S.
Shewell Wm. cor. E. T. and 2 S.

SILVER JOSEPH,
es. E. T.

WALLACE & EVANS,
E. T. bet. 1 and 2 S.

WALKER BROS.
E. T. bet. 1 and 2 S.
Woodmansee Bros. E. T. bet. 1 and 2 S.

ZION'S WHOLESALE CO-OPE-
RATIVE INSTITUTION, E. T.

Guns and Sporting Apparatus.

BARKER & WELLS,
ws. 2 S. bet. E. T. and 1 E.

FREUND & BRO.
es. E. T. bet. 1. and 2 S.
Hague James, ws. E. T.
Whitmore & Alt, ns. 2 S.

Hairdressers.

CLARK GEORGE,
ss. 2 S. bet. E. T. and 1 E.

HENNEFER WILLIAM,
ws. E. T. near 2 S.
Gill & Limer, ns. 2 S.

DIEHL & RHEINBOLD,
Salt Lake House
Russell Robert, sr. ns. 2 S. bet. 1 E. and E. T.
Moriss B. es. E. T. below 2 S.

SQUIRES JOHN,
es. E. T. bet. S. T. and 1 S.
Wright T. H. 1 S. near E. T.

Hardware Dealers.

BASSETT & ROBERTS,
E. T. near 1 S.

CRONYN & PERRIS,
E. T. bet. 1 and 2 S.
Cunnington John, cor. F. T. and 2 S.
Callahan M. B. ws. E. T.

KIMBALL & LAWRENCE,
E. T. cor. 1 S.

MAIBEN JOHN B.
cor. E. T. and 1 S.

MITCHELL F. A.
1 S. near E. T.
Reggel L., E. T.

WALKER BROS.
E. T. bet. 1 and 2 S.

WATTS, SLEATER & CO.
1 S. bet. E. and W. T.

Harness Makers.
(See Saddlery.)

Clark A. J., Railroad shop, 13th wd.

BOWRING & CROW,
E. T. bet. S. T. and 1 S.
Brooks J. G., E. T. near 2 S.
Hague James, ws. E. T.
Langly C. 2 S. near 1 E.
McKinnon A., E. T. bet. 1 and 2 S.
Moss W. J., Railroad shop, 13th wd.
Nelson C. J. ss. 2 S.
Seegmiller & Platt, ss. 2 S. near E. T.
Railroad Shops, 3 E. above 1 S.

Hats, Caps, Furs, etc.

AUERBACH F. & BRO.
ws. E. T.

COHN LOUIS & CO.
ws. E. T.

DUNFORD GEORGE & SON,
es. E. T. bet. 1 and 2 S.

KAHN BROS.
es. E. T. bet. 1 and 2 S.

KIMBALL & LAWRENCE,
E. T. cor. 1 S.

MAIBEN J. B.
cor. E. T. and 1 S.

MITCHELL F. A.
1 S. near E. T.

SHIPP A. & CO.
E. T. below 1 S.
Siegel Bros. E. T. near Salt Lake House
Walker Bros., E. T. bet. 1 and 2 S.

WOODMANSEE BROS.
E. T. bet. 1 and 2 S.

Hatters.

Merrill A. 1 W. bet. 1 and 2 N.
Shelmerdine James, 3 S. bet. 2 and 3 E.

Hides and Leather.

Jennings William & Co. E. T. cor. 1 S.

Hotels.

California House, 1 S. near E. T.

DELMONICO HOTEL,
E. T. near 2 S.

MANSION HOUSE,
cor. 3 S. and 1 E.

ALL SORTS OF NOTIONS, CHEAP, AT H. E. PHELPS' VARIETY STORE.

| ICE | 163 | LIQ |

MANSION HOUSE,

E. TUFTS, Proprietor.

Ready to accommodate the Public with good rooms well furnished. The table set with every variety the market affords. This House is retired and also the Cheapest Hotel in the city.

Also attached to the premises is a large

Stable and Good Corrall

FOR TEAMS.

TWO BLOCKS S. OF THE THEATRE.

PACIFC HOUSE,
E. T. bet. 2 and 3 S.

PACIFIC HOUSE,

F. REICH, Proprietor,

EAST TEMPLE STREET,

Between 2d and 3d South,

SALT LAKE CITY.

Good Accommodations and Board by the Meal, Day or Week on Reasonable Terms.

Revere House, ns. 2 South
Salt Lake House, E. T.
SOUTHWORTH'S H. L.
1 S. east of Exchange building

H. L. SOUTHWORTH'S

HOTEL and BOARDING HOUSE,

FIRST SOUTH STREET,

EAST of EXCHANGE BUILDING,

SALT LAKE CITY.

Good Accommodations and a Well Supplied Table are offered to the Public.

Townsend House, cor. W. T. and 1 S.

Ice Cream.

CLIVE & REID,
2 S. bet. 1 E. and E. T.
CLAWSON JOHN R.
1 S. near E. T.
FIELD & KELSON,
E. T. bet. 1 and 2 S.
McDONALD JOHN,
E. T. bet. 2 and 3 S.
WALLACE & EVANS,
E. T. bet. 1 and 2 S.

Ice Dealer,

CLAWSON JOHN R.
1 S. near E. T.

Insurance Companies.

Connecticut Mutual Insurance Co. N. P. Wood, agent, with William Sloan & Co.
Pacific Insurance Co. Walker Bros.

NATIONAL LIFE INSURANCE
CO. E. L. Sloan, agent
New England Mutual Insurance Co. John Meeks, agent
Occidental Insurance Co. of San Francisco, M. B. Callahan, agent, E. T. bet. 1 and 2 S.

Indian Interpreter.

Huntington D. B. 2 N. cor. 3 W.

Iron and Steel.

Callahan M. B. ws. E. T.
ZION'S WHOLESALE CO-OPE-
RATIVE MERCANTILE INSTITUTION, E. T.

Jewelry, Watches, etc.

Asmussen Carl, E. T. bet. 1 and 2 S.
Daynes John, 1 S. near E. T.
JONES WILLIAM,
1 S. opp. Theatre
Kidgell Chs., Sr. 2 S. bet. E. T. and 1 E.
MEEKS JOHN,
es. E. T.

PIONEER
JEWELRY STORE,

J. MEEKS, Proprietor,

E. Temple Street,

SALT LAKE CITY.

Jewelry, Watches, Clocks, etc., of the Finest Quality and Best Styles. A First Class Watchmaker constantly employed.

Watters I., E. T. near 2 S.

Joiners.

(See also Carpenters.)

Taylor J., Mountain, cor. Fir
Walling Warren, Sugar House wd. County road

Junk and Second Hand Dealers.

Lashbrook Charles, 1 S. bet. E. T. and 1 E.
Showell Thomas, ss. 2 S. near E. T.
Showell George, es. E. T. below 2 S.

Lawyers.

(See Attorneys and Counselors.)

Leather Dealers.

Jennings Wm., E. T. cor. 1 S.
SLOAN WM. & CO.
E. T. near 2 S.

Lime.

Findley Hugh, E. T. bet. S. T. and 1 S.
Muir Thomas, 5 S. bet. 4 and 5 E.
McD- ff J. & Sons ws. E. T. below 2 S.
Pascoe J. F. P., N. T. bet. 1 and 2 W.

Liquors, Wines, Etc.

City Liquor Store, es. E. T. below 2 S.
GODBE & CO.
cor. E. T. and 1 S.

M. L. DAVIS,

SURGEON & PHYSICIAN

7th Ward, 3rd South Street,

Between East and West Temple,

SALT LAKE CITY.

OFFICE AT

GODBE & CO.'S,

Exchange Buildings.

The long experience which Dr. DAVIS has had in the treatment of the various diseases incidental to the human system, enables him to treat them with more than ordinary success.

Clive & Reid, Idaho Bakery, aim at obtaining customers, and then retain them.

LIV   165   NUR

PYPER A. C. & CO.
E. T. bet. S. T. and 1 S.
Walker Bros. E. T. bet. 1 and 2 S.

Livery, Feed and Sale Stables.
CALIFORNIA STABLES,
A. C. Sprague, propr. cor. 2 S. and W. T.

CALIFORNIA STABLE,
A. C. SPRAGUE, Propr.
SADDLE HORSES
AND
CARRIAGES
Furnished on the Shortest Notice.
SECOND SOUTH, COR. W. TEMPLE,
SALT LAKE CITY.

Faust & Houtz, 2 S. near E. T.
Great Western, near Mansion House
Monte & Hanson, rear Salt Lake House
U. P. RAILROAD STABLES,
—— Pratt, propr. 2 S. bet. E. and W. T.

Locksmiths.
Clayton John, ws. E. T. below 2 S.
Toms J. ws. E. T. below 2 S.

Lumber.
Decker Charles, 9th wd. 6 S. cor. 5 E.
Little Feramorz, 1 S. bet. 1 and 2 E.
Wells D. H. cor. S. and E. T.
Woolley S. A. 3 E. cor. 4 S.
Young J. A. cor. E. T. and S. T.

Machinists.
Edginton W. W. 11th wd.
Kidgell Charles jr. 5 E. bet. 5 and 6 S.
Lawson James, 2 W. bet. N. T. and 1 N.
Lyngburg C. 5 S. bet. 3 and 4 E.
Pierpont Thomas, 1 S. cor. 1 W.
Reid Peter, at Theatre
Sawdon William, 5 E. cor. 4 S.
Silver W. J. cor. Central and Peach
Tremaine W. H., S. T. bet. 5 and 6 E.
Tuckfield J. W. Elm, cor. Bluff
Thomas D. G. 6 E. cor. 4 S
Tibbett William, 5 E. cor. 7 S.
Webster Thomas, 5 E. cor. 4 S.

Manufactories and Companies.
Pacific Woolen Mills, San Francisco, Cal., William Jennings & Co. agents
Mission Woolen Mills, San Francisco, Cal., William Jennings & Co. agts.
Champion Reaper & Mower, Nalsbett & Hindley, agents
Blandy's Celebrated Steam Saw Mill and Engine, Cronyn & Perris, agents
Farg J. A. & Co.'s wood working machinery, Cronyn & Perris, agents
Woolen Factory, Sugar House wd. Brigham Young, propr.
Pall Wooden Ware, Parley's Canon, E. D. Woolley, 18th wd. 1 E. bet. 1 and 2 S.
STEAM WOOD WORKING CO.
Folsom, Romney & Co. proprieters, S. T. bet. 1 and 2 W.
STEAM WOOD WORKING CO.
Smith Bros. 1 E. bet. 3 and 4 S.
Carding Machine, 1°th wd.
Paper Mill, Sugar House wd., Geo. Q. Cannon
Woolen Factory, Sugar House wd. Smoot & Co. proprietors
Silk Cocoonery, 2 miles south of Salt Lake City, Brigham Young, proprietor

Cotton Factory, Washington, Washington Co., Brigham Young, proprietor
Ogden Woolen Mills, A. Randall, 1 W. bet. 1 and 2 N.
Co-operative Pottery Association, Croxall & Co.

Market.
City Market, 1 S. bet. E. T. and 1 W.

Masons, Plasterers, etc.
Cowan A. 4th wd. 3 W. bet. 6 and 7 S.
Cooper Chs. ws. E. T. bet. S. T. and 1 S.
Cotterell Chs. 14th wd. S. T. bet. W. T. and 1 W.
Coult James. 11th wd. 7 E. bet. 1 and 2 W.
Harford Thos. 13th wd. 3 E. bet. 2 and 3 S.
Keir David, 6 S. cor. 2 W.
Keysor Guy, 3 E. bet. 4 and 5 S.
Jones William, S. T. bet. 5 and 6 W.
Lyons Joseph, 5 E. bet. 2 and 3 S.
Morgan William, 6 W. cor. 1 S.
McFall J. 3 S. bet. 1 and 2 E.
Nutt James, 4 S. bet. 3 and 4 W.
Nowell William, 2 S. bet. 3 and 4 E.
Nelmeyer William, 3 S. bet. 5 and 6 E.
Pasby A. 7 E. bet. 5 and 6 S.
Reid George, 6 W. bet. N. and S. T.
Rummell N. 2 S. bet. 6 and 7 E.
Rummell J. H. 1 S. bet. 1 and 2 E.
Sproul A., S. T. cor. Ash
Taysum A. J. Oak, cor. Garden
Williams T. 15th wd. 2 S. cor. 5 W.

Matches.
Cornwall Thomas, es. E. T. below 2 S.
Fielding Amos, 8 W. bet. 7 and 8 S.
Findley Hugh, E. T. bet. S. T. and 1 S.
Nelbaur H. 2 E. bet. 2 and 3 S.

Medicines.
(See Drugs and Medicines.)

Milliners.
Colebrook Mrs., E. T. bet. S. T. and 1 S.
Day Mrs. 2 S. bet. 1 E. and E. T.
Dewey Mrs. F. ½ block e. of Washington Square
Engigo Mrs. & Pratt Mrs. S. T. bet. W. T. and 1 W.
Rancell S. ns. 2 S.
SMITH JOB,
ws. E. T. below 2 S.

Millinery Goods.
(See Fancy Goods)

Millwrights.
Ensign Samuel, 3 S. bet. 2 and 3 E.
Kesler F., N. T. cor. 3 W.
Wells P., S. T. bet. 4 and 5 E.

Newspapers, Periodicals, Etc.
Deseret News, daily, semi-weekly and weekly, George Q. Cannon, editor
Juvenile Instructor, George Q. Cannon, editor, Deseret News buildings.
Telegraph, daily, semi-weekly and weekly, T. B. H. Stenhouse, propr. and editor, 1 S. bet. E. T. and W. T.
Salt Lake City Directory and Business Guide, E. L. Sloan & Co.
Utah Magazine, E. L. T. Harrison, editor, Exchange buildings

Notaries Public.
Clayton William, at Eldredge & Clawson's
Caine John T. office at Theatre
LYNCH PATRICK,
office, at James Hagues' gun store, E. T.
Phelps W. W., W. T. bet. S. T. and 1 S.

Nurserymen.
Derr William, 16th wd. 1 N. bet. 1 and 2 W.
Fowler Samuel, 1 S. bet. 6 and 7 E.
Hemmingway L. S. 1 W. cor. 6 S.
Hartwell Elliott, 6 E. bet. 1 and 2 S.
Miller E. 2 S. bet. 4 and 5 E.
Reading John, 2 S. cor. 2 E.

Boys' Clothing, in any quantity, low, sold by HELLMAN & CO, Salt Lake City.

ORG   167   PRO

Fenton Thomas, 4 W. bet. 4 and 5 S.
Wagstaff William, 1 E. cor. 6 S.
Wallace G. B. 2 W. cor. 1 N.

Organ Builder.
Ridges J. 3 N. bet. 3 and 4 W.

Oyster Dealer.
SIMMONS J. M.
under Revere House

Painters and Glaziers.
Fagan M., Railroad shops, 13th wd.
Lambourne A. 20th wd. Wall, cor. Fir
Mathews John, 2 S. bet. 1 E. and E T.
MIDGLEY & EVANS,
2 S. w. of E. T.
Morrow & Bain, es. E. T. below 2 S.
MORRIS WILLIAM V.
1 S. bet. 4 and 5 W.
Phillips W. J. 2 S. w. of E. T.
Pickering John, 20th wd.
Pitt M. cor. Central and Peach
Pitt William, N. T. cor. 1 W.
Piggott Geo. W., 6 S. bet. 2 and 3 E.
Richards P., W. T. bet. 2 and 3 S.
Smith George, Maple, cor. Garden
Shaw O., N. T. bet. 1 and 2 W.
TULLIDGE & MACAVOY,
2 S. bet. 1 and 2 E.

TULLIDGE & MACAVOY,
PAINTERS.

GRAINING, SIGN WRITING,
HOUSE PAINTING, Etc.,
EXECUTED IN THE BEST STYLE WITH
Promptness and Dispatch.
Office, 2d South, bet. 1st and 2d East Sts., Salt Lake City.

Turner H., Wall, cor. Spruce
Toone John, Spruce, cor. Garden
Woods William, W. T. bet. 5 and 6 S.

Paints, Oils and Glass.
Marrow & Bain, es. E. T. below 2 S.

Paper Hangers.
Lambourne W. 20th wd. Wall, cor. Fir
Neve & Thornberg, es. E. T. below 2 S.

Periodical News Dealers.
Carter R. 2 S. bet. E. T. and 1 E.
Cooper Charles, ws. E. T. bet. S. T. and 1 S.
DWYER JAMES,
s. of Post Office buildings

JAMES DWYER,
RAILROAD NEWS DEPOT,
SOUTH OF POST OFFICE BUILDING.
Dealer in all kinds of
NEWSPAPERS, MAGAZINES, BOOKS,
Stationery, Play Books,
CHEAP PUBLICATIONS, ETC.
Salt Lake City.

Elliott & Co. E. T. bet. S. T. and 1 S.

Phonographers.
Evans David W., News office
Sloan Edward L., S. T. cor. Elm

Photographists. Etc.
CARTER CHARLES,
es. E. T. bet. 1 and 2 S.
Cannon M. 17th wd. 1 W. bet. N. and S. T.
Martin Edward, es. E. T.
OLSEN JOHN,
1 S. bet. E. and W. T.
SAVAGE & OTTINGER,
E. T. bet. S. T. and 1 S.

Physicians and Surgeons.
ANDERSON W. F.
2 E. bet. 2 and 3 S.
Baker ——, 13th wd. 2 E. bet. 2 and 3 S.
Bernhisel J., N. T. opp. Temple block
CUNNINGHAM J. N.
1 S. near Theatre
Crockwell John D. M. 1 S. near E. T
DAVIS M. L.
at Godbe's drug store
Gerber John, 15th wd.
Hyler M. R., Bench, bet. 8 and 9 S.
Hovey O. D. 5 N. cor. 1 W
FOWLER ALLEN,
E. T. bet. 1 and 2 S.
Kenner R. H., S. T. bet. E. and W. T.
Lee E. cor. 3 N. and 2 W.
Newton S. E. 2 S. bet. 3 and 4 E.
ORMSBY J. S.
cor. E. and 2 S.
Sprague S. L. 1 E. bet. S. T. and 1 S.
TAIT WILLIAM,
at Bauman & Bros. E. T. bet. 1 and 2 S.

W. H. TAIT, M. D., M. R. C. S. L.,
SURGEON & PHYSICIAN,
OFFICE AT
BAUMAN BROS,' DRUG STORE,
EAST TEMPLE STREET,
SALT LAKE CITY.

Potteries.
Allwood M. 2d wd.
CO-OPERATIVE,
cor. E. T. and 5 S.
Reese William, 1 W. bet. 1 and 2 S.

Produce and Grain.
Cunnington J. cor. E. T. and 2 S.
Dunbar W. C., E. T. bet. 1 and 2 S.
Day David, E. T. bet. 1 and 2 S.
Goddard George, E. T. bet. 1 and 2 S.
Hall T. C., E. T. below 2 S.
PYPER A. C. & CO.
E. T. bet. S. T. and 1 S.
STUBBS & KIRKWOOD,
ws. E. T.
Stringfellow & Bro. E. T. near 1 S.

SILVER JOSEPH,
es. E. T.
Showell William, cor. E. T. and 2 S.
Maltese S., E. T. below 2 S.

Provision Dealers.
(See General Merchandise.)

Restaurants, etc.
CLAWSON JOHN R.
1 S. near E. T.
Doty B. L. 2 S. bet. 1 E. and E. T.
Field & Dawson, ss. 2 S. near E. T.
Greenwald N., Delmonico Hotel
Montana Restaurant, ss. 2 S.
Star Restaurant, J. W. Dawson, es. E. T. below 2. S.

Rope Makers.
Cripes Chas. 16th wd. 6 W. bet. 1 and 2 N.
McMaster William, 9 E. bet. 1 S. and S. T.

Saddlery.
(See also Harness Makers.)
BOWRING & CROW,
E. T. bet. S. T. and 1 S.
Breckbank Isaac, 8th wd. 1 E. cor. 4 S.
Curtis Foster, 7th wd. E. T. bet. 3 and 4 S.
Eastman A. 2 W. opp. Union Square
Jenkins William, S. T. bet. 1 and 2 W.
Jones D. W. ss. 2 S. bet. E. T. and 1 E.
McKinnon A. es. E. T. below 2 S.
Nelson C. J. ss. 2 S.
Seegmiller & Platt, ss. 2 S. near E. T.

Saddletree Makers.
Jackman Levi, 5 W. cor 1 N.
Thorp T., Pine, bet. High and Prospect

Saloons.
BILLIARD SALOON,
E. T. bet. 1 and 2 S.
Merchants' Exchange, Wagner & Co. ns. 2 S.
OYSTER SALOON,
under Revere House
RAILROAD SALOON,
E. T. bet. 1 and 2 S.

Salt Lake City Guide and Business Directory for 1869.
SLOAN E. L. & CO.
Post Office lock box 370

Saw Mills.
Little Feramorz,office, 1 S. cor. 2 E. mills in Big Cotton-
wood Canon
Neal W. O. cor. Currant and Plum
Saw Mill, Big Cottonwood Canon, D. H. Wells, propr.
office. nw. cor. E. T. and S. T.
Saw Mill, Mill Creek, 1st wd. J. J. Thayn, propr.
Steam Saw Mill, N. Mill Creek Canon, J. A. Young,
propr.
Steam Saw Mill, Lambs' Canon, J. A. Young, propr.

Shoe Dealers.
(See Boots and Shoes.)

Sewing Machines.
MITCHELL F. A.
1 S. near E. T.
GODBE & CO.
cor. E. T. and 1 S.
BASSETT & ROBERTS,
agents, Singers' Sewing Machines

Sewing Machine Manufacturers.
Sawdon & Webster, 9th wd.

Seeds, Vegetables and Flowers.
LONG JOHN V.
13th wd.

Sexton.
Taylor J. E. 1 S. bet. 2 and 3 E.

Soap Manufacturers.
Foster William, 8 S. bet. 3 and 4 W.
ORNSTEIN & POPPER,
1 S. bet. E. T. and 1 E.
Torbet A. 8 W. bet. 7 and 8 S.

Stage Offices.
BOISE,
J. Leach & Co. ss. 2 S. bet. 1 E. and E. T.
Southern, office, ns. 2 S. bet. 1 E. and E. T.
EASTERN, WESTERN AND
NORTHERN, Wells, Fargo & Co. E. T. bet. 1 and 2·

Stationers.
Brown T. D. & Son, E. T. bet. 1 and 2 S.
Calder D. O., Council House, cor. E. and 3. T.
Elliott O. H., E. T. bet. S. T. and 1 S.
SAVAGE & OTTINGER,
E. T. bet. S. T. and 1 S.

Stone Cutters.
Mitchell B. F. 1 S. bet. 1 and 2 W.
Williams T. 15th wd. 2 S. cor. 5 W.

Storage.
TRUMBO J. K.
E. T. bet. 1 and 2 S

Stoves, Ranges, Tinware, etc.
(See also Tin and Sheet Iron Workers.)
ALLEN J. M. & CO.
ws. E. T. near 2 S.
Best Alfred, E. T. opp. Salt Lake House
Callahan M. B. ws. E. T.
Hawkins Thomas, E. T. opp. Salt Lake House
MITCHELL F. A.
1 S. near E. T.
PYPER A. C. & CO.
E. T. bet. S. T. and 1 S.
SHARKEY R. C.
(executors of) ws. E. T.
WATTS, SLEATER & CO.
1 S. bet. E. and W. T.
ZION'S WHOLESALE CO-OPE-
RATIVE INSTITUTION, E. T.

Tailors and Drapers.
(See also Clothing Stores.)

Cowley William, ws. E. T. opp. Salt Lake House
Erskine A. 20th wd.

JONES CHARLES R.
ns. 2 S.

Manning John, 2 S. bet. 1 E. and E. T.
Ninde A. 2 S. bet. 1 E. and E. T.
Sproat C. 1 S. bet. E. T. and 1 E.
Suter F. W. ss. 2 S. bet. 1 E. and E. T.

TAVEY PETER,
2 S. near 1 E.

Treseder R. 6 E. bet. S. and 1 S.
Thermlog & Anderson, ns. 2 S.

TAYLOR JOHN & BRO.
1 S. bet. 1 E. and E. T.

JOHN TAYLOR & BRO.,

MERCHANT TAILORS,

Have constantly on hand a fine assortment of

CLOTHS, CASSIMERES,

VESTINGS, ETC,

**1st South St., nearly opposite Theatre,
Salt Lake City.**

Taylor G. E. G. 3 S. cor. 5 E.
Treseder R. es. E. T. below 2 S.
Thomson John, 2 S. bet. 1 E. and E. T.
Treseder C. M. 19th wd.

THIRKILL & EARL,
1 S. near E. T.

Western James, es. E. T. below 2 S.

Teachers, Public and Private Schools.

Careless George, 4 S. bet. W. T. and 1 W.
Cook Mrs., S. T. bet. 1 and 2 W.
Calder D. O. cor. S. T. and E. T.
Dickson R. 14th wd. 2 S. bet. 1 and 2 W.
Doremus H. I., Union Academy, 17th wd.
Haskins T. W. Rev. Independence Hall
Lyne T. A. 1 S. bet. 4 and 5 E.
Lichtenburg Paul, 5 W. bet. 2 and 8 N.
McLean A. 1 S. bet. E. and W. T.
Morgan J. es. E. T. below 2 S.
Maeser K. G., Elm, cor. Fruit
Mutch L. F., W. T. bet. N. T. and 1 N.
Needham A. S., W. T. bet. 3 and 4 S.
Priestley W. H. 1 S. bet. W. T. and 1 W.
Pratt Orson jr. W. T., bet. S. T. and 1 S.
Rager Mr. 2 S. bet. 1 and 2 E.
Sproat C. 1 S. bet. 1 E. and E. T.
Strickland A. 5 E. bet. 4 and 5 S.
Taylor George J., Deseret University
Tripp B. 16th wd.
Willes William, 4 E. bet. S. T. and 1 S.

Tanners.

Golding Robert J. 1 N. bet. 1 and 2 W.
Jennings William, 15th wd.
Margets R. n. of Union Square
Pug-ley Phillip, 19th wd.
Pickard James, 1 block s. of Court House

SLOAN WM. & CO.
E. T. near 2 S.

Tripp E. B., N. T. cor. 2 W.

Type Founder.

Rance Samuel, 5 S. bet. 6 and 7 E.

Tea Dealers.

Cunnington John, cor. E. T. and 2 S.

MITCHELL F. A.
1 S. near E. T

Ping Chong, 2 S. near E. T.

PYPER A. C. & CO.
E. T. bet. S. T. and 1 S.

WALKER BROS.
E. T. bet. 1 and 2 S.

ZION'S WHOLESALE CO-OPE-
RATIVE INSTITUTION, E. T.

Telegraph Offices.

DESERET TELEGRAPH LINE,
office, S. T. e. of E. T.

WESTERN UNION TELE-
GRAPH CO. es. E. T. bet. S. T. and 1 S.

Tin and Sheet Iron Workers.
(See also Stoves, Ranges and Tinware.)

ALLEN J. M. & CO.
ws. E. T. near 2 S.

Best Alfred, E. T. opp. Salt Lake House
Boaz William, 2 S. bet. E. T. and 1 E.
Callahan M. B. ws. E. T.
Hawkins Thomas, E. T. opp. Salt Lake House

JONES CHARLES F.
2 W. bet. 2 and 3 S.

PYPER A. C. & CO.
E. T. bet. S. T. and 1 S.

SHARKEY R. C.
(executors of) E. T.

Stevenson Edward, 1 S. bet. E. and W. T.

Turners.

Bird James, 2 S. near 1 E.
Cast E. M. 1 E. bet. 2 and 3 S.
Foster Wm. H., E. T. bet. 2 and 3 S.
Hulse James, 20th wd. Spruce, cor. Prospect

Traders and Street Brokers.

Charles T. W. 12th wd. 2 S. cor. 5 E.
Goddard S. 2 E. bet 2 and 3 S.
Harris William, 11th wd.
Johnson W. D., S. T. bet. 3 and 4 W.
Johnson L. L. 3 S. bet. 3 and 4 W.
Livingston O. M. 1 W. cor. 5 S.
Latey William, 8 S. bet. E. and W. T.
Myer I. W., Spruce, cor. Wall
Reese Col. John, nw. cor Court House block
Reese Enoch, E. T. bet. N. T. and 1 N.
Savage G. N. 3 E. bet. 1 and 2 S.
Stewart George, 8th wd.
Young B. H. 3 E. cor. 1 S.

Undertakers.

DINWOODEY HENRY,
E. T. bet. S. T. and 1 S.

Taylor J. E. 1 S. bet. 1 and 2 E.

Umbrella Manufacturer.

Hawkes Thomas, 11th wd. 2 S. bet. 6 and 7 R.

Upholsterers.

Neve & Thornburg, E. T. bet. 2 and 3 S.

Veterinary Surgeon.

Pitt William, 4 W. bet. 4 and 5 S.

Wagon Makers.

Blazard J. H. 1 S. bet. E. and W. T.
Bringhurst S. 8th wd. 3 S. bet. E. and 1 E.
Carlisle John, 2 W. opp. Union Square
Hayward G. 1 N. bet. 5 and 6 W.
Hartog Herbert, 1 E. bet. 1 and 2 S.
Little J. C. 13th wd. 2 E. cor. 1 S.

NAYLOR BROS.

1 E. bet. 1 and 2 W.
Pusey H, 13th wd. Railroad Shops
Stahl D. W. 13th wd. Railroad Shops
Wiggill Ely, 1 E. bet. 2 and 3 S.

Watch Makers and Repairers.

(See also Jewelry, Watches, Etc.)
Asmussen C. ws. E. T. bet. S. T. and 1 S.
Barlow J. M. 15th wd. 1 S. cor. 3 W.
Ballan William, ws. E. T. bet. S. T. and 1 T.

DAYNES JOHN & SONS,
ss. 1 S.

ELIASON & CO.
ws. E. T.
Harvey Andrew, 1 S. bet. 1 E. and E. T.
Higley W. G., E. T. bet. 1 and 2 S.
Kidgell Charles, ns. 2 S.

MEEKS JOHN,
E. T. near 2 S.
Nelson S. ss. 1 S.
Riser Henry, E. T. opp. Salt Lake House
Watmough William, Quince, cor. Apricot
Watters I., E. T. near 2 S.

Well Diggers.

Calton W. F. 7 E. bet. 2 and 3 S.
Hunter Stephen, E. T. cor. 4 S.

Wheelwrights.

Broadhurst Samuel, 14th wd. 1 S. bet. 1 and 2 W.
Blazard J. H. 14th wd. 1 S. bet. E. and W. T.
Stahl D. W., Railroad Shops, 13th wd.
Sinclair P. 1 E. cor. 7 S.
Walker Chs. 7 S. bet. 3 and 4 E.

Whips.

Huskinson W. ws. E. T.
Scherewe D. 2 S. bet. 1 and 2 E.

Willow Ware.

SMITH JOB,
ws. E. T. below 2 S.

Wines.
(See Liquors.)

Zion's Co-operative Mercantile Institutions.
(Retail.)
Allen J. M. & Co. ws. E. T. nr. 2 S.
Brown John, E. T. bet. S. T. and 1 S.
Bunting James L., E. T. bet. S. T. and 1 S.
Bassett & Roberts, E. T. near 1 S.
Best Alfred, E. T. opp. Salt Lake House
Cronyn & Perris, E. T.
Cooper Samuel & Bros. E. T.
Co-operative Pottery, cor. E. T. and 5 S.
Colebrook Charles, E. T. bet. S. T. and 1 S.
Day David, E. T. bet. 1 and 2 S.
Dinwoodey Henry, E. T. bet. S. T. and 1 S.
Dunbar W. C. ws. E. T.
Davis George W., E. T. bet. S. T. and 1 S.
Grenig Daniel, es. E. T. near 2 S.
Godbe & Co. cor. E. T. and 1 S.
Hawkins Thomas, E. T. opp. Salt Lake House
Hague James, E. T.
Ivins A., E. T. bet. S. T. and 1 S.
Kimball & Lawrence, cor. E. T. and 1 S.
Martin Edward, ws. E. T.
Morgan O. J. ws. E. T.
Malben John B. cor. E. T. and 1 S.
Mitchell F. A. 1 S. near E. T.
Naisbitt & Hindley, E. T. opp. Salt Lake House
Needham S. H. 1 E. bet. 2 and 3 S.
Phelps Henry E., E. T. bet. S. T. and 1 S.
Pyper A. C. & Co. E. T. bet. S. T. and 1 S.
Shipp A. & Co. E. T. below 1 S.
Stringfellow & Bro. E. T. below 1 S.
Silver Joseph, es. E. T.
Stubbs & Kirkwood, E. T.
Taylor T. & W., E. T.
Wilkinson W. B., E. T.
Woodmansee Bros., E. T. bet. 1 and 2 S.

RATES OF INTEREST IN THE UNITED STATES.

ALABAMA.—Eight per cent.; forfeit interest and usury.

ARKANSAS.—Six per cent.; by agreement as high as ten ; forfeit usury and contract void.

CALIFORNIA.—Where there is no express contract in writing, ten per cent. Parties may agree in writing for the payment of any rate whatever on money due or to become due on any contract.

CONNECTICUT.—Legal interest six per cent.; forfeit all interest, but allows the original amount lent.

DELAWARE.—Six per cent.; forfeit of the whole debt.

FLORIDA.—Legal interest six per cent.; may agree to give eight; forfeit the whole interest paid.

GEORGIA.—Seven per cent.; usurious contracts forfeit all interest paid.

ILLINOIS.—Six per cent.; contracts for money loaned ten per cent.; forfeit threefold the amount of the whole interest.

Views of the Overland Route, at Carter's Gallery, adjoin'g Wells, Fargo & Co.'s.

172   RATES OF INTEREST IN THE UNITED STATES.

INDIANA.—Six per cent.; forfeit all the interest paid.

IOWA.—Six per cent.; by agreement as high as ten per cent.

KENTUCKY.—Six per cent.; forfeiture of excess of interest paid.

LOUISIANA.—Five per cent.; eight per cent. on special contracts; forfeiture of all interest received or paid; usurious interest may be recovered back.

MAINE.—Six per cent.; forfeit of the claim for usury.

MARYLAND.—Six per cent.; no longer any penalty.

MASSACHUSETTS.—Six per cent.; forfeit of thrice the usury.

MICHIGAN.—Seven per cent.; on special contracts ten per cent.; and all above that may be recovered as any other debt.

MISSISSIPPI.—Six per cent.; by agreement as high as eight per cent. on money loaned; forfeit the usury.

MISSOURI.—Six per cent.; beyond this forfeit of all interest.

NEW HAMPSHIRE.—Six per cent.; forfeit of thrice the amount unlawfully taken.

NEW JERSEY.—Six per cent.; forfeit of the whole debt.

NEW YORK.—Seven per cent.; usurious contracts void.

NORTH CAROLINA.—Six per cent.; contracts for usury void, and forfeit double the usury.

OHIO.—Six per cent.; by special contract, ten per cent.; forfeiture of all the interest paid above six per cent. This is the rule established by the courts; the statutes prescribe no penalty.

OREGON.—Ten per cent.; by contract, twelve per cent.; for illegal interest, forfeit to school fund debt and all interest.

PENNSYLVANIA.—Six per cent.; forfeit of the whole debt.

RHODE ISLAND.—Six per cent.; forfeit of usury above six per cent.

SOUTH CAROLINA.—Seven per cent.; forfeit of all interest taken.

TENNESSEE.—Legal interest six per cent.; liable to an indictment for misdemeanor; if convicted, to be fined a sum not less than the whole usurious interest taken and received, and no fine to be less than ten dollars; the borrower and his judgement creditors may also, at any time within six years after usury is paid, recover it back from the lender.

TEXAS.—Eight per cent.; by special contract, twelve per cent.; forfeiture of all the interest paid or charged.

VERMONT.—Six per cent.; recovery in an action with cost.

VIRGINIA.—Six per cent.; all contracts tainted with usury void.

WISCONSIN.—Seven per cent.; by contract any amount agreed upon by the parties, not exceeding twelve per cent. Excess, forfeiture of the entire debt.

In England and France legal interest is five per cent., in Ireland six.

CAMP DOUGLAS.

THIS post is situated about two and a half miles east of Salt Lake City, and is pleasantly located on the eastern "bench," not far from the base of the mountains. It is well laid out, with buildings neatly and tastefully finished. The quarters are capable of holding about 3,000 troops. The following is a list of the

OFFICERS AND STRENGTH OF COMMAND.

January, 1869.

Name	Rank	Bvt. Rank	Kind of Duty	No. of Men
W. H. Lewis	Maj.	Lt. Col.	Com'dg Post	
John H. Knight	Capt.	Lt. Col.	Com'dg Co. A	59
A. E. Woodson	1st Lt.		Co. A	
Charles Hay	2d Lt.		Co. A	
D. W. Benham	Capt.	Maj.	Com'dg Co. C	74
H. M. Benson	1st Lt.		Adjt. and A. C. S.	
J. S. Proctor	Capt.		Com'dg Co. D	53
Wm. Harmon	1st Lt.		Co. D	
W. L. Foulk	1st Lt.		Com'dg Co. G	60
D. B. Abrahams	2d Lt.		Co. G	
Geo. L. Tyler	Capt.		Com'dg Co. K	63
A. H. Wands	1st Lt.		Co. K	
W. L. Clark	2d Lt.		Co. K	
C. A. Reynolds	Capt.	Lt. Col.	A. Q. M., U. S. A.	
F. Meacham	Capt.		Asst. Surgeon U. S. A.	

CIVILIANS.

Butler H. C. clerk in Q. M. Department
Cram E. S. blacksmith
Dow Alexander, tinsmith
Hutchinson Daniel, wagonmaker
Henderson Jerry (col'd), with Col. Lewis
Johnson Daniel, bds. with Wm. Unsworth
Kane S. harnessmaker
King Thomas, blacksmith
Peacock James, clerk with post trader
Rogers T. J. clerk in commissary
Stokes O. P. clerk in Q. M. department
Schmidt Henry, lab.
Sawrenson Peter, lab.
Silvey Manuel, with Col. Lewis
Taylor Abraham, fruit vender
Zabriskie E. B. post trader

Ice Cream, and the et ceteras in the Season, at the Idaho Bakery, 2d South St.

175   SALT LAKE CITY DIRECTORY.

TOWNS IN THE VICINITY OF SALT LAKE CITY.

SOUTH.

South of Salt Lake City, in Salt Lake county, are a number of settlements; and a considerable portion of the county is cultivated and inhabited, the dwellings being more or less scattered, as in an old settled farming country. The first city on the direct road is

LEHI,

In Utah county, thirty-one miles south of Salt Lake City. It is pleasantly situated on a plain, about three miles north of Lake Utah, a beautiful sheet of fresh water nearly thirty miles in length from north to south, by about fifteen miles in width from east to west. The streets of Lehi, as in all the cities and towns of Utah Territory, are wide, fringed with shade trees, with water running down by the sidewalks, used for irrigation purposes. Present population about 1,000.

AMERICAN FORK

Is four miles from Lehi; L. E. Harrington, Mayor and Postmaster. It was incorporated in 1853, and is a thriving little city. The hay lands surrounding it afford a considerable quantity for the Salt Lake market. It has a co-operative mercantile association, of which Mayor Harrington is President, which owns a respectable store doing considerable business. Population 1,200.

PLEASANT GROVE

Is three miles from American Fork, and is laid out one mile square, with the streets running at right angles. It has a co-operative mercantile association. Thomas Wooley is Mayor. Population about 600.

PROVO

Is the county town of Utah county. It is forty-eight miles from Salt Lake City, and lies on the northeast side of Lake Utah, situated a little south of the Provo, or Timpanogos, river, and not far from the mouth of Provo cañon. It has fine facilities in water power, farming lands, timber, the fisheries in Lake Utah, and in location, for becoming a place of considerable importance in the future. It has a beautiful church, which was opened for public worship in the summer of 1868; a brick court house; a theatre; a dancing hall, in which social parties are held; five district schools and a number of private schools. A. O. Smoot is Mayor. Population about 4,000.

THE IDAHO BAKERY, SECOND SOUTH STREET, IS THE PLACE TO GO TO.

176   TOWNS IN THE VICINITY OF SALT LAKE CITY.

SPRINGVILLE,

Six miles south of Provo, is a neat town, pleasantly situated, with a population of 1,200.

SPANISH FORK

Is twelve miles south of Provo, and not far from the mouth of Spanish Fork canon, up which is the most direct road to Uintah valley, in the Uintah range of mountains. Three miles from it, on the road to Payson, was the Indian reservation till the treaty made here by Government with the chiefs of the Utah tribes in June, 1865. Spanish Fork has a population of 1,200.

NORTH.

The first settlement north of Salt Lake City is

BOUNTIFUL,

In Davis county, with a population of nearly 2,000, scattered over an area of several miles as a farming community. It has a very neat and elegant church, which is ten miles from Salt Lake City.

CENTREVILLE

Is three miles north of Bountiful, lying in a fruitful part of the country, with a farming population of 600.

FARMINGTON

Is the county seat of Davis county. It has a large adobe court house, the upper story of which is used for meetings and other public purposes; a substantial rock church, and a hotel. Its population is about 1,100. Distance from Salt Lake City, 18 miles.

KAYSVILLE,

Four miles north of Farmington, has a population of about 600; a substantial built church with a capacious basement story; also a hotel.

OGDEN

Is thirty-nine miles from Salt Lake City, and lies between the Weber and Ogden rivers, near the mouth of Ogden canon. It was located and a settlement formed in September, 1850. Situated in the centre of a farming country, with thriving settlements around and contiguous to it, Ogden has natural advantages which cannot fail to make it a place of no little importance. It will be a station for the Union Pacific and Central Pacific railroads, and the point of junction of the two great lines which, connected, span the continent from the Missouri to the Pacific. The rapid and largely increasing trade of Ogden since the first of January shows that business men have a keen eye to its rising importance, and that its growth is likely to be rapid. It has nearly 5,000 inhabitants, with North Ogden six miles distant to the north;

Lynne three miles distant to the northwest; Slaterville about two miles from Lynne; and, following on the same road, Plain City, some ten miles from Ogden. These settlements present, in the summer season, a beautiful prospect, the fields waving with heavy grain, the orchards bearing a wealth of excellent and luscious fruit, and the shade trees covered with a dense foliage.

Ogden is the county seat of Weber county. The Mayor is Hon. Lorin Farr, who has been a member of the Territorial Legislature for several sessions. Bishop C. W. West is Postmaster, and his energy and enterprise have done much to aid the growth and development of the city.

It has a large tabernacle, for public worship, besides a number of meeting houses, in different parts of the city.

The officers of Weber county are:

Probate Judge—F. D. Richards.
Sheriff—Gilbert Belnap.
Deputy Sheriff—Wm. Brown.
County Clerk—W. Thompson.
Coroner—Wm. N. Fife.
County Recorder—W. Thompson.
County Surveyor—Jos. A. West.
Superintendent of Common Schools—Wm. W. Burton.
Assessor and Collector—Sanford Bingham.
Selectmen—L. J. Herrick, R. Ballantyne, H. Holmes.
County Poundkeeper—Robert McQuarrie.

WILLARD,

Fourteen miles north of Ogden, is a rapidly growing settlement, situated about a mile east of Great Salt Lake, and half a mile from the base of the mountains east. It has a population of over 800; Alfred Cordon, Postmaster.

BRIGHAM CITY,

The county seat of Box Elder county, is a little over seven miles north of Willard, and is one of the handsomest towns of its size in Utah. Under the fostering care and energy of the Hon. L. Snow, it is steadily growing in influence, size and importance. The houses are mostly handsome and neat structures, although but few of them are of pretentious appearance. Brigham City lies at the mouth of the Box Elder canon, up which the road passes to reach the southwest part of Cache valley, the canon opening into that valley a little distance from Wellsville, one of the principal settlements in Cache county. It is also three miles from Bear river, where the Union Pacific railroad crosses it. As a station of the U. P. R. R., it offers facilities for becoming a distributing point for the growing settlements of Cache county, and for Montana and a portion of Idaho. It has a very fine court house, in which public meetings are held, and a large and substantial tabernacle in course of erection. Its population is close upon 4,000.

9

BRIEF AMERICAN HISTORY.

The following has been prepared from the most authentic sources in order to show at a glance in what year each of the original thirteen States was settled and by whom; also the year in which each of the present States was admitted into the Union, together with its population in 1860.

	Year.	Population.
Virginia, first settled by the English	1607	1,556,318
New York, " " " Dutch	1613	3,880,735
Massachusetts, " " " English Puritans	1620	1,231,066
New Hampshire, " . " " " "	1623	326,073
New Jersey, " " " Dutch	1627	692,035
Delaware, " " " Swedes and Danes	1627	112,216
Maryland, " " " English	1634	687,049
Connecticut, " " " English Puritans	1633	460,147
Rhode Island, " " " Rodger Williams	1636	174,620
North Carolina, " . " " English	1650	992,622
South Carolina, " " " Hugonots	1670	703,708
Pennsylvania, " " " William Penn	1682	2,906,165
Georgia, " " " English	1733	1,057,286
Vermont, admitted into the Union	1791	315,098
Kentucky, " " " "	1792	1,155,684
Tennessee, " " " "	1796	1,109,801
Ohio, " " " "	1802	2,339,502
Louisiana, " " " "	1812	709,002
Indiana, " " " . "	1816	1,350,428
Mississippi, " " " "	1817	791,395
Illinois, " " " "	1818	1,711,951
Alabama, " " " "	1819	964,201
Maine, " " " "	1820	628,279
Missouri, " " " "	1821	1,182,012
Arkansas, " " " "	1836	435,450
Michigan, " " " "	1837	749,113
Florida, " " " "	1845	140,424
Texas, " " " "	1845	640,215
Iowa, " " " "	1846	674,699
Wisconsin, " " " "	1848	775,871
Minnesota, " " " "	1848	379,994
California, " " " "	1850	172,023
Oregon, " " " "	1859	52,465
Kansas, " " " "	1861	107,206
West Virginia, " " " "	1862	No census
Nevada, " " " "	1864	6,051
Nebraska, " " " "	1866	28,841

TERRITORIES.

	Organized.	Capital.
Arizona	1863	Tucson.
Colorado	1861	Denver.
Dacotah	1861	Yankton.
Idaho	1863	Boise.
Montana	1864	Helena.
New Mexico	1850	Santa Fe.
Utah	1850	Salt Lake City.
Washington	1853	Olympia.
Wyoming	1868	

OGDEN CITY
BUSINESS DIRECTORY.

ATT   179   ·   GRO

Attorney.
Blair S. M., office at Ogden House

Baker.
JOST JOHN A.
es. Main

Blacksmiths.
Ford & Nicholas, C. P. R. R. blacksmith shop, es. Main
Fowler & Pearce, es. Main
Nicholas John, es. Main
Rees J. T. es. Main
Shupe A. J. es. Main
Williamson C. C., Montana blacksmith shop, es. Main

Boarding Houses.
McGAW JAMES,
  private boarding house, es. Main
Williams W. D. propr. Weber House, es Main
Woodworth A. J., U. P. R. R. House, es. Main
Wright Wilson A. es. Main

Boots and Shoes.
Eggleston & Sons, es. Main

Butchers.
Douglas Ralph, es. Main
Pool John R. es. Main

Cabinet Makers.
Delmore & Bro. s. end Main

Clothing and Gents' Furnishing Goods.
Gotlieb Joel, es. Main
Mendelsohn & Co. ws. Main
Orchard & Kohn, ws. Main

Cooper.
CHILD ORVILLE R.
es. Main

Drugs.
GODBE W. S. & CO.
  wholesale and retail, ws. Main
Pidcock Wm. es. Main
WEBER COUNTY CO-OPERA-
TIVE ASSOCIATION, ws. Main
WHITE & BROWN,
es. Main

Dry Goods.
FARR LORIN,
  es. Main
Peery & Herrick, ws. Main
READ BROTHERS,
Cash store, es. Main
STAYNER THOMAS J.
es. Main
WHITE & BROWN,
es. Main

WOODMANSEE CHARLES,
ws. Main

**SALT LAKE STORE,
OGDEN.
CHAS. WOODMANSEE,
PROPRIETOR.
DRY GOODS,
GROCERIES,
AND GENERAL MERCHANDISE
AT REASONABLE PRICES.**

Feed Stables.
Leavitt N. es. Main
Nelson Bros. es. Main

General Merchandise.
Haswell T. es. Main
HORROCKS JAMES,
  ws. Main
Mendelsohn & Co. ws. Main
Nelson Bros. es. Main
Peery & Herrick, wholesale and retail, ws. Main
Pidcock Wm. es. Main
READ BROTHERS,
Cash store, es. Main
STAYNER THOMAS J.
es. Main
Stewart Isaiah, ws. Main
WEBER COUNTY CO-OPERA-
TIVE ASSOCIATION, Geo. W. Turner, salesman, ws. Main
Wheat Horace, ws. Main
WHITE & BROWN,
es. Main
WOODMANSEE CHARLES,
ws. Main

Grist Mills.
Farr Lorin & Co. n. of city
West & Young, n. of city

Groceries.
FARR LORIN,
ws. Main
HORROCKS JAMES,
ws. Main
Perry & Herrick, ws. Main
STAYNER THOMAS J.
es. Main
WHITE & BROWN,
es. Main

California Woolen Goods, for Men's Wear, at the CASH STORE, Ogden.

HAR   180   WOO

WOODMANSEE CHARLES,
ws. Main

Hardware.

HORROCKS JAMES,
ws. Main
Johnson L. ws. Main

Hairdressers and Barbers.
Holbrook W. S. at U. P. R. R. House, es. Main

ROBINSON J. R.
next door to Cramer's Restaurant, es. Main

THOMAS THOMAS R.
at Ogden House, es. Main

Hotel.
Ogden House, es. Main

Milliner and Fancy Goods.

HILL ELIZABETH,
home made straw hats, ws. Main

Paint Shop.
Nelson D. es. Main

Photographer.

VAUGHAN C.
es. Main

Physicians.
McIntyre W. L., Main
Wheeler P. es. Main
Williams Dr. Main

Restaurants.

CRAMER J. H.
es. Main

KELLY & DEE,
Star & Eagle, ws. Main

Saddles and Harness Makers.
Dwiggins James, es. Main

STOKER WM.
es. Main

Stoves and Tinware.
Johnson L. ws. Main

PEARCE CHARLES,
ws. Main

Tanner.
Browning Jonathan, ws. Main

Watchmaker.

LOCK ROBERT,
ws. Main

Woolen Factory.
Randall & Co. northeast of city

THE UNION PACIFIC RAILROAD.

THE construction of a railroad across this continent, so as to unite with a continuous line of track the Atlantic and Pacific oceans, and open a new and more rapid means of communication between the nations of Europe and those of the far east, was a project discussed by advanced minds soon after the advantages of the locomotive were practically demonstrated. Then the country to be traversed west of the Missouri river was a *terra incognita*, and for years afterwards was vaguely described on the maps as the "Great American Desert." Faint rumors, gathered from mountain trappers, occasionally reached the eastern states that there were vast mountain ranges lying east of the Pacific coast, with deep and rugged gorges, almost impassable to man or animal, dividing their huge bases and towering summits; while impenetrable deserts and wonders startling and innumerable heightened the perils of a region to be dreaded by civilized man.

The explorations of Fremont, while they disabused the public mind of many previously entertained erroneous impressions, did not by any means elucidate the practicability of an overland railroad. Nor were they calculated to encourage hope that the country through the Rocky Mountains and in the Great Basin could ever be made profitable in supporting by its products a civilized population. When in 1846-7 the Mormons were compelled by mobocratic violence to leave Nauvoo and betake themselves to the far west for shelter, safety and a home, so popular was the opinion that it was impossible for a civilized white population to exist there, that the idea prevailed that they would perish of hunger or fall a prey to wild beasts and savage nomads. In July of 1847 their pioneers entered the valley of the Great Salt Lake; and having been firmly imbued with a belief in the future construction of an overland railroad, during the whole of their tedious journey they carefully kept it in view, and endeavored to find a practicable route for it. It is worthy of remark here, that the line which they marked, and subsequently pointed out, in a memorial to congress, as the best adapted for the talked of railroad, has been very closely followed in the construction of the line for over seven hundred miles. Yet even when they had demonstrated their ability to live and prosper in the Great Basin, and when the overland railroad project had grown to be looked upon as perfectly feasible, its construction and completion were placed away in the future to nearly the close of the present century. How rapidly events occur in this age! How fast we grow! What unlooked-for yet natural combinations of circumstances have occurred to hasten the completion of a work so vast, so important and involving and fostering so many overwhelming interests! The discovery of gold in the Occident State; the rush of people to the auriferous shores laved by the mighty Pacific; the vast travel overland, following in the track of the pioneer Mormons; the thousands of nameless graves studding the prairie billows of the great plains, or marking at brief intervals, through the Black Hills and Rocky Mountains, the last earthly resting places of eastern-born brave and adventurous spirits; the shining gold brought from California, awakening interest and cupidity; with fresh discoveries of the precious metals in other regions, turned the attention of eastern capitalists and the people of the Republic to this land of dangers and desert, as it had been described; and not the feasibility but the necessity of an overland railroad now claimed and received serious consideration. The discovery of rich mines in the regions now composing Nevada, Montana and Idaho; with the rapidly growing settlements and increasing prosperity of Utah—which was a base of supplies for the surrounding mining regions—hastened the inception of the work. While the rich discoveries of the precious metals in the Pike's Peak region, now Colorado, and the up-springing of numerous towns and cities which soon claimed an importance in the great centres of commerce of the country, undoubtedly stimulated to the early commencement of the Union Pacific line; the development of the vast mineral resources of Nevada, Montana and Idaho, causing a great and growing commerce between those points and the east and west, as surely stimulated to the commencement of the Central Pacific, and to the putting forth of energies by each company which have challenged and obtained the admiration of the world, for the unparalleled progress made in a work of such magnitude:

GOVERNMENT GRANTS.

The proposed undertaking, however, was so great that private capital was doubtful of being able to accomplish it, and hesitated to enter upon the organization of a company for the construction of the line. But the necessity of having such a road daily assumed graver proportions; and finally the government, while having a terrible and unparallelledly expensive war on its hands, agreed to lend the national aid to the undertaking. The grants given to the Union Pacific and Central Pacific lines were alike; that to the former including, in government six per cent. currency interest thirty-year bonds, $16,000 per mile, for 517 miles from the Missouri river to the base of the Rocky Mountains; $48,000 per mile, for 150 miles westward from the eastern base of the Rocky Mountains; and $32,000 per mile for the rest of the distance until it should meet with the Central Pacific. To this government added, as a grant, every alternate section of land for twenty miles on each side of the railroad, or 12,800 acres for each mile, worth at the government price of $1,25 per acre, $16,000 a mile; but as an act of congress, signed March

7th, 1868, provides that the government alternate sections shall not be sold for less than $2,50 per acre, it is but fair to estimate the sections granted to the railroad at the same price. Government also granted the companies the right to issue their own mortgage bonds to an amount equal to the bonds issued by the United States to the company; with the rights of way and material, including the necessary public lands for track, stations, depots, etc.

DIFFICULTIES IN THE WAY.

A charter for the construction of the road was granted in July of 1862; and in October of 1863 a preliminary organization was made, followed soon after by a formal organization with a board of fifteen directors to which was added five government directors. In the following August the first contract for constuction was let; and the work proceeded slowly till January 1866, at which time but forty miles of track were laid. Difficulties of no ordinary character had to be encountered from the outset. Among these financial difficulties that would have disheartened men less energetic and and persevering than those who had the work in hand, had to be met and overcome. These conquered, others presented themselves. On this subject, a correspondent of the Boston *Journal* treating upon it has said:

"The Company commenced operations at Omaha, then a small town, destitute alike of the skill necessary for the practical construction of such a public work, and destitute even of the mere manual force necessary. Mechanics were needed, laborers were needed; if they were summoned from abroad, boarding places must be found, and some kind of homes extemporized. There were no shops in which, and no tools with which, to labor. Shovels, spades, picks, plows, axes and other implements were to be purchased in Chicago, Buffalo, Boston, New York or Philadelphia, wherever they could be found best in quality and cheapest in price, and transported to this new point of departure. And here again was another obstacle to be contended with, for as yet no rail track had been laid nearer than about 150 miles of the east bank of the Missouri river. Over this distance, therefore, all men and materials had to be transported by the slow and expensive process of wagon trains. The engine of 70 horse power, now propelling the Company's works at Omaha, was thus carried in wagons from Des Moines, on the river of that name, that at the time being the only available means of getting it through. Again, west of the Missouri river the country is almost entirely destitute of trees, and excepting a limited supply of cottonwood, similar in fibre and strength to the old Lombardy poplar of the east, there was nothing from which railroad ties could be obtained. East of the Missouri the forest conditions were quite similar, so that in a short time it came to pass that the

THE IDAHO BAKERY, SECOND SOUTH STREET, IS THE PLACE TO GO TO.

SALT LAKE CITY DIRECTORY. 185

very ties on which the railroad has been constructed had to be cut in Michigan, Ohio, Pennsylvania and New York, and teamed over the country at an expense sometimes of two dollars and seventy-five cents per tie. Then it should be added that the supplies necessary for the support, clothing and maintenance of the laborers were also to be purchased far east and transported as before. In less than a year these difficulties were confronted and conquered, and the great work begun in serious earnest."

CONSTRUCTION OF THE ROAD.

The forty miles laid in January, 1866, had stretched into 305 in the January of 1867; and in January, 1868, 540 miles were completed. In March, 1869, the cars had reached and passed Ogden, 1,032 miles west of the Missouri River, about 500 miles of track having been laid in the later fourteen months. The astonishing triumph of railroad building on the great overland line so far exceeds anything previously accomplished of a similar work that no rival parallel can be drawn. The Union Pacific Company now runs their cars direct to Ogden, within a short distance of Salt Lake, with a schedule time of thirty hours from Ogden to Cheyenne, fifty hours to Omaha, seventy-eight hours to Chicago and five days to New York.

ALONG THE LINE.

A number of towns have sprung up along the line and others have grown to be places of importance with a rapidity commensurate with the prosecution of the work of construction. Omaha, which a few years ago, was but a small outfitting point for emigrant and freighters' wagon trains starting westward, has now some fifteen thousand inhabitants, with energetic, pushing business men who are in full sympathy with the growth of the city, ambitious to see it rise in importance, and already stretching out to secure a full share of the trade of the western territories. Its position on the western bank of the Missouri river; the converging lines of railroad which meet on the opposite side of the river at Council Bluffs and which carry to the great Union Pacific the commerce and traffic of the south and east; and the broad Missouri bearing on its bosom from St. Louis and other points almost a nation's ransom of freight, give to Omaha natural advantages which can not fail to make it a city of great importance and size in a very few years.

Fremont, North Platte, Cheyenne, and other towns along the line have natural advantages and central positions which cannot fail to make them places of much importance as the country around them becomes settled and developed.

One interesting feature connected with travel on the line of the Union Pacific Railroad, and one, too, as novel as it is interesting, is found in the herds of antelope and buffalo which are offten passed

Views of Echo Kanyon, at Carter's Gallery, adjoining Wells, Fargo & Co.'s.

186   SALT LAKE CITY DIRECTORY.

through. The lithe and graceful antelopes, startled with the snorting of the locomotive, erect their heads as if in astonishment, and seeing the strange looking monster speeding away from them often start out in full career to outrun the huge thing that rushes along so swiftly and steadily in a direct line. They will sometimes run thus for two or three miles, keeping pace with the train of cars and gracefully flinging back their heads as if in proud defiance of the tireless engine with which they vainly try to compete. Large herds of buffaloes are occasionally seen, scattered in wild confusion, cross the track, toss up the earth on either side of the line, shake their shaggy manes, and wildly dash across the prairie.

THE DENVER BRANCH LINE,

Running from Cheyenne to Denver, will connect Colorado with the Union Pacific Railroad, and open up rapid communication between that point and the east and west. A system of wooden railroads, proposed and chartered some time ago by enterptising citizens of Colorado, is rapidly growing in favor there, and their construction will probably be commenced at an early day. When conpleted, they will place the rich mineral and timber lands of the principal parts of the Territory in close communication with Denver, aid in the development of the whole Territory, and centralize its wealth at a point in close connection with the great overland route.

THE SCENERY

Along portions of the Union Pacific is most attractive, and in places sublime. Reaching the Wasatch range, and passing down the wild gorges known as Echo and Weber Canons, a constant successions of bold, beautiful and magnificently picturesque scenery opens to view. The towering, rocky sides, fashioned by the hand of time in wierd looking and fantastic shapes, astonish and awe the beholder. Tourists and travelers will find in the scenery through which the great overland railroad passes, enough to turn the attention of those who love and seek the sublime, picturesque and beautiful from the oft-trodden scenes of Europe to the "back bone" of the American Continent. Passing through the Wasatch Range, Salt Lake Valley is entered, and the

GREAT SALT LAKE

Stretches away to the north and south, with islands rising out of its bed which have the proportions of lofty mountains. The waters of the Lake hold in solution an extraordinary amount of saline matter, varying at different points, according to their contiguity to the rivers emptying into it or distance from them, from fifteen per cent. to twenty-six per cent. An abundance of salt is consequently obtained from it, an article of a coarse quality being got in such quantities at times on the shores that it can be shoveled into wagons; while by boiling an excellent table salt is

Best Bread, Pies and Crackers, by Clive & Reid, 2d' South St., Salt Lake City.

SALT LAKE CITY DIRECTORY. 187

procured. The line of railway passes up the eastern side of the Lake, northward, with the giant peaks of the grand Wasatch range to the right; and after crossing Bear river, stretches away to the west towards Promontory Point.

THE CENTRAL PACIFIC.

The western portion of the line has been constructed with a rapidity, engineering skill and energy in overcoming difficulties which challenges admiration no less than the Union Pacific. Cutting a roadway and laying a line of track across the Sierras, along the side of mountain declivities where yawning precipices. drop down into frightful depths, and through passes seemingly impassable is an engeering triumph which cannot well be appreciated by those who have not passed over the line. The two great companies have fairly won the honors which accrue to them in having built the greatest railroad line in the world, bringing the connecting points together, from a distance of about seventeen hundred miles in a little over three years from time the work was fairly entered upon; for the short distance laid, up till the January of 1866, can scarcly be taken into account.

The developement of the great west consequent upon the completion of this work; the vast traffic which will pass over it; the closer linking of the old nations of Eastern Asia with those of Western Europe; the growth of a power in the west that will speedily rival in all the essentials of greatness the older and eastern States of the Union; and the important results growing out of this truly national work, in which the Republic may justly take pride, are points which the most sanguine can scarcely overestimate.

DIRECT ROUTE EAST.

The travel from the Pacific coast and the Great Basin, when they reach the terminus of the Union Pacific Railroad at Omaha, can travel eastward by a direct line on the

CHICAGO AND NORTHWESTERN

Railroad, the distance between Chicago and Omaha by it being 493 miles. This line is in excellent condition, with splendid cars, Pullman's palace sleeping coaches, and every requisite convenience and comfort. By it, too, they can make connections, at COUNCIL BLUFFS, with the Council Bluffs and St. Jo Railroad for Plattsmouth, Nebraska City, St. Jo, etc.; at BOONE, with stages to Des Moines and Fort Dodge; and at DIXON with the Illinois Central Railroad for points north and south. The line passes through the flourishing towns of Council Bluffs, Dun lap, Boone, Cedar Rapids, Clinton, and Dixon.

CHICAGO.

ITS GROWTH AND TRADE.

Less than forty years ago the place where Chicago now stands was a prairie, bordering on Lake Michigan, on which a log fort garrisoned by two companies of United States troops; a fur agency; three taverns; two stores; a blacksmith's shop; a house for the interpreter of the station; and one occupied by Indian Chiefs, were the only habitations and evidences of the white man's having selected it for an abiding place. To-day it has probably 350,000 inhabitants. The history of growth to greatness contained in this single statement places the "Garden City" above all competitors in rapid developement and progressive prosperity. Its miles of stately avenues, where palatial residences present most varied and artistic architectural beauties; its streets stretching miles on miles in length; the broad and noble boulevards which will soon wind along its magnificent parks; its long lines of wharves, where hundreds of large vessels, lake steamers and smaller craft, discharge their freight or receive their loading, all mark a young but giant municipality whose inhabitants are filled with a laudable ambition to make their city not merely the metropolis of the great States to which it is a naturally geographical and central mart, but one of the leading cities of the world.

To notice in detail and describe all the points of interest which Chicago presents to a visitor, would require much more space than can be devoted to it here; indeed it would fill a volume of respectable size to do them justice.

PLACES OF INTEREST.

THE LAKE TUNNEL

Is a work which, did any other one not exist to prove it, would be sufficient evidence of the enterprise and energy which have made Chicago what it is. The turbid waters near the shore of Lake Michigan, as the city grew in extent and population, were mixed with the contents of the miles of sewerage which traversed the city limits. The "villainous compound" could not be endured for drinking, culinary purposes and ablutions. Yet the lake was the only available source for any abundant supply, and to obtain pure water it was determined to work a tunnel under the bed of the lake to a distance where it could be obtained, and thus bring it clear and sparkling from the body of the lake into the city. Ground was broken for the tunnel on the 17th of March, 1864. A shaft nine feet in diameter was sunk, at a point selected close to the lake, to a depth of sixty-five feet.   The tunnel was then commenced and carried for a distance of two miles beneath the bed of the lake to a point determined upon ; where an immense " crib," constructed at an expense of over one hundred thousand dollars, and built like a ship, was taken and securely weighted down and moored.   In the centre of this crib was a well open at bottom and top, down which another shaft was run into the bed of the lake, and the work of tunneling was carried on from both ends. On the 24th of November, 1866, the tunnel was completed ; and since then Chicago has enjoyed an abundance of pure water.

At the water-works are three powerful engines, the largest of which is capable of pumping from the tunnel eighteen million gallons of water in twenty-four hours ; and a building is erected and being finished in which will be placed two more very large and powerful engines.

THE WASHINGTON STREET TUNNEL,

Which passes underneath an arm of the Chicago river is another engineering triumph and an object of interest.   The immense traffic over the bridges which are thrown across the river was so much impeded by the passage of vessels up and down, causing the bridges to be kept open often for a length of time, that the arrangements of business men were largely interfered with, and it became so great an inconvenience, that it was determined to tunnel under the river.   This has been successfully done, and there is now a passage way under the water, arched with brick, floored with timber, lighted with gas, which will greatly facilitate business communications between the two sides of the river.   The Washington Street Tunnel is well worthy the attention of visitors to the " Garden City."

At the corner of Western and Chicago Avenues are two artesian wells, which will well repay a visit from those who have the time at their disposal.   One is about a thousand feet deep, and the other about seven hundred.   They were bored by oil speculators, who expected to obtain petroleum but found water instead.   A million gallons a day of water is discharged from them.   They are near together, with a bore of about six inches each.

The large Court House, to which extensive additions were being made in April; the Chamber of Commerce building; the Post Office; the Dearborn Observatory; the parks; the various buildings devoted to benevolent and charitable purposes, etc.; and the stock yards, four miles south of the city, are objects of interest, and evidences of the spirit and enterprise of the citizens.

THEATRES.

Chicago may congratulate itself upon its theatres.   Besides numerous other places of amusement and entertainment, it possesses four excellent temples of the drama, in which varied tastes can be gratified.

CROSBY'S OPERA HOUSE

Is the largest, having a seating capacity to accommodate about 2,400 persons. It is the building which was made famous throughout the United States by the Crosby Opera House lottery scheme. It is situated on Washington street, between State and Dearborn, with a frontage of 143 feet on Washington. On the main floor is the parquette and orchestra stalls; on the second floor is the dress circle, the centre being divided into fifty boxes. The family circle is on the third floor, which conveys a covert insinuation that families must climb considerably to obtain operatic and theatrical enjoyment. The stage is not quite so large as that of the Salt Lake City Theatre. The auditorium is 86x95 feet, with a ceiling 65 feet high, the latter being decorated with portraits of leading composers. The style of drama produced partakes more of the sensational and "leg" character than of the legitimate.

M'VICKER'S THEATRE,

On Madison street, between Dearborn and State, is the next largest theatre in the city. It is managed by Messrs. McVicker & Myers, the former named gentleman owning the theatre and Mr. Myers principally managing it, besides occupying with his lady the leading position among the company. The building is 80 feet between the walls and 160 feet deep. It is capable of seating some 1,800 persons. It is tastefully finished and well arranged, and has a very pleasing appearance inside. On the main floor are the parquette and reserved seats; on the second floor the dress circle and balcony reserved seats; while the third floor is devoted more particularly to those who aspire to the dignity of theatrical deities. In this theatre the sensational and legitimate drama find place for exposition, and all the leading stars of the country are secured that their specialties may be presented to the public. Mr. Myers is a courteous and affable gentleman who plays with much ability and manages the theatre most admirably.

COL. WOOD'S MUSEUM,

Situated on Randolph street, between Clark and Dearborn, combines natural history with the drama, and presents the visitor with an excellent collection of mineralogical, orinthological, animal and collected specimens illustrative of the natural world and of savage and civilized art. The catalogue of birds, reptiles, quadrupeds and insects comprises some twelve hundred specimens, from all parts of the world, to which additions are being constantly made. Geological and relic rooms contain most interesting geological and mineralogical specimens. The funeral bier and memorable relics of Lincoln; wax work figures of the last supper and trial before Pontius Pilate of our Savior Jesus Christ, which are made to move by machinery; a model of the Capitol at Washington; one of the Parthenon; a grotto of Antiparos; illustrated views of California; two cosmoramic saloons; and the mummies around which the papyrus was rolled on which the Book of Abraham—published in the Pearl of Great Price—was inscribed, form a collection of specimens worthy the attention of all and the admiration of the student of nature. The mummies were sold by those who had them in charge after the death of the Prophet, Joseph Smith, and were afterwards obtained for the Museum—so the printed catalogue states.

Besides the attractions named is another, which cannot be overlooked, in the reproduction of a denizen of primeval days, which has received the name of *Zeuglodon Macrospondylus*, one of an extinct species to which the generic name of *Hydrachen* has been given. The skeleton of this monster was found in the state of Arkansas; and its length, as it sported in the wilds of primitive earth, was ninety-six feet.

With the museum is a fine, large, roomy theatre, under the management of J. W. Blaisdell, Esq., where the sensational and standard drama finds correct interpretation. The company is a very good one; the pieces produced are mounted and put upon the stage with much care and taste; and the patronage bestowed upon the Museum and theatre is most liberal and well deserved.

THE DEARBORN THEATRE,

Or "Aiken's Dearborn Theatre," is a perfect *bijou* of a place, principally devoted to the intellectual and refining of the standard modern comedies. The company at this theatre is most excellent, the actors and actresses being conversant with their business and manifesting an appreciation of the higher requirements of their profession instead of seeking the silly and vain clap-trap applause of the ignorant and uncultivated. Mr. Aiken is a gentleman of culture, who is devoted to his profession, and who is not governed alone by the mere mercenary objects of gathering "dollars and dimes" into the treasury. He is doing more to elevate the tastes of the people to an appreciation of refined and intellectual dramatic representations than, perhaps, any other manager in the eastern states. A good actor, a popular manager, and a general favorite, he has surrounded himself with ladies and gentlemen of congenial tastes; and the consequence is that at all times a treat may be anticipated in witnessing a performance at the "Dearborn." From a lengthy article in a Chicago paper, reviewing Mr. Aiken's career as "manager, actor and man," we make the following extract—premising that it is not near so eulogistic as other paragraphs in the article:

"But little that we can say will add to the knowledge possessed by the majority of our readers in regard to the career of Mr. Frank E. Aiken, whether as actor or manager. If we would praise, we have but to name one whose reputation is identical at once with excellence in a great variety of the most exquisite parts which the standard drama contains, and with tact, enterprise, liberality and conscientious fidelity both to matters of taste and of morals in theatrical management. In short the Chicago public, who have known him for five years, know all that we could possibly relate of a professional career, whose previous years were those of hard study and incessant practice in an art which is indeed ' long ' in comparison with the most extended life the most earnestly and busily occupied in mastering it."

Comedy, in the Dearborn theatre, finds a fitting temple, and in the company faithful interpreters. The house is not large, but it is chastely elegant; and while the characters are presented with a rare fidelity to nature in this season of sensation and " broad effects," the pieces are mounted in a style that manifests the taste of a student and the culture of an artist. The business manager, Mr. Mann, the stage manager, Mr. Keller, and the treasurer, Mr. Marsh will be found gentlemen by all who meet them. We commend the "Aiken's Dearborn Theatre " to the extensive patronage of a cultivated public.

In addition to those noticed are the German theatre, the Theatre Comique, Farwell Hall, Turner Hall, Arlington Hall, Crosby's Music Hall, and a number of other places devoted to amusement and entertainment.

HOTELS.

Chicago is well supplied with good hotels capable of affording accommodation to a very large number of guests.

THE BRIGGS HOUSE,

B. H. Skinner, proprietor, situated on the corner of Randolph and Wells streets, is a favorite first class hotel. It is in close proximity to the Court House, the Chamber of Commerce and the leading business portion of the city; and is within convenient distance of the theatres and other places of amusement. The superintendent, G. H. French, Esq., and the clerks, are gentlemanly and courteous, the waiters obliging and attentive, and the *cuisine* admirable, while the tables are furnished in a sumptuous manner. The house is large, five stories high, and can afford accommodation for about four hundred and fifty guests. Parties from the west will find this an excellent and comfortable stopping place.

The Sherman House, corner of Clark and Randolph streets ; the Tremont House, corner of Lake and Dearborn ; the Matteson House, corner of Dearborn and Randolph ; St. James Hotel, on State, corner of Washington ; the Revere House, on the north side, corner of North Clark and Kinzie ; the Adams House, corner of Lake street and Michigan avenue ; the Richmond House, corner of South Water street and Michigan avenue ; the Metropolitan, southwest corner of Randolph and Wells ; the Barnes House, corner of Randolph and Canal ; and the City Hotel, corner of Lake and State, are all popular hotels and extensively patronized.

10

LEADING BUSINESS HOUSES.

The trade of Chicago is very large, and daily growing larger. The leading merchants who have made the city their home are men of enterprise, a large per centage of them being young and with all the energy which young blood possesses when imbued with the spirit of this really " go-a-head " age. We can recommend the following firms in their several lines, as first-class houses that have the determination, and are striving assiduously for it, to wrest from the eastern sea-board cities the trade of the great west.

AGRICULTURAL IMPLEMENTS.

Austin & Boal, 221 and 223 South Water street, are a firm well known, firmly established, and doing a large and paying business. In agricultural implements, farmers' tools, stoves and hollow ware, wagon and carriage stock, etc., they are heavy manufacturers and jobbers. Buyers in their line of goods, visiting Chicago, will do well to pay them a visit.

ALES AND PORTERS.

On the north side of the river, and close to the Water Works, are Lill's brewery, J. Bromfield, secretary ; and that of the Sands' Ale Brewing Co., F. A. Wheeler, secretary. So popular are the ales manufactured in these two establishments that signs announcing the fact of one or the other of them being sold inside are placed over most of the saloons in Chicago.

Lill's brewery has a frontage of about 200 feet and runs 1000 feet from front to rear, including the necessary offices, coopers' shop, etc. It is supplied with every requisite for producing the best articles of ales and porter in demand ; and has a storage capacity in its cellars for about 120,000 gallons. It enjoys a large and profitable trade, and the business is being rapidly extended westward.

The Sands' Ale Brewing Company is the first establishment that has yet shipped ales west of the Wasatch range, having filled an order last Fall for the Salt Lake City Billiard Rooms. F. A. Wheeler, Esq., the secretary of the company, is an enterprising, wide-awake gentleman, who is determined to maintain the high reputation which the brewery has gained for producing a most superior quality of ales, porter and beer. The establishment turns out an enormous quantity for the market and has a very large trade extending into the surrounding States and away to the far west.

BOOTS AND SHOES.

The firm of T. B. Weber & Co., is a leading house in the boot and shoe trade. Occupying very extensive premises, six stories high, at No. 9 Lake street, which are filled with manufactured goods and materials ;

they are compelled by increasing business to move in July into a still larger building, and will occupy 3, 5 and 7 Lake street from that date. Keeping a large number of excellent workmen constantly employed their stock is always complete; and the amount of their sales annually reach a very high figure. That their trade is rapidly growing is simply a natural result of selling a superior and warranted quality of goods at a very low margin of profit.

The firm of M. D. Wells & Co., 38 Lake street, is also a leading house in the boot and shoe business, manufacturing their own goods; keeping a large and complete stock on hand; and selling at figures that present strong inducements to buyers, the secret of their success can be easily understood.

CLOCKS.

The American Clock Co., 115 Lake street, W. F. Tompkins, agent, has already done considerable business in Utah, and their trade is steadily increasing. They keep supplied with a most complete assortment of American clocks; and are sole agents for the E. N. Welch Manufacturing Co., the New Haven Clock Co., and Seth Thomas Clock Co. For quality, variety and price they occupy a first position, and are, perhaps, the most extensive dealers and jobbers in their line in the United States. They have a house in New York, at 3 Cortlandt street, and another at San Francisco, 310 Sausome street.

CLOTHS.

Charles Beardslee, Bros. & Co., 87 and 89 Michigan avenue, take rank as one of the first houses in the cloth business in Chicago. Their stock of goods is most complete, comprising the best quality of foreign and domestic manufactures.

CLOTHING.

For a line of ready made clothing we can confidently recommend the firm of Young, Brothers & Co., 98 and 100 Michigan avenue. An old established firm in New York and St. Louis, they do a thriving business, and job at the lowest possible margin of profits. Ever keeping supplied with an immense stock of goods suitable for the season, they are prepared to meet the trade and give figures to western buyers which will command sales. W. F. Adams, Esq., of this house, will be found by those who make his acquaintance, a gentleman who is determined to do business and secure trade for the firm.

CRACKERS.

The cracker manufactory of C. L. Woodman & Co., 230 and 232 Kinzie street, is a notable feature of Chicago. Mr. Woodman has enjoyed Aldermanic honors; is an enterprising, spirited gentleman; and stands high in the estimation of his fellow citizens. He has the only

cracker factory of the kind in the United States; and to give the figures
of the quantity of crackers turned out in his establishment in a day
would be equal to inviting discredit to the statement.   On the opening
of his cracker manufactory the Chicago *Journal* said: "Henceforth the
world will know that until some other city may beat Chicago, the latter
possesses the largest bakery in the world, and she throws down the
gauntlet of comparison.   Yesterday this gigantic establishment was
formally opened by the proprietor, whose name, Charles L. Woodman,
is already famed in the north, south, east and west, over this vast continent."   Details of the building follow; and the opening was hailed by
the Chicago press as an "event" in the annals of city enterprise.   The
building is extensive and adjoining the freight depot of the Chicago and
Northwestern Railway, where goods can be easily and readily shipped.
The whole machinery of the establishment is run by steam; and prices
at which the various kinds of plain and fancy crackers are jobbed show
that the business must be enormous to make them pay.   The baking is
done in two of Vale's rotary ovens, an ingenious invention which is
worthy of elaborate description.   The concern is in a most flourishing
condition.

DRY GOODS.

The name of J. V. Farwell & Co., is so closely associated with the dry
goods trade in Chicago, and with the prosperity of the city, that it has
come to be viewed as a synonym for enterprise and honorable dealing.
Farwell Hall is named after the senior member of the firm, and is a token
of the honorable esteem in which he is held.   The trade done by this
house is immense and growing; so much so that this season they design
erecting a new store a short distance south of their present location, with
a capacity to do a business of twenty-five millions.   The premises now
occupied by them are situated on Wabash avenue, Nos. 42, 44 and 46,
and are owned by the firm who are thus relieved from the heavy burden
which they would have to carry did they rent, and this places them in
a position to give buyers the benefit of proportionately lower expenses,
in a smaller margin of profit required on sales.   The vast pile of goods
on hand in the saleroom are but indications of what are to be found on
the floors where the stock is kept in bulk; and the regiment of employees
are ever busy in business hours.   Their trade is exclusively wholesale.

Bowen, Whitman & Winslow, in the same line, are situated on Randolph street, Nos. 15 and 17.   With an immense stock of dry goods
constantly on hand, bought in the best markets, they are in a position
to make figures advantageous to the buyers; and their trade is a healthy
and growing one.   George S. Bowen, Esq., of the firm, is president of
the Wool Manufacturers and Wool Growers Association of the Northwest, and as such is philanthropically interested in the development of
the highly important branch of domestic manufactures which the society
represents.   The firm is a first class one, and invite inspection of their
stock.

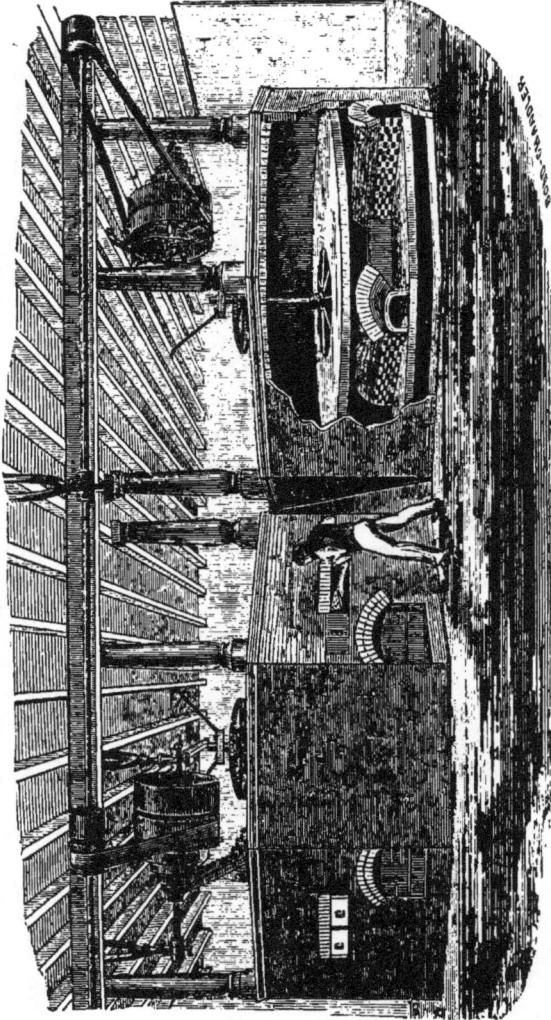

DRUGS.

In drugs, Burnham & Van Schaack, 1 and 3 Randolph street, deservedly hold a first place. Wholesale drug and paint dealers, with a full line of goods, and most extensive premises filled from basement to sixth story, they are in a position to promptly fill any invoice that may be ordered; while being heavy shippers direct from the manufacturers, they can make figures which smaller buyers could not reach down to. The house has only to extend their acquaintance to secure proportionately increased business. They also manufacture a warranted and strictly pure white lead; and have a full stock of the best selected and imported wines and liquors. We commend the house to western druggists and those engaged in the trade.

FILE MANUFACTURERS.

Abbott & Howard, 21 Dearborn street, are the agents for the celebrated files of Thomas Firth & Sons, steel and file manufacturers, Sheffield, England. The celebrity of these goods, only requires that the agents' names and business place should be known.

FURNITURE.

The completion of the line of railroad through to Utah will have a tendency to open up several branches of business which have been comparatively unnoticed before. Among these will doubtless be the importation of furniture to that region. W. W. Strong, furniture manufacturer and dealer, 203 Randolph street, possesses excellent advantages for meeting the demand, being able to furnish furniture in every desirable style, of excellent quality, and at rates that will successfully meet competition.

GROCERIES.

The largest grocery establishment in the west is that of Day, Allen & Co., 34 and 36 Randolph street. They are heavy importers of all kinds of groceries; and where they do not import they purchase in such quantities that they have many advantages in freight and other things over smaller buyers. Their sales for 1868 were about $2,500,000; for 1869 they are expected to reach over $3,000,000. In March of 1869 they amounted to $290,000 for that month alone. Buyers will gain by calling on the firm.

HARDWOOD.

With the development of the manufacture of sleighs, wagons, carriages and furniture in the west, arises the necessity of importing hard woods, such as ash, oak, hickory, black walnut, cherry, etc. Messrs. Hatch, Holbrook & Co., 265 Archer avenue and corner of Erie and Kingsbury streets, keep supplied with a very large stock of hard wood lumber; and with a yard covering a wide area where land is so very valuable, they have excellent facilities for seasoning. Their yard is edging the river,

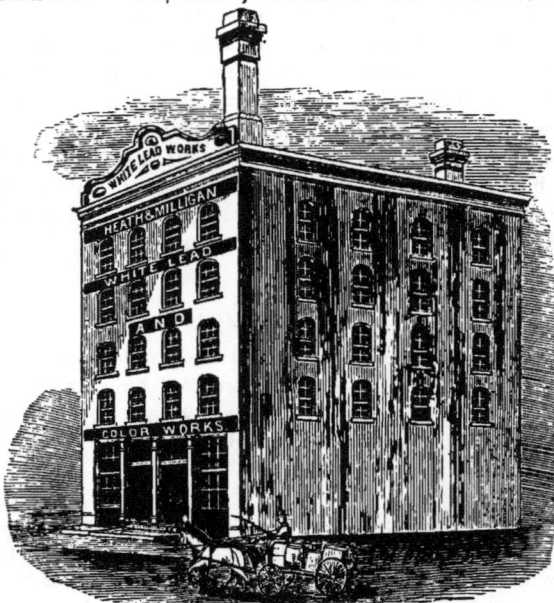

and a wharf where vessels can lay end to end, affords them accommodation for discharging the ship loads of lumber which come to them from so many different points. The firm is a first-class one.

HATS, CAPS, ETC.

In this line of business Fitch, Williams & Co., occupy a leading position. With extensive premises fronting on Lake street, Nos. 33 and 35 and having a front as well on Wabash avenue, the large and airy show rooms are excellently lighted, and the immense stock of goods can be seen to fine advantage. The latest styles and novelties in hats and caps, straw goods, and everything in that line of business, are kept in quantity to meet the requirements of a heavy jobbing trade; and the figures at which the firm do business are well calculated to divert the western trade in this branch of business from leading cities farther east. Merchants visiting Chicago and designing to make purchases in their line will do well to call on this firm.

IRON WORKS.

At Richards' Iron Works, 190 and 192 Washington street, can be found a magnificent assortment of machinery of various kinds, including some of the most valuable patents in the United States, a result of the inventive and constructive powers of Mr. Richards. Their suction and force pumps, adapted for planing mills, saw mills, grist mills, elevators, warehouses, hand fire engines, etc., etc., have been tested under the most trying circumstances, such as in the construction of the Washington Tunnel, under the Chicago river, and have met the most unqalified endorsement by those best capable of judging of their merits. Portable steam engines; Mr. Richards' own patent of a corn sheller and cleaner; belting, buckets, shafting and pulleys, iron and Burr stone mills, smut machines, wheat separators, etc., are manufactured by this firm, of excellent quality and have a wide range of usefulness.

JEWELRY.

B. F. Norris & Co., 123 Lake street, up stairs, as a first-class wholesale jewelry house, enjoy an enviable reputation. Doing an extensive business in their line, they offer superior inducements, to buyers of jewelry and watchs. Everything in diamonds, jewelry, watches, fine plated goods, which the wants of the western market demand, will be found at this house; and an acquaintance with Mr. Norris will be equivalent to a certainty of purchasing from him, for he is determined to meet competition on legitimate grounds. The goods kept on hand by this firm contain so much that is beautiful and unique, that an examination would be a treat for an artistic eye and refined taste.

LIQUORS.

Morse & Co., South Water street, are exclusively wholesale dealers in liquors and imported wines; and having a heavy stock constantly on

hand in warehouse and in bond, do a large business with the trade. Their wines comprise the most esteemed brands; and their spirits are of the finest known on the continent. The drug trade who wish pure liquors and the best quality of wines will profit by an acquaintance with the house.

MILLINERY, FANCY GOODS, ETC.

The heaviest importers of French flowers, velvets, bonnet silks and millinery in the United States, are, undoubtedly, Keith Brothers, 68 and 70 Wabash avenue. It is a rare treat, open to all interested in the trade, to pass through their extensive rooms, where masses of goods are arranged with artistic skill. With two fronts to their building, the Main one Wabash avenue, and the rear facing Dearborn park, there is a flood of light in every story from the basement up. They occupy five floors, each 165 feet by 50, besides a high basement, 195 by 50—all admirably adapted to their business, which is exclusively wholesale. The wide avenue in front and the street in the rear afford ample room for shipping and receiving, while the open park and lake view beyond, besides rendering the outlook unusually pleasant to the visiting merchant, afford him a better light for examining stock than is usually to be had in such stores.

Possessing capital which places them above the necessity of buying "on time," they go into the first markets of the world where ready cash is the *vade mecum* to the best bargains, and thus they are enabled to purchase the choicest goods on the best importers' terms; and for this purpose they keep a buyer in the Parisian and other principal European markets. By this means, and by shipping in such bulk, they can meet any competitors in the United States markets.

Velvets from Lyons; silks and ribbons from Basle; new styles in bonnets and dress hats from Paris; caps from Glasgow; laces from Nottingham; and other goods from the places where they are manufactured in Europe, are purchased by their European buyer, who is thoroughly conversant with the trans-Atlantic trade. Their importations independent of their domestic purchases, which are proportionately large, reach in the neighborhood of half a million annually.

But their business includes, as well, straw-goods, hats, caps and furs making a heavy wholesale trade in these articles. Every desirable variety of hat and cap, in style, finish and make, can be had from them; and all so arranged in the department devoted to them, that they can be examined and any selection made without disturbing the admirable arrangement which exists throughout, and without trouble.

NOTIONS, HOSIERY, ETC.

In this line of business unquestionably the firm of C. A. & C. H. Barnum & Co., have no successful competitors. The partners of the firm, Messrs. C. A. Barnum, C. H. Barnum, J. D. Mason and J. B. Staring, are young men, full of energy and enterprise, attention to business, courteous and gentlemanly, who are determined to do business on legitimate principles, and have already secured a large and lucrative trade in the surrounding states and in the great west. Their stock of goods is most complete, and through long experience in buying they can figure down exceedingly low, being satisfied with a small margin, knowing that such a course by making a heavily increased business always pays. In hosiery, gloves, white goods, linens, hoop skirts, corsets, handkerchiefs, veils, bereges, velvet ribbons, belt ribbons, shirts, thread, umbrellas, parasols, perfumery, etc., etc., they keep in stock a full line and are prepared to job on advantageous terms to buyers. We heartily commend C. A. & C. H. Barnum & Co., to intending purchasers.

PIANOS.

The influence of music upon society is daily becoming more and more recognized ; but in no place are its refining and elevating influences more appreciated or better recognized than among the people who inhabit the valleys of Utah. J. Bauer & Co., manufacturers and importers of musical instrument and wholesale dealers in pianos and organs, of 69 Washington street, stand in the front rank of music and musical instrument dealers in Chicago. With a house at 650 Broadway, New York, and their extensive one in Chicago, they are prepared to supply choirs, bands, harmonic societies, and similar associations with the most approved instruments, pianos and organs.

PRINTERS, BOOKBINDERS, ETC.

Rounds & James, of 46 State street, have made themselves a character for excellence of execution, promptness in dispatch, and quality of material, in job printing, bookbinding, electrotyping, and furnishing printers' materials, which places them in the front of the business houses in their line in Chicago. With a full supply of type and printers' materials, capital workmen, most excellent taste, and fine business facilities, they can give satisfaction in anything from printing a business card to furnishing a first class newspaper or jobbing office. We know of no house in their line of business that we can so well recommend.

SASH, THIN CEILING, ETC.

The Garden City Planing Mill is situated on Canal street. The mill was burned down in March ; but with the recuperative energy which is a characteristic of Chicago under such adverse circumstances, in about two weeks from the terrible fire which destroyed it, and with it the lives of several firemen engaged in attempting to extinguish the flames, the machinery was again working and the business of the company suffered but a very temporary interruption. The quality and quantity of sash turned out ; the amount of planing, groving, tongueing and beading done, and work generally turned out of this mill would seem almost fabulous to those unacquainted with the magnitude of such a business, were the figures given. One article produced here commends itself to special attention, in the "thin ceiling" produced, which is calculated to work a revolution in hard finished plastering and ceiling, by offering a superior and elegant article of wood finish, at very low figures, to take the place of plastering work. The superintendent, W. Wisdom, Esq., is confident that he can ship goods by rail for the west at rates that will secure buyers.

SEEDS, ETC.

In seeds, bulbs, roots, etc., the firm of Hovey & Heffron, 57 State street, have but to be named. Their stock is selected with the utmost care, and comprises the choicest varieties of foreign and domestic seeds, flowers, roots, etc. To this is added a most extensive stock of English, French, German, and Italian ornamental goods, in parian, bronze, etc., for house, garden and lawn. A visit to the establishment will more than amply repay the time occupied in it.

SHIP CHANDLERS.

For everthing in this line, we refer our readers to Messrs. Gilbert, Hubbard & Co., ship chandlers and sail loft, 205 and 207 South Water street, corner of Wells.

SAFES.

In this department of business we recommend Messrs. Herring & Co., of 40 State street, whose champion fire and burglar proof safes have won a reputation through the country which recommends them to every business man who desires to have a protection for his books and cash on hand, which will secure them against the effort of burglars and the ravages of fire. The factory is on Fourteenth street, corner of Indiana avenue.

STOVES.

Messrs. Ransom & Co. of 205 Randolph street, in their show rooms have one of the finest stock of stoves for inspection to be found in the United States. With everything that can make a stove excellent applied in their manufacture; with numerous most valuable patents; and selling at prices which invite increasing trade, they are prepared to do a business to any amount in most desirable and serviceable office stoves, parlor ranges, and wood and coal cook stoves. The works are at Albany, New York, and are in constant and rapid communication with the Chicago house.

WAGONS.

The number of wagons which have crossed the plains during the last twenty years, and which have been put into service in the west has alone made a heavy trade in them. Yet there are peculiarities about western travel and the working of wagons in the west, which eastern manufacturers do not well understand. These are being made a special study by Bishop & Prindle, wagon manufacturers, 16 South Jefferson street, who are manufacturing an article especially for the Utah trade. From an examination of their stock, the quality of material employed in the construction of their wagons, and the method adopted to secure a certain and complete seasoning of the timber used, there is no question but their wagons will rapidly grow in public favor throughout the west.

WHITE LEAD, ETC.

Heath & Milligan, 170 and 172 Randolph street, produce an excellent quality of articles at their white lead, zinc and color works. We recommend dealers in these and kindred articles to give them a call. They are also agents for the LaSalle Glass Company.

WINES (DOMESTIC.)

John Exton, 27 Washington street, makes a speciality of California wines, brandy and champagne, receiving the best brands direct from the makers, and on terms which enable him to sell at prices as low as they can be bought either in the New York market or at the vineyards where made. Every wine of celebrity, of California make, California brandy, and the best article of wine bitters he keeps constantly and largely in stock, received from the California Wine Company expressly for the drug and family trade. He also keeps on hand a large stock of the best Kentucky and Canada whiskies.

WOOL AND WOOLEN GOODS.

Messrs. Sturges, McAllister & Co., 80 and 82 Wabash avenue, are the leading firm in wool and woolen goods not only in Chicago but in the west. Their sales from January 1st to December 31st, 1868, amounted $1,007,854.80, as we find by the *Chicago Live Stock Reporter*. Making a speciality of domestic manufactured goods over foreign importations, the energies of the firm have been directed to the development of home woolen manufactures, but more particularly in Illinois and the adjoining states. They are agents for the sale of goods manufactured in sixty mills in the United States, and of that number twenty-three are in the state of Illinois. The quality of the goods produced in those mills shows the progress which they have made in woolen manufactures, for the immense stock of Sturges, McAllister & Co. contains fabrics that will claim equality, and in some instances superiority, over the best imported goods of the same kind. The firm are also agents for the manufuactures of ten cotton mills; and offer to the trade most excellent fabrics made by them. The wool trade of the west has received much aid form this firm who are largely interested in it.

11

Chicago Business Houses.

Agricultural Implements, Wholesale.
TILTON, LIBBY & HITCHCOCK, 187 S. Water

Agricultural and Seed Warehouse.
ELLINWOOD, STAFFORD & CO. 171 Lake

Architects' and Engineers' Stationery.
MIDDLETON J. W. & CO. 196 Lake

Auctioneers.
BUTTERS WM. A. & CO. 5, 7, 9 and 11 Randolph

Baking Powder.
ROYAL BAKING POWDER CO. Wm. M. Clarke, 185 S. Water

Banks.
MARINE CO. OF CHICAGO, 156 Lake, cor. LaSalle
MECHANICS' NATIONAL BANK, 154 Lake

Baskets, Wholesale.
VERGHO, RUHLING & CO. 104 Lake

Bedding and Upholstery Goods, Whol.
FAXON E. G. L. & Co. 74 and 76 Lake

Belting, Hose, Packing. Etc.
HALLOCK & WHEELER, 143 Lake

Billiard Table Mnfrs.
BRUNSWICK J. M. & BRO. 47 and 49 State
SCHULENBURG C. & CO. 84 Randolph

Bird Cages.
VERGHO, RUHLING & CO. 104 Lake

Blank Book Mnfrs.
MIDDLETON J. W. & CO. 196 Lake

Book Binder.
SONNE CHAS. 47 LaSalle

Booksellers and Stationers.

W. B. KEEN.   D. B. COOKE.

W. B. KEEN & COOKE,

PUBLISHERS,

Wholesale and Retail

BOOKSELLERS AND STATIONERS,

113 and 115 State Street,

CHICAGO, - - - ILL.

Boot and Shoe Mnfrs. and Whol. Dealers.
DOGGETT, BASSETT & HILLS, 29 and 31 Lake
KIRTLAND, ORDWAY & CO. 43 Lake
LYMAN, ALDRICH & LINCOLN, 27 and 29 Randolph
PHELPS, DODGE & PALMER, 48 and 50 Wabash av.
WATSON J. L. & CO. 54 Lake
WEBER T. B. & CO. 35 and 37 Lake. (See adv't inside front cover)
WELLS M. D. & CO. 38 Lake

M. D. WELLS & CO.

Chicago Manufacturers and Jobbers of

BOOTS AND SHOES,

38 Lake Street, Chicago.

We invite the Trade to a careful Examination of our

CHICAGO MADE GOODS.

WHITNEY BROS. & YUNDT, 22 Lake

Breweries.
LILL'S CHICAGO BREWERY CO. W. Lill, pres. J. Bromfield, sec. Chicago av. cor. Pine. (See adv't page 210)
SANDS' ALE BREWING CO. Pearson, cor. Pine. (See adv't opp. back paster)

Brush Works, Steam.
GERTS, LUMBARD & CO. 204 Randolph

Buffalo Robes and Raw Furs.
BOSKOWITZ J. & A. 241 Lake

Builders' Hardware and Tools.
HULBURD, HERRICK & CO. 163 Randolph

Buggy and Wagon Stock.
FLINT & AYER, 16 and 18 Wells

Burning Brands.
KOCH GUSTAV, 49 S. Wells

Cabinet Furniture, Mnfr. and Dealer.
LIEBENSTEIN HENRY, 167 and 169 Randolph

Cancelling Stamps.
MIDDLETON J. W. & CO. 196 Lake

Candles (Star and Tallow) and Soap, Whol.
SCHNEIDER E. & CO. 20 LaSalle

Carpets, Whol.
ALLEN & MACKEY, 89 S. Clark
HOLLISTER & PHELPS, 114 and 116 State. (See adv't page 202)
SPEAR, PRINCE & CO. 84 and 86 State

Carriage Hardware.
HUNTER N. D. 202 Lake

Carriage Dealers.
COAN & TEN BROEKE CARRIAGE MNFG. CO. 67 and 69 Adams

Carriage Goods.
HAYDEN & KAY, 45 and 47 Lake

Carriage Mnfrs.
COAN & TEN BROEKE CARRIAGE MNFG. CO. 65 and 69 Adams

Cheese Dealers, Whol.
BOGARDUS H. A. & CO. 181 S. Water

Children's Carriages, Whol.
VERGHO, RUHLING & CO. 104 Lake

China and Glassware.
HINRICHS & SONTAG, 56 Lake

Cigars and Tobacco, Whol.
PARTRIDGE JOHN C. & CO. 48 Dearborn

Cloaks and Cloakings.
GRISWOLD J. W. & CO. 48 and 50 Wabash av.

Cloaks and Shawls, Whol.
FIELD, LEITER & CO. State, cor. Washington

Clock Mnfrs. and Dealers.
AMERICAN CLOCK CO. W. F. Tompkins, agt. 115 Lake. (See adv't inside back cover)

Clothes Wringers, Whol.
DUVALL HARRY, 164 Lake

Clothing, Whol.
CLEMENT, OTTMAN & CO. 27 and 29 Randolph
KELLOGG CHAS. P. & CO. 24 and 26 Lake
KOHN A. & H. & CO. 86 Michigan av.

LOVEJOY WM. B. & CO. 102 and 104 Michigan av.
YOUNG BROS. & CO. 98 and 100 Michigan av. (See adv't page 214)
WADSWORTH PHILIP & CO. 34 and 36 Lake
WHITE BROS. & CO. 43 and 45 Wabash av.

Cloths, Cassimeres, and Vestings.
BEARDSLEE CHARLES, BROS. & CO. 87 and 89 Michigan av. (See adv't page 214)

Coach and Saddlery Hardware, Whol.
BUCHANAN, CARPENTER & CO. 179 Lake

Commission Merchants.
CLOUGH & ELLIS, 79 and 81 State
SMITH & DEXTER, 121 S. Water

Confectioners, Whol.
PAGE M. E. & CO. 24 Michigan av.
SANFORD C. W. 88 Randolph

Copying Presses.
MIDDLETON J. W. & CO. 196 Lake

Cotton Batting, Carpet Warps, etc.
BENHAM & BROWN, 42 and 46 Randolph

Cracker Mnfrs.
WOODMAN C. L. & CO. 230 and 232 Kinzie. (See adv't page 200)

Crockery and Glassware.
JAEGER F. & E. 73 Wabash av.
KETCHUM & MORTIN, 40 Randolph

Crockery, Importers and Jobbers.
BOWEN IRA P. & CO. 170 Lake

Cutlery and Guns.
JOHNSON, SPENCER & CO. 44 Lake and Sheffield, England

Cutlery Mnfrs.
CHICAGO CUTLERY MANUFACTURING CO. 202 Lake

Dress Goods, Whol.
BOWEN, WHITMAN & WINSLOW, 15 and 17 Randolph. (See adv't inside front cover)
FARWELL JOHN V. & CO. 42, 44 and 46 Wabash av. (See adv't opp. front paster)

Dry Goods, Com. Mers.
BUTTERS WM. A. & CO. 5, 7, 9 and 11 Randolph
CHICKERING & NEW, 83 State

Dry Goods, Fancy.
HARMON, AIKEN & CO. 23 and 25 Randolph

Dry Goods, Whol.
BOWEN, WHITMAN & WINSLOW, 15 and 17 Randolph. (See adv't inside front cover)
CARSON, PIRIE & CO. 60 and 62 Wabash av.
FARWELL JOHN V. & CO. 42, 44 and 46 Wabash av. (See adv't opp. front paster)
FIELD, LEITER & CO. State cor. Washington
HUNT, BARBOUR & HALE, 35 and 37 Lake and 75 to 79 Michigan av.
JACKSON S. D. & CO. 52 and 54 Wabash av.
KEITH D. W. & A. & CO. 76 and 78 Wabash av.
STETTAUERS & WINEMAN, 15 and 17 Lake

Druggists, Whol.
BURNHAM & VAN SCHAACK, 1 and 3 Randolph
DWYER E. P. & CO. 92 and 94 Lake

Engines.
COOPER C. & J. & CO. 88 Michigan av.

Engravers, Corporate, Notariel and Wax Seal.
MIDDLETON J. W. & CO. 196 Lake

Engravers, General.
MIDDLETON J. W. & CO. 196 Lake

Engravers, Wedding and Visiting Card.
MIDDLETON J. W. & CO. 196 Lake

Engravers, Wood.
MIDDLETON J. W. & CO. 196 Lake

Envelope Warehouse.
MIDDLETON J. W. & CO. 196 Lake

Fancy Goods.
HINRICHS & SONTAG, 56 Lake
VERGHO, RUHLING & CO. 104 Lake

Farming Tools, Stoves and Hollow Ware.
AUSTIN & BOAL, 221 and 223 S. Water. (See adv't front of Chicago Department)

Fruit Dealer, Whol.
ROBERTS S. C. 89 S. Water

Fruits and Fancy Groceries.
BENNET, FULLER & CO. 15 Dearborn

Fruits, Pickles, Jellies, etc.
THOMAS & CO. 91 S. Water

Furnishing Goods, Ladies.
FISK D. B. & CO. 53 and 55 Lake

Furnishing Goods, Whol.
FIELD, LEITER & CO. State, cor. Washington
PRICE, ROSENBLATT & CO. 42 Lake

Furniture Mnfrs. and Dealers.
BEIERSDORF J. 172 Lake
HALE A. L. & BRO., Canal, near Randolph
STRONG WM. W. 208 Randolph. (See adv't page 198)
TOBEY CHARLES, 87 to 91 State

Gas Fixtures, Whol.
FOSTER E. W. & CO. 166 Lake

Garden Seeds.
CARPENTER, JOHNSON & COLES, 196 Randolph

Gents' Furnishing Goods.
BROWN & PRIOR, 98 Wabash av.
WHITE BROS. & CO. 43 and 45 Wabash av.

German Bookseller.
SONNE CHAS. 47 LaSalle

Glassware, All Kinds.
HINRICHS & SONTAG, 56 Lake

Grindstones, Whol. and Ret.
HALE THOMAS, 480 to 484 N. Water

Grocers, Whol.
BECKWITH C. H. 112 and 114 S. Water
DAY, ALLEN & CO. 34 and 36 Randolph. (See adv't page 212)
DURAND BROS. & POWERS, 131 S. Water
GRAFF M. & CO. 87 S. Water
GRANNIS & FARWELL, 19 and 21 Randolph

Guns, Pistols and Sporting Apparatus.
FOSTER JAMES H. & CO. 186 Lake

Guns, Whol.
FOLSOM BROTHERS & CO. agency for Henry & Sons' Rifles, 194 Lake

Hair Dealer, Wig Maker, Hair Jeweler, Etc.
CAMPBELL M. 81 S. Clark. (See adv't page 186)

Hardware, Whol.
BRINTNALL, TERRY & BELDEN, 175 Lake
GREENEBAUM SONS, 240 Randolph
MARKLEY, ALLING & CO. 51 Lake
WAYNE J. L. & SON, 190 Lake

WAYNE J. L. & SON, dealers in General and Cabinet Hardware, Coffin Trimmings and Undertakers' Goods. 190 Lake Street.

Hat and Cap Mnfr,
LOOMIS J. M. 95 S. Clark

Hats, Caps and Furs.
CARHART, LEWIS & TAPPAN, 43 and 45 Wabash av.
FITCH, WILLIAMS & CO. 33 and 35 Lake. (See adv't page 212)

GIMBEL, LINDAUR & CO. 64 and 66 Wabash av.
KEITH BROS. 68 and 70 Wabash av.
KENT, WELSH & CO. 22, 24 and 26 Randolph
SATTERLEE, SIVYER & FOWLER, 46 Lake
SWEET, DEMPSTER & CO. 102 and 104 Michigan av.

Hoop Skirt Mnfrs.

OSBORNE & CHEESMAN COMPANY, 48 and 50 Wabash av.

Hoop Skirts and Corsets.

PRIDE OF THE WEST HOOP SKIRTS AND CORSETS, W. W. Houghton, agt. 56 and 58 Wabash av.

Horticultural Seed Warehouse.

HOVEY & HEFFRON, 57 State. (See adv't page opp. front paster)

Hotels.

BRIGGS HOUSE, Randolph, cor. Wells. (See adv't page 216)
ST. JAMES' HOTEL, Merseral & Libby, proprs. State, cor. Washington

Iron Foundry.

NORTHWESTERN MANUFACTURING CO. 10 N. Jefferson

Iron, Nails and Steel, Whol.

FLINT & AYER. 16 and 18 Wells
KIRK, COLEMAN & CO. 189 S. Water. (See adv't page 210)

Iron Works.

CHICAGO IRON WORKS, F. Letz & Son, proprs. 84 to 92 Franklin

Japanese and Chinese Goods.

HAUGHEY W. P. 35 Madison

Lamps and Glassware.

BOWEN IRA P. & CO. 170 Lake
CASE & SAVIN, 97 Michigan av.

Lanterns and Signals.

CHICAGO MANUFACTURING CO. 43 and 45 Franklin. (See adv't page 218)
DANE, WESTLAKE & COVERT, 95 Michigan av.

Lard Oil Mnfrs.

FAIRBANK, PECK & CO. 14 LaSalle

Law Book Publishers.

CALLAGHAN & COCKCROFT,

LAW BOOKSELLERS,

PUBLISHERS & IMPORTERS,

Our stock of Law Books is the largest in the West, and our facilities for collecting scarce Law Books are unequalled.

Catalogues sent Gratis upon application.

80 Dearborn Street,

CHICAGO, - - - ILLINOIS.

MYERS E. B. & CO. 87 Washington

Leaf Tobacco and Cigars.

CASE S. S. & CO. 149 S. Water

Linen Shirts, Bosoms, Collars and Cuffs.

GEO. CHURCHILL, OF TROY, N. Y., Chickering & New, sole western agts. 83 State

Liquor Dealers, Whol.

MORSE & CO. 117 S. Water. (See adv't inside front cover)
SWETT & LEONARD, 111 S. Water, cor. Dearborn

Lithographers.

MIDDLETON J. W. & Co. 106 Lake

Leather and Findings.

KALTENEGGER & SCHUMANN, 49 Franklin
UNION HIDE AND LEATHER CO. 207 Lake. (See adv't page 198)

Lumber; Hardwood.

HATCH, HOLDBROOK & CO. 265 Archer av. and Kingsbury, cor. Erie. (See adv't page 194)

Machinery.

HAWKINS & JAMES, dealers in Machinery, 193 S. Water St., Chicago.

Machine Shop.

NORTHWESTERN MANUFACTURING CO. 10 N. Jefferson

Malleable Iron Foundry.

NORTHWESTEN MANUFACTURING CO. 10 N. Jefferson

Melodeons.

KIMBALL W. W. 63 Washington

Merchandise Brokers.

MARSH V. A. & CO. Special attention given to purchasing of groceries for the wholesale trade west. 82 S. Water

Mill Furnishing.

NOYE WILLIAM F. 228 and 230 Washington. (See adv't page 204)

Millinery and Straw Goods, Whol.

FISK D. B. & CO. 53 and 55 Lake
WEBSTER & GAGE, 78 Lake

Mouldings, Frame and Picture Dealers.

RICE & THOMPSON, 123 S. Clark

Music Publishers and Dealers.

ROOT & CADY, 67 Washington

Neatsfoot Oil Mnfrs.

FAIRBANK, PECK & CO. 14 LaSalle

Neck Ties and Neck Wear.

DAMON, TEMPLE & CO. 22, 24 and 26 Randolph

Newspapers.

CHICAGO TRIBUNE, Dearborn, cor. Madison. (See adv't page 218)
CHICAGO EVENING JOURNAL, 46 Dearborn. (See adv't page 198)
CHICAGO EVENING POST, Madison, near Dearborn. (See adv't page 218)
CHICAGO REPUBLICAN, 93 Washington

Notions, Whol.

BAKER, GREIG & CO 42 Randolph
BARNUM C. A. & C. H. & CO. 49 Lake. (See adv't front cover)
BOWEN, WHITMAN & WINSLOW, 15 and 17 Randolph. (See adv't inside front cover)
FRANK & CO. 20 Lake, up stairs
FARWELL JOHN V. & CO. 42, 44 and 46 Wabash av. (See adv't page opp. front paster)
FIELD, LEITER & CO. State, cor. Washington
JACKSON S. D. & CO. 52 and 54 Wabash av.
KEITH D. W. & A. & CO. 76 and 78 Wabash av.
PRICE, ROSENBLATT & CO. 42 Lake
STETTAUERS & WINEMAN, 15 and 17 Lake
STINE J. M., KRAMER & CO. 28, 30 and 32 Randolph

Oils, Paints, Glass, Varnishes, etc.

CHASE, HANFORD & CO. 179 S, Water

Organs and Melodeons.

KIMBALL W. W. 63 Washington
PRINCE GEO. A. & CO. 89 Washington

Packers of Lard in Caddies.

FAIRBANK, PECK & CO. 14 LaSalle

Paints, Oils and Glass, Whol.

HOOKER & WEARE, 127 S. Water
LEWIS HAM & CO. 90, 92, 94 and 96 S. Water

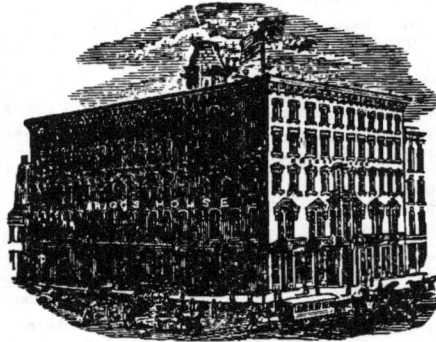

Paper Collars and Cuffs.
KEYSTONE COLLAR CO. 88 Michigan av.
UNITED MANUFACTURING CO. of Troy, N. Y.;
  CHICKERING & NEW, sole western agents, 83
  State

Paper Hangings and Window Shades.
FAXON F. G. L. & CO. 74 and 76 Lake
SPEAR, PRINCE & CO. 84 and 86 State

Paper Mnfrs. and Dealers.
BRADNER, SMITH & CO. 133 S. Water

Paper Warehouse.
JONES J. M. W. 42 and 44 Dearborn

Piano Stool Mnfr.
KIMBALL W. W. 63 Washington

Pianos.
KIMBALL W. W. 63 Washington

Pianos, Organs and Melodeons.
BAUER J. 69 Washington. (See adv't opp. inside
  back cover)
KIMBALL W. W. 63 Washington

Pickles, Sauces, etc.
DINGER S. & BRO. 71 State

Planing Mills.
GARDEN CITY PLANING MILL, 41 to 47 S. Canal.
  (See adv't page 194)

Plated and Britannia Ware.
JAEGER F. & E. 73 Wabash av.

Printers, Stationers and Binders.
SPALDING & LAMONTES, 138 Lake

Printers, Job and Commercial.
MIDDLETON J. W. & CO. 196 Lake

Provision Dealers, Whol.
STILES, GALDY & McMAHAN, 285 S. Water

Pumps, Lift and Force.
BIGNALL & McDONALD, 232 Lake

Railroads.
CHICAGO AND NORTH-WESTERN. (See adv't
  page 220)

Railroad Stationery.
MIDDLETON J. W. & CO. 196 Lake

Reapers and Mowers.
WALTER A. WOOD MOWING AND REAPING MA-
  CHINE CO. Chas. E. Whitman, agent, 206 Lake

Republic Paper.
REPUBLIC MILLS, First Class Writing Paper, J. W.
  MIDDLETON & CO. 196 Lake

Rubber Goods, all Kinds.
HALLOCK & WHEELER, 143 Lake

Safe Mnfrs.
HERRING & CO. 40 State. (See adv't back fly leaf)
HALL'S SAFE AND LOCK CO. 93 Dearborn

Sash, Doors and Blinds Mnfrs.
FARSON, BRAYTON & CO. Lake, cor. Market
MEYERS CHARLES J. S. 28S Lake

Saw Mnfrs.
BRANCH, CROOKES & CO. 214 Lake

Scales and Balances.
FORSYTH & CO. 88 Michigan av.
TILTON, LIBBY & HITCHCOCK, Buffalo Scale Co.'s,
  187 S. Water

Seeds, Whol. and Ret.
HOVEY & HEFFRON, 57 State. (See adv't opp. front
  paster)

Sewing Machines.
ELLIPTIC SEWING MACHINES, Hilder & Thomp-
  son, agents, 121 Wabash av.
WILLCOX & GIBBS' SILENT SEWING MACHINE
  Cornell, Ward & Comings, agents, 133 Lake

Ship Chandlers.
FOSTER GEORGE F. 217 S. Walnut
GILBERT HUBBARD & CO. Wells, cor. S. Water.
  (See adv't page 204)
PURINGTON & SCRANTON, 209 S. Water

GRANT & McLEAN, 209 Lake
HAYDEN & KAY, 45 and 47 Lake

Shipping Tags.
MIDDLETON J. W. & CO. 196 Lake

Shirt Front Mnfrs.
TOMLINSON E. H. & E. S. 80 State

Silver Plated Goods, Whol.
BOWEN IRA P. & CO. 170 Lake

Slates, Slate Pencils and Marbles.
HINRICHS & SONTAG, 56 Lake

Soap Makers, Eagle and Dexter Brands.
HAYES J. & CO. 220 Washington

Spool Cotton.
J. M. TAFT & CO.'S celebrated 3 cord spool cotton,
  CHICKERING & NEW, sole western agts. 83 State

Stationers.
MIDDLETON J. W. & CO. 196 Lake

Stationers and Blank Book Mnfrs.
JONES J. M. W. 42 and 44 Dearborn
SONNE CHAS. 47 LaSalle

Steam Engine Builders.
NORTHWESTERN MANUFACTURING CO. 10 N. Jefferson

Steam Heating Apparatus.
NORTHWESTERN MANUFACTURING CO. 10 N. Jefferson

Steam Pumps.
NORTHWESTERN MANUFATURING CO. 10 N. Jefferson

Steel and Files, Mnfrs.
ABBOTT & HOWARD, agts. for Thos. Firth & Sons, 21
  Dearborn. (See adv't page 210)
FIRTH THOMAS & SONS, 21 Dearborn. (See adv't
  page 210)

Stoves and Hollow Ware.
DANE, WESTLAKE & COVERT, 95 Michigan av.
RANSOM S. H. & CO. 205 Randolph. (See adv't page
  194)
RATHBONE JOHN F. & CO. 98 and 100 Michigan av.

TUBULAR KEROSENE LANTERN.

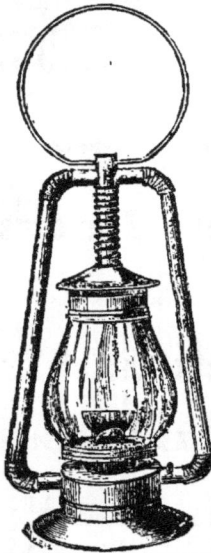

Our "Tubular" Kerosene Lantern is entirely unlike all other Kerosene Lanterns in use. It is new in principle, and free from ALL the objections which hitherto have made Kerosene Lanterns so unpleasant and dangerous. By the aid of the bell over the globe, and the tubes leading therefrom to the burner, the flame is supplied with a strong blast of air, which renders the combustion complete, giving a pure white light free from smoke and smell, like that of a chimney lamp, and also imparting to the flame great power to endure wind and motion.

But a still greater advantage in this Lantern is the fact that the oil cup never heats or takes fire, there being two strong currents of cool air between the oil and flame. Also, the singular principle on which the Lantern is constructed prevents all over-burning, and like a "governor" on a steam engine, it shuts off the flame the instant it becomes too high or too hot. On this account the Lantern has attracted great attention among Scientific men, Insurance agents and Lantern experts. It is very simple in construction, very firm and durable; will, in every way, be satisfactory to the consumer, and affords a better margin to the Trade than any other Lantern in the market. It is sold by all the Jobbers at our lowest rates.

Chicago Manufacturing Co.,

43 & 45 Franklin Street.

P. S.—We still manufacture our celebrated Champion Lanterns, for Lard and Whale Oil, in silver, brass and tin.

FOR 1869.
THE CHICAGO EVENING POST!
TO-DAY, THE
LEADING EVENING PAPER IN THE WEST.
Radical, Fearless, Honest, Independent, Live, Spicy, Readable, Progressive.
THE CHEAPEST PAPER PRINTED, AND THE BEST.
Markets Full, and Perfectly Reliable.

THE WEEKLY is the BEST FAMILY NEWSPAPER Published in the West, and is furnished in clubs at only

ONE DOLLAR A YEAR!

TERMS:
DAILY, per year, **$10.00. WEEKLY,** Single Subscribers, per year, **$1.50;** Clubs of Ten, or more, per copy, **$1.00.**

POST PRINTING COMPANY,
CHICAGO, - - ILLINOIS.

THE
CHICAGO TRIBUNE.
PRE-EMINENTLY
The People's Paper,
IS THE
Best Newspaper Published,
AND UNEQUALED AS
An Advertising Medium.
SEND FOR SPECIMEN COPIES.
TRIBUNE COMPANY,
CHICAGO, - ILLINOIS.

Stove Mnfrs.
PRATT, WENTWORTH & CO. 196 Lake

Stoves, Whol.
TILTON, LIBBY & HITCHCOCK, 187 S. Water

Straw Goods.
FITCH, WILLIAMS & CO. 33 and 35 Lake

Surgical Instruments, Whol.
BLISS & SHARP, 144 Lake

Tailors, Merchant.
BROWN & MATHEWS, 93 Wabash av.
NEWMAN & PERRY, 84 Dearborn

Tailors' Trimmings.
PHILLIPS T. F. & CO. 22, 24 and 26 Randolph

Teas, Choicest Stock in the West.
BECKWITH C. H. whol. grocer, 113 and 115 S. Water

Teas, Whol.
HIBBEN & CO. 235 Randolph

Theatre.
DEARBORN THEATRE, Frank E Aiken, propr. Dearborn, near Washington. (See adv't page 209)

Threshing Machines.
BIRDSALL H., SON & CO. 93 and 95 W. Lake

Tinware, Stamped, Japanned and Planished.
DANE, WESTLAKE & COVERT, 95 Michigan av.

Tinware, Whol.
SEAVEY T. B. & H. M. 82 Randolph

Tobacco and Cigars, Whol.
HIBBEN & CO. 235 Randolph

Toys, Whol.
HINRICHS & SONTAG, 56 Lake
VERGHO, RUHLING & CO. 104 Lake

Toys and Fancy Goods.
SCHWEITZER E. & CO. 184 Lake. (See adv't page 202)

Trimmings, Dress and Cloak.
GRISWOLD J. W. & CO. 48 and 50 Wabash av.

Trunk Mnfr. and Dealer.
WALKER GEO. H. 96 State

Trunks, Valises and Traveling Bags.
VOGLER H. & CO. 19 and 21 Randolph

Upholstery Goods.
SPEAR, PRINCE & CO. 84 and 86 State

Varnish Mnfrs.
CHICAGO VARNISH CO. 194 and 196 Pine. (See adv't on view of Salt Lake City)

Velocipede Mnfrs.
MERRILL O. E. & CO. 13 LaSalle

Wagon Makers.
BISHOP & PRINDLE, 16 S. Jefferson. (See adv't page opp. front paster)

Wall Paper Mnfrs.
HOWELL M. A. JR. & Co. 117 and 119 State.

Watches, Clocks and Jewelry.
NORRIS B. F. & Co. 123 Lake. (See adv't inside back cover)

White Goods.
BAKER, GREIG & CO. 42 Randolph

White Lead, Zinc and Colors, Mnfrs.
HEATH & MILLIGAN, 170 and 172 Randolph. (See adv't page 202)

Wigs and Ornamental Hair.
GRAY J. 77 S. Clark

Window Shade Mnfrs.
BELLAMY & HASKINS, 90 Randolph

Window Shades.
SPEAR, PRINCE & CO. 84 and 86 State

Wines and Liquors, Whol.
AMMON E. & CO. 233 Randolph
BECKWITH C. H. 113 and 115 S. Water

Woolen Goods.
BOWEN, WHITMAN & WINSLOW, 15 and 17 Randolph. (See adv't inside front cover)
FARWELL JOHN V. & CO. 42, 44 and 46 Wabash av. (See adv't page opp. front paster)

Wool and Woolen Goods.
STURGES, McALLISTER & CO. 80 and 82 Wabash av. (See adv't page 216)

Wrapping Paper Mnfrs. and Dealers.
McCANN & FITCH, 129 S. Water

Wrought Iron Pipe and Fittings.
NORTHWESTERN MANUFACTURING CO. 10 N. Jefferson